# THE CO

## *From the Carmelite Convent to the Crosses at Auschwitz*

Edited by

**Alan L. Berger**
**Harry James Cargas**
**Susan E. Nowak**

**Studies in Judaism**

**University Press of America,® Inc.**
Lanham · New York · Oxford

Copyright © 2004 by
University Press of America,® Inc.
4501 Forbes Boulevard
Suite 200
Lanham, Maryland 20706

12 Hid's Copse Rd.
Cumnor Hill, Oxford OX2 9JJ

Library of Congress Control Number: 2003117060
ISBN 0-7618-2803-6 (paperback : alk. ppr.)

# Studies in Judaism

# TABLE OF CONTENTS

# ACKNOWLEDGMENTS

This book evolved from our long-standing conviction that informed and honest dialogue is essential in seeking even a partial mending of Christian-Jewish relations after Auschwitz. The task is daunting because of the tortured history involved, and owing to vastly different understandings of basic terms and principles such as "forgiveness," "history," and "repentance." Moreover, political, psychological, and theological triumphalism are far from being vanquished. However, the winds of change seem to be blowing at least in certain quarters of the Roman Catholic Church. And while we reject the assumption of a moral equivalency between the history of Catholic Christian antisemitism and the attitude of Judaism towards their frequent persecutors, we note the appearance of a more nuanced understanding of Catholicism emerging in sectors of the Jewish community.

We are indebted to the contributors to this volume, Jews and Roman Catholics, from America and Poland. Their willingness to share their struggles with the crucial and painful issues that continue to plague Christian-Jewish dialogue are paradigmatic for all who wish seriously to engage in this enterprise. Precipitated by the twin crises of the Carmelite convent and the crosses at Auschwitz, the issues involved go beyond these two events and, unless faced openly and honestly, threaten to undermine the future of Jewish and Christian interchange. The contributors know that there is a long road ahead. Their essays, which were written during various phases of the crises, reflect the challenges Catholics and Jews face in heeding the lessons of the Holocaust. These contributions are signposts along the way for those interested in mature dialogue.

Special thanks go to Barbara Appelbaum of the Center for Holocaust Awareness and Information and to Professor Christine Bochen of Nazareth College for their helpful comments in the drafting process. We are indebted to Professor Abe Shenitzer for his lucid translations of several Polish documents. Konstanty Gebert's article originally appeared in *Gazeta*

*Wyborcza* (April, 1999). We are grateful to the author for translating this article into English. We are also pleased to acknowledge SIDIC for their permission to reprint "A Convent and Cross in Auschwitz," and "The Cross in Jewish-Christian Relations." We want additionally to express our gratitude to the Florida Atlantic University Foundation, the Sisters of St. Joseph of Rochester, and the Religious Studies Department of Nazareth College, for their support of this project.

Earlier portions of the manuscript were typed by Mary Elizabeth Drew, Susan's mother, and by Evelyn Mermonstein. Bonnie Lander, Alan's assistant, typed the entire text and was indefatigable in preparing the work for publication. Whatever the task, she is patient, prepared, and skillful. Martha Zubrow is owed a debt of thanks for indexing this volume.

This book is dedicated to the memory of Professor Harry James Cargas, a leading figure in Catholic-Jewish relations.

# CONTRIBUTORS

**Abe Shenitzer** is the translator of German, Russian, and Polish books and articles.

**Alan L. Berger** holds the Raddock Eminent Scholar Chair of Holocaust Studies, at Florida Atlantic University, where he directs both the Holocaust and Judaic Studies B.A. program and the Center for the Study of Values and Violence after Auschwitz. Among his books are *Crisis and Covenant, Children of Job, Judaism in the Modern World* (editor), co-editor with his wife Naomi of *Second Generation Voices*, winner of the 2002 B'nai Zion Media Award, and co-editor of *Encyclopedia of Holocaust Literature*, which received *Booklist* Best Reference Book of 2002 and Outstanding Reference Source 2003 – Reference and User's Services Association of the ALA Awards.

**Rachel Feldhay Brenner** is Professor of Modern Hebrew literature at the University of Wisconsin-Madison. She has published numerous articles on the representations of the Holocaust in Canadian and Israeli literatures. She is the author of *Writing as Resistance: Four Women Confronting the Holocaust* (Penn State, 1997).

**Harry James Cargas** (d. 1998) was professor emeritus of language and literature at Webster University (St. Louis, Missouri). He was the author of many books, including *Voices from the Holocaust, Problems Unique to the Holocaust, Conversations with Elie Wiesel,* and *Exploring Your Inner Space.* Cargas is also the author of numerous articles in, among others, *Christian Century, New York Times, Jewish Spectator, Commonweal, America,* and *Negro American Literary Reflections of a Post-Auschwitz Christian,* and *Shadows of Auschwitz: A Christian Response to the Holocaust.* He was honored for his remarkable humanitarian effort by the Tree of Life Award and 5,000 trees planted near Jerusalem in the Harry James Cargas Parkland. He was also recipient of the Eternal Flame Award from the Anne Frank Institute, the Micah Award from the American Jewish Committee, and the Human Rights Award from the United Nations Association.

**Eugene J. Fisher** is Associate Director of the Secretariat for Ecumenical and Interreligious Affairs, U.S. Conference of Catholic Bishops, and a Consultor to the Holy See's Commission for Religious Relations with the Jews. He has published, often in collaboration with Jewish scholars, some twenty books and over 300 articles.

**Reverend Edward H. Flannery** (d. 1998) was a pioneer in interreligious efforts who served as Director of the Secretariat for Catholic-Jewish Relations, National Conference of Catholic Bishops as consultant to the Vatican Secretariat of Catholic-Jewish Relations, and as Associate Director of the Institute of Judeo-Christian Studies at Seton Hall University. He is the author of *The Anguish of the Jews*, a study of antisemitism. Reverend Flannery was a staunch supporter of Israel and, as president of the National Christian Leadership Conference for Israel, he publicly expressed his commitment to the American-Israel friendship.

**Konstanty B. Gebert** (b. 1953), former underground activist, is an international reporter and columnist for the liberal daily *Gazeta Wyborcza* and editor of the Jewish monthly *Midrasz* in Warsaw.

**Cardinal Józef Glemp** is Primate of Poland.

**Jan Karski** (d. 2000) was a member of the Polish underground resistance in World War II. He met with Churchill, Roosevelt, and other statesmen in an unsuccessful attempt to stop the Holocaust. His 1944 book *The Story of a Secret State* tells of his experiences. Yad Vashem designated him one of the righteous among the nations.

**Stanisław Krajewski,** Ph.D. in mathematics, teaches at the Department of Philosophy of the University of Warsaw. Member of the Board of the Union of Jewish Communities in Poland, he is co-chairman of the Polish Council of Christians and Jews, and has been a member of the International Council of the Auschwitz-Birkenau Museum and Memorial from its creation. He is also the Polish consultant to the American Jewish Committee.

**Stanisław Musiał, S.J.** (b. 1938) is an essayist and former editor of *Tygodnik Powszechny* (a Catholic weekly). He studied philosophy and theology in Cracow, Warsaw, and also in Italy, Germany and France. In 1986-95 he was Secretary of the Polish Bishops' Conference Commission for Dialogue with Judaism. He participated in the Geneva meetings (1986, 1987) concerning the Carmelite Convent at Auschwitz.

**Jacob Neusner** is Research Professor of Religion and Theology and Senior Fellow, Institute of Advanced Theology at Bard College, Annandale-on-Hudson, New York 12504.

**Susan E. Nowak** is Assistant Professor of Religious Studies at Nazareth College. She lectures and writes on Jewish-Christian relations, women and the Holocaust, and the impact of feminist theory on interfaith relations.

**David Patterson** holds the Bornblum Chair in Judaic Studies at the University of Memphis. He is a winner of the Koret Jewish Book Award and has written numerous books, including *Along the Edge of Annihilation, Sun Turned to Darkness, Greatest Jewish Stories, When Learned Men Murder, Exile, Pilgrimage of a Proselyte, The Shriek of Silence, In Dialogue and Dilemma with Elie Wiesel,* and others. He is co-editor of *Encyclopedia of Holocaust Literature,* which received *Booklist* Best Reference Book of 2002 and Outstanding Reference Source 2003 – Reference and User's Services Association of the ALA Awards, and translator of *The Complete Black Book of Russian Jewry.*

**John T. Pawlikowski,** O.S.M. is Professor of Social Ethics and Director of the Catholic-Jewish Studies Program at the Catholic Theological Union. He has served on the United States Holocaust Memorial Council by presidential appointment since its inception in 1980. He has recently co-edited and contributed to *Ethics in the Shadow of the Holocaust* (Sheed & Ward).

**Marvin Prosono** received his B.A. from Stanford University in Psychology and his Ph.D. from the University of California, San Francisco in Sociology. He has traveled extensively throughout Europe, published numerous papers on Holocaust-related themes and is presently a professor of sociology at Southwest Missouri State University in Springfield, Missouri.

**Timothy M. Thibodeau** is Professor of History at Nazareth College. He earned a Ph.D. in Medieval History at the University of Notre Dame, and has published a variety of books, essays and articles on Medieval Christianity.

**Elie Wiesel** is University Professor and Andrew W. Mellon Professor in the Humanities at Boston University. He is the author of more than forty books. Among his works are *Night, The Gates of the Forest, A Beggar in Jerusalem,* (which won the *Prix Médicis*), and his two volume autobiography, *All Rivers Run To The Sea,* and *And the Sea is Never Full.*

# INTRODUCTION

Auschwitz, the largest killing center established by National Socialism, ceased operating on January 17, 1945. Ten days later it was occupied by troops of the Soviet Army. As the full scope of the mass systematic extermination process became known - approximately one and a half million people, most of them Jewish, were murdered there by the Nazis - individuals of conscience saw in the death camp a symbol of the inevitable end result of antisemitism and racism. This vast necropolis was viewed as a lesson to all humanity. The clearest warning of the relationship between the fate of the Jewish people and the possible human future is found in the words chiseled on the memorial at Auschwitz-Birkenau:

FOREVER LET THIS PLACE BE
A CRY OF DESPAIR
AND A WARNING TO HUMANITY
WHERE THE NAZIS MURDERED
ABOUT ONE AND A HALF MILLION
MEN, WOMEN, AND CHILDREN
MAINLY JEWS
FROM VARIOUS COUNTRIES
OF EUROPE
AUSCHWITZ-BIRKENAU
1940-1945

Yet, nearly six decades later this anguished warning appears unheeded. The tragic paradox is that it is on the grounds of Auschwitz itself where new religious tensions have burst forth.

Auschwitz was the name given to three camps. Auschwitz I, the *Stammlager* (main camp), established in June 1940 initially to punish Polish political prisoners, had been a First World War Austro-Hungarian military barracks. Approximately eighty thousand Poles, many Russians, and some Jews were murdered there. Auschwitz II (Auschwitz-Birkenau), three kilometers away, was ready to receive victims in Spring 1942. It is estimated that over one million Jews and approximately three hundred thousand Roma (Gypsies), and Russian prisoners of war were murdered at this site. Auschwitz III, Monowitz/Buna, was the industrial section of the camp where slave laborers toiled until being sent to the gas chambers. Given this grizzly record, Auschwitz should serve to unite rather than to divide people in their determination to put an end to hatred and violence. Moreover, in 1979 UNESCO designated Auschwitz-Birkenau a "World Heritage site." Thus the death camp is entrusted with a mission to preserve the memory of the dead as a warning to the living. If Auschwitz cannot serve to bring people together, then nothing will. But competing Jewish and Polish memories continue both to wound and to divide.

## THE CONTEMPORARY CRISES

The issue was joined in the late twentieth century by two events centered on the festering wound of Auschwitz. The first of these was the 1985 establishment of a Polish Carmelite convent in the *Theatregebäude* (Old Theater) on the grounds of Auschwitz I.[1]    During the Holocaust this building served as a warehouse, storing possessions stolen from the victims, as well as canisters of *Zyklon B*, the gas used to poison the prisoners. It also housed the camp commandant. At the gravel pit behind the convent the Carmelite nuns erected a twenty-one foot high "Papal Cross," which is not, in fact, a papal cross (see p. 32 *et passim*). There ensued demonstrations, mutual recriminations, and accusations that seemed straight out of medieval times. An international interfaith commission was established to resolve the issue. It was agreed that the convent would be closed by 1989 and that an Interfaith Center for prayer and dialogue be established outside the grounds of Auschwitz. Although the nuns eventually, but only reluctantly, abandoned the convent in response to a papal decree issued well past the 1989 deadline, they left behind the cross and heated controversy.

Through negotiations between Jewish and Polish groups, the matter was temporarily resolved by largely political and diplomatic means. Although negotiated by religiously motivated individuals, the underlying theological issues were, however, not specifically addressed. For example, the symbolic meaning of the cross is very different for Polish Catholics and for Jews. For Poles, the cross bears theological and political significance. Theologically, it is the sign of redemptive suffering. Politically, it is a regime in Poland, which like their Nazi predecessors, had sought to suffocate the Catholic Church. Jews, however, have historically been persecuted and murdered under the sign of the cross. Far from being a sign of hope, the cross has too often been used as a persecutive sword. Further, there was much heated debate concerning the appropriateness of *any* religious symbol at Auschwitz. These symbols frequently united only the members of their own communities while simultaneously demonizing those of other communities. Similarly, the role of prayer was differently understood by Catholics and Jews. For example, is it appropriate to continue doing theological business as usual after the *Shoah*? Can religious observance and spiritual practices be understood or invested with the same meaning and significance after the Holocaust? Is not a fundamental reinterpretation demanded?

The second upheaval began in 1986 with the initial appearance of crosses and *Mogen Davids* (Stars of David) *inside* Auschwitz-Birkenau. Polish Boy Scouts, intending no harm, placed these symbols in memory of all the victims. Soon, politics and theology again joined to create an ugly situation, with conditions in certain sectors approaching a holy war. In late 1997 the Auschwitz Museum removed all religious symbols from within the camp's barbed wire fences, but not before a firestorm of protests and mutual acrimony had occurred. Once again the grim scenario of missed opportunities, mixed signals, and demonizing of the *Other* came into play.[2] The Catholic Church, the Polish government, and Jewish organizations joined in discussions which were exacerbated by extremism on both sides, especially by right wing xenophobic Polish nationalism which portrays Jews as the implacable enemy of Catholic Poland, and by a parochial right wing Jewish ideology which claims that all Poles are antisemites. At this time, a familiar pattern emerges: a political/diplomatic, rather than a theological, resolution of the problem is being sought. Yet we know that which is suppressed returns with fury.

Although separated in time, these two crises involve at best competing, when not actually antagonizing, symbols, politicization, and a breakdown of consultation. Both crises involve failure to recognize the humanity of the *Other* and inability to respond compassionately to the *Other's* experience. We are struck by the emergence of nothing less than the language and, to an extent, actions reminiscent of a religious war at the end of the twentieth century. Long unresolved tensions became manifest in their full ugliness. For example, as during the *Shoah*, Polish Jews were again defined and condemned as non-Poles, i.e., non-Christians who did not belong in Poland. Antisemitic canards uttered by the Polish Cardinal, Józef Glemp, resurrected the hatred expressed in the writings of the *Adversus Judaeos* tradition, in which early church fathers such as St. John Chrysostom excoriated and demonized the Jews, in the language and symbols of the twentieth century. For example, the Cardinal accused a group of American Jews who had scaled the walls of the Carmelite convent of attempting to murder the nuns. He also contended that Jews had too much influence over the press, and that the Jews were meddling in Polish affairs. Yitzhak Shamir, then the Israeli Prime Minister, some of whose family were murdered in the *Shoah*, contended that Poles imbibe antisemitism with their mothers' milk. And yet there were also some hopeful signs. Voices of moderation committed to honest interfaith dialogue, led by Father Musiał, Cardinal Jean-Marie Lustiger, Theo Klein, and Stanisław Krajewski, among others, began to be heard. These are the voices which must be heeded, for they understand the force of the theological issues upon Catholic, Jewish, and Polish sensibilities as these groups confront the legacy of the Holocaust and the contemporary meaning of Auschwitz.

## THEOLOGICAL BACKGROUND

Theological repudiation. Ecclesiastical domination. Socio-religious persecution. These words chronicle the course of Jewish-Christian relations in general from the early part of the Common Era through the late twentieth century and into the beginning of the new millennium. Historically linked, with Christianity evolving out of Judaism, and theologically intertwined, the *raison d'etre* of each tradition being its covenantal relationship with God, the relationship between the two traditions has been tragic. Jewish-Christian relations expose in graphic detail the lethal effects of theological supersessionism when religious triumphalism is supported by the cultural, socio-economic, and political powers of the day. We are shown the ways in which fear, hatred, and violence corrupt the journey toward theological self-understanding when a tradition is unable to embrace religious pluralism or tolerate any creed but its own. For two millennia, Christianity has struggled to articulate its faith experience, beliefs, and mission in ways which confirm its existence as a religious tradition separate and distinct from Judaism. Plagued by theological uncertainties made worse by the continuing development of Judaism as a religion, Christian commentaries and treatises declared Judaism's covenantal relationship with God had been superseded and eclipsed by that of Christianity.

Despite Christianity's irrevocable historical connection to its Jewish matrix, all too often Christian self-understandings have been solidified by *negating* Judaism, especially its claim to a special covenantal relationship with God as the deity's chosen people.

Christian claims stress the superiority of Christianity's "spiritual" nature in contrast to "carnal" Judaism, emphasizing its recognition of Jesus as the One sent by God over against his "rejection" by the Jewish people. Moreover, Christianity's claims underscored its status as the locus of God's presence in the world compared with that of the "reprobate, stiff-necked people" of the "Old Covenant." In particular, theological antisemitism has enabled the Church to reconcile the observable gulf between its claims to a realized eschatology and the unredeemed behaviors of Christians, both ecclesiastical leaders and laity. Utilizing a dynamic of projection, the failings of the historical church have been projected upon Judaism and the Jewish people, thereby relieving Christian believers from responsibility for repairing the *disparity* between its theological assertions and its actual behaviors.

By delegitimizing the Jewish covenant, vilifying Jewish observance, and demonizing the Jewish people, Christian preaching and teaching have been a primary source of the suffering experienced by the Jewish people throughout the Common Era. Distorted readings of both the Hebrew and Christian scriptures justified Jewish segregation in ghettos, exculpated Christian violence against Jewish men, women, and children, and reinforced a belief in Judaism's theological bankruptcy. At the same time they promoted Christianity's theological claim as the "New Israel of the New Covenant" who has received from God what Judaism, the holder of the "Old Covenant," forfeited. Furthermore, theological antisemitism proved a potent force for quieting Christian self-doubts concerning the legitimacy of its own covenantal status, the credibility of its scriptural interpretations, and the efficacy of its sacramental practices. Theological self-justification united harsh theological polemics demonizing Jews and Judaism to Christianity's power over cultural, national, and economic institutions, thereby reducing Jews, individually and collectively, to the status of socio-economic, political, and religious pariahs.

The Holocaust, the most virulent expression of Jew hatred, fed by a long tradition of Christian theological antisemitism, reveals irrevocably the inherent hatred and intolerance of theological imperialism and lays bare the violence and brutality condoned by theological supersessionism. While scholars debate whether Christian theological antisemitism would ever in and of itself have initiated a genocidal attack on Jews and Judaism, the *Shoah* is indisputable evidence that genocide is the logical end when theological and racial antisemitism combine with technological sophistication and bureaucratic domination. *Supersessionary theological claims* promote a view of Jews as a religiously marginalized people outside the universe of moral obligation. *Racial antisemitism* portrays Jews as if they were a contagion that, if not eradicated, necessarily leads to cultural disintegration, moral decay, and race suicide. Both worldviews consider Judaism an anachronistic, bankrupt religion devoid of vitality, moral force, and revelatory power.

The implications of this distorted theologico-racial worldview have not only exempted Jews and Judaism from Christian "teachings of respect," but also justified the infamous tradition which Jules Isaac labeled the "teaching of contempt." During the Nazi reign of terror, this enabled many Christians to remain indifferent to the racial antisemitism propagated by Nazi leaders while allowing others to embrace Nazism's racial ideology. So pervasive – and seemingly logical – was this modern expression of traditional Christian anti-Judaism that only a small percentage of the Christian faithful discerned the danger. These few understood with indisputable clarity that the lives of Jewish men, women, and children hung in the balance as the Christian churches – Orthodox, Protestant, and Roman Catholic – for the most part acquiesced to the forces of idolatry and apostasy.

Almost sixty years after the Holocaust there are encouraging signs that some Christian churches are beginning to confront and eradicate this odious tradition. One needs only a cursory knowledge of the unprecedented statements professing sorrow for past antisemitic beliefs, practices, and behaviors to recognize that this tragic history weighs heavily upon some contemporary Christians, leadership and laity alike. Beginning with Pope John XXIII's convening of Vatican II in 1963, and continuing with Pope John Paul II's 1998 papal document, *We Remember: A Reflection on the Shoah,* and his extraordinary pilgrimage to Israel where he spoke movingly at Yad Vashem and inserted a prayer for peace in the stones of the Western Wall, the modern church began a long delayed theological self-critique.

Furthermore, on the political level, at the urging of the Pope, the Vatican has established diplomatic relations with Israel. The significance of these papal initiatives is intensified by groundbreaking statements issued, in particular, by Polish, German, French, and Italian bishops, as well as official guidelines for preaching and teaching about Jews and Judaism issued by the United States National Council of Catholic Bishops.

However, the insidious influence of the legacy of antisemitism remains strong and continues to reveal itself in Christian preaching, sacramental celebration, and religious teaching, despite sincere efforts to eradicate its hold on Christian self-understandings. For example, the year 2001 has seen the same Pope John Paul II remain silent in the face of two vicious assaults on the church's official position of viewing Judaism as its elder brother. The first instance was the crude public antisemitic tirade by Syrian President Bashir al Assad, uttered as the Pope stood by the dictator's side. Neither John Paul II nor, subsequently, the Vatican official spokesperson Joaquim Navarro-Valls, issued any clear unambiguous refutation. The second case was provided by the issue of the Jedwabne massacre. In 1941 sixteen hundred Jews in this small village were murdered by their Polish neighbors.[3] Polish President Alexander Kwaśniewski offered an apology and asked forgiveness from the souls of the dead and their families. However, Poland Primate Cardinal Glemp issued a public denunciation of his country's willingness to accept responsibility. The question remains whether the church can and will honestly confront the role which antisemitism has played in Christianity's struggle to construct a viable theological self-understanding in the face of Judaism's continued vitality, growth and development.

## CONTEMPORARY LESSONS

The establishment of a Carmelite convent and the presence of the Cross/es at Auschwitz, the canonization of Edith Stein as St. Teresa Benedicta a Cruce (St. Teresa Blessed by the Cross) and the persistent advocacy of Pope Pius XII's canonization by Pope John Paul II each highlight the continuing influence of theological antisemitism in Jewish-Christian relations. This book is committed to furthering the often painful process of identifying and eliminating the antisemitic elements of Christian theologies in order to begin the equally arduous process of theological reconstruction. To this end, the editors invited Jewish and Christian scholars to join us in this venture. Our initiative arose after the three of us presented papers at a panel addressing the Auschwitz Convent controversy. To our surprise, the room was packed to capacity, some of our colleagues standing in the hallway in an effort to be part of this discussion. The intensity of the discussion reinforced our belief that what was a stake was much more than a disagreement over the site of a Carmelite convent, even if that site happened to be Auschwitz.

The dictates of theological antisemitism continue to stop up the ears and harden the hearts of many Christians, leaders and laity, crippling intellectual faculties, reducing them to mechanisms used to bolster defensive – and frail – self-understandings. Ultimately, theological antisemitism disables Christians individually and collectively. Consequently, the Church and its sons and daughters cannot adequately articulate a self-understanding that honors its faith experiences, beliefs, and mission without denigrating Judaism as a religion and degrading Jews as a people.

On the Jewish side, there has been a tendency to view all Poles as murderers, as if they and not the German Nazis had built the death camps. Furthermore, Jews discovered that they needed to know much more about the nuances of Christianity. Both sides needed to work through stereotypes of the *Other.*

It is our hope that the essays in this book will effect at least a partial *tikkun*, or mending, of this poisonous legacy and its debilitating effects on Jewish-Christian relations. At the outset of the twenty-first century, with its promises and perils, it is critical that we spare no effort in confronting the poison of antisemitism, and the dangers inherent in not knowing and respecting each other's story. Our collective energies need to be channeled into mending the current course of interfaith relations. Only then can we hope for the necessary change in Christian theological self-understandings, which will make every plea for forgiveness credible because it is given visible expression through Christian behavior and practice.

While we believe that the papers in this volume need not be summarized, it is nevertheless accurate to state that each from its own particular perspective urges a three-fold course of action. *Politically*, the authors call for mutual consultation between Christians and Jews considering any type of memorial in Auschwitz. Berger, Neusner, Prosono, Musiał, and Krajewski each evaluate the relationship of nationalism and theology. Alan L. Berger calls for a post-Auschwitz interfaith paradigm rooted in the *Shoah* as "our common text" and demanding "nothing less

than reconstituting our world." This paradigm, he argues, can emerge only
when Christians and Jews acknowledge a shared spiritual partnership, honor
the sanctity of human life, repudiate triumphalistic readings of scripture and
religious teaching, and listen so "as to hear the humanity of the voice of the
*Other.*" Jacob Neusner, in reviewing the impact on Poland of religious
dialogue between Judaism and Christianity, finds a scarcity of influence on
"the profound animosity that poisons Judeo-Christian interchange in
Poland." His proposed program of dialogue arises from the monotheistic
beliefs Judaism and Christianity share to hinge on a dynamic notion of story
and define an emerging human task: "to seek in the religious experience of
the other, the stranger and outsider, that with which we, within our own
work, can identify." From a sociological perspective, Marvin Prosono
applies a notion of symbolic territoriality to examine the conflict emerging,
first, over the Carmelite convent and later, in response to a "possibly more
polarizing controversy," over the presence of crosses. He advocates a
reconceptualization of the function of symbols at Auschwitz in such a way
that the Auschwitz complex becomes "the symbol by preventing
interference from any competing symbolization." Wary of the efficacy of
speculative analysis by itself, Prosono generates a series of finely honed
questions to guide such a reconceptualization.

   Polish voices extend the analysis of this section. Rev. Stanisław
Musiał examines the incident revolving around another Polish cleric,
Henryk Jankowski, whose antisemitic sermons resulted in his being banned
from the pulpit for one year, to offer a penetrating analysis of
contemporary antisemitism in Poland. With candor bred of anguish, Musiał
outlines ecclesiastical responses to the incident, finding in them a
banalization of evil "that lulls the conscience and blurs the boundary
between good and evil." Challenging church officials to acknowledge
publicly Jankowski's statement as not only antisemitic, but as "antisemitism
at its worst – Hitler style," he calls upon the Polish church to define
antisemitism as a sin or risk losing its credibility before the Polish people
and the world. Stanisław Krajewski helpfully chronicles the history of the
large cross near the Carmelite convent. He rightly terms the placing of this
cross "a step in the religious war over the convent." Krajewski notes
further the complex relationship between the cross and Polish nationalism,
which works to limit the possibilities of action by the Polish president.
*Psychologically,* the message is one of attempting to listen to the voice of the
*Other*. Achieving this task will help avoid the tendency on both sides to

demonize each other. On the *theological* plane, it is abundantly clear that further study of doctrines and texts is absolutely essential. Furthermore, it is imperative that those doctrines and passages in texts, which condone or encourage hatred, must be exposed to critical scrutiny.

The transformation called for by the authors contributing to Section III, *Psychological and Theological Dynamics,* amounts to nothing less than a Copernican revolution for both Judaism and Christianity. Harry James Cargas, of Blessed Memory, offers a profound theological reflection, illuminating the inherent connection between the symbolic value of Auschwitz and the establishment of the Carmelite convent at the death camp. He argues that because the symbolic value of Auschwitz has "penetrated our souls," the Church, which "is nothing if not an institution of symbols," cannot ignore the symbolic valence of the convent. Rev. John Pawlikowski and Dr. Eugene J. Fisher each pursue the notion of memory and memorialization, keenly aware that these notions powerfully influenced perceptions, interaction, and negotiations during both crises. Pawlikowski speaks directly to the importance of maintaining memory, especially as it directs memorialization, hoping to promote a constructive atmosphere to repair the breach of trust, understanding, and sensitivity vital to improved Jewish-Christian relations. Fisher focuses upon "the larger Catholic 'memory' of the *Shoah,*" specifically, *We Remember,* the statement by the Holy See's Commission on Religious Relations with the Jews, and *Catholics Remember,* statements of local churches on the Holocaust. The similarities and differences between the papal and episcopal statements, as well as among the local church statements, are carefully laid out.

Jewish memory is different. For example, the Polish-born Rachel Feldhay Brenner offers a personal meditation based on her first visit to Poland after a 43-year absence. Encountering both the dynamic world of contemporary Polish Jewish life and the continuing presence of Polish antisemitism, she reflects on Polish Catholic uses and abuses of Holocaust memory. For Brenner, the only way Holocaust memory should be used is by those in Poland who keep Holocaust memory alive by contraposing it to the "forces of hatred that produced" the *Shoah.* From Poland, the Jewish intellectual Konstanty Gebert meditates on the frequently contentious ritual of the "March of the Living" which, until recently, encouraged hatred towards Poles and Poland. He calls, on the one hand, for calm negotiations, which test the limits of possible compromise. On the other hand, however, he underscores the fact that Jews in Christian Europe should harbor no illusions: the experiences and world-views of Christians and Jews are different. He speaks of the defeat suffered by both Jews and Europe when Auschwitz — instead of being a place everyone should approach with terror in the heart — became domesticated. It is, Gebert movingly writes, "the lack of horror that should elicit our horror."

The respective chapters of Susan E. Nowak, David Patterson, and Timothy M. Thibodeau, for their part, address the implications of the ongoing controversy for the development of systematic theology and liturgical practice. Each explores the impact of supersessionary theological worldviews upon religious self-understanding and liturgical practice, calling for a fundamental transformation of teachings distorted by theological triumphalism and observances fueled by religious intolerance. The section closes with Alan L. Berger's interview of Elie Wiesel. Eloquently and directly, Wiesel reflects upon the events which have fueled — and continue to fuel — this controversy. Through his voice we hear clearly the continuing agony that undermines efforts to resolve the convent/crosses controversies: inconsistencies of word and deed, insensitivity towards Holocaust victims, and refusal to acknowledge moral failure during a time of extremity. With an authority born of experience, he challenges us each to honor our own memory and confront our own conscience, recognizing that "somehow, they all fuse into one past. All memories merge into one, and that is God's memory." Perhaps these reflections may help Catholics and Jews understand each other's stories, thereby contributing to a partial *tikkun* of the world.

## ENDNOTES

1. For a valuable study of this issue see Carol Rittner and John K. Roth, Editors. *Memory Offended: The Auschwitz Convent Controversy.* (New York: Praeger Publishers, 1991.)
2. On the issue of Mixed Signals see Alan L. Berger "Catholic-Jewish Relations After Auschwitz: Mixed Signals and Missed Opportunities," in *Remembering for the Future: The Holocaust in an Age of Genocide.* Edited by John K. Roth and Elisabeth Maxwell (London: Palgrave Publishers Ltd., 2001), pp. 661-672.
3. See Jan T. Gross *Neighbors: The Destruction of the Jewish Community in Jedwabne, Poland.* (Princeton: Princeton, University Press, 2001), and *Thou Shalt Not Kill: Poles on Jedwabne. Więź,* Special Issue. March 2001. Warsaw. Towarzystwo.

# POLITICAL DYNAMICS

# THE CARMELITE CONVENT AT AUSCHWITZ: NATIONALIZING THEOLOGY

## Alan L. Berger

"What have we and you in common? If we take the question literally, a book and an expectation."

Martin Buber.[1]

Fima, the Israeli protagonist of Amos Oz's novel by that title, offers a reading of the Auschwitz Convent controversy that draws a stark portrayal of *types* and *stereotypes* which is, at least on one level, the fundamental if frequently unstated aspect of Jewish-Christian dialogue that appears most resistant to change. Responding to news of the convent controversy, Fima observes:

> Who the hell needs all this? We've gone out of our minds. We've gone right off our rockers. What are we doing squabbling with the Poles about who owns Auschwitz? It's already beginning to sound like an extension of our usual story about "ancestral rights" and "ancestral heritage" and "we shall never hand back territory that we have liberated"...What makes Auschwitz a Jewish site anyway? It's a Nazi site. A German site. As a matter of fact, it really ought to become a *Christian site* [emphasis added], for Christendom in general and Polish Catholicism in particular. Let them cover the whole death camp with convents and crosses and bells...With a Jesus on every chimney. There's no more fitting place in the world for Christendom to commune with itself. *Them* [emphasis added], not us. Let them go on pilgrimages there, whether to beat their breasts or to celebrate the greatest theological victory in their history...It's quite right that a Jew who goes there to commune with the memory of the victims should see a forest of crosses all around him and hear nothing but the ringing of church bells. That way he'll understand that he's in the true heart of Poland.

3

The heart of hearts of Christian Europe. As far as I'm concerned, it would be an excellent thing if they'd move the Vatican there. Why not? Let the pope sit there from now to the Resurrection on a golden throne among the chimneys...[2]

Fima's overwrought response is quite different from Buber's interfaith position, and not likely to open further the doors of Polish-Jewish, Jewish-Catholic, and interfaith dialogue – openings which are, in any case, highly elusive and fraught with ambiguity. Several questions emerge upon reflecting on Fima's words. For example, what is at stake for Jews and Catholics and for Jews and Poles at Auschwitz, in particular, and for Jewish-Christian relations and in remembering the Holocaust, in general? Why should a group of Carmelite nuns declaring that it is their religious duty to pray for the souls of the victims of Auschwitz and to do penance have aroused or, better, re-ignited such a firestorm? What is the significance of an eight meter high cross on the building used to store canisters of the poison gas *Zyklon* B?

In what follows, I stress a literary and a theological point of view which, while not ignoring the history and politics of the situation, focuses instead on what may have been learned from this entire sorry and sorrowful episode. Further, in the process I hope to show why the Jewish-Catholic dialogical enterprise is such a slender reed in spite of the hopes inspired by the bright theological dawn envisioned by Vatican II, *Nostra Aetate*, and, more recently, the papal document *We Remember: A Reflection on the Shoah*.

## A NOTE ON HISTORICAL THEOLOGY

The controversy engendered by the Carmelite Convent at Auschwitz and the Jewish-Christian dialogical enterprise both bear heavy theological baggage. While this is not the place to rehearse the long and baleful history of Jewish-Christian relations, for purposes of illumination it is instructive to focus briefly on the issue of chosenness as it exemplifies the underlying tension between two great historical religions. The Jewish people as God's elect is a fundamental teaching of Jewish theology. The precise meaning of this election has occupied thinkers from biblical to contemporary times. For instance, the enigmatic pronouncement in the Book of Amos captures the ambiguity of election: "You only have I known of all the families of the earth: therefore I will punish you for all your iniquities." [Amos 3:2]. The fact that rabbinic tradition taught that God chose the Israelites out of love rather than national merit did little to take the edge off chosenness as viewed by others outside the Jewish tradition. Broadly put, many Jews understand chosenness as the instrumental part of the covenant. In other words, Jews are to bear witness to the Oneness of God. The deity, in turn, is to insure the physical continuity of the chosen people.

Commencing with the theological ambiguity towards his own Jewish matrix displayed in the writings of Paul [epitomized in Romans 9-11], continuing with the increasing theological tension of the Synoptic Gospels, and culminating in the hostility of the Gospel of John [especially John 8:39-47], the growing estrangement between Judaism and Christianity comes to a head by the second century of the common era. Both Jews and Christians interpreted historical events through a theological prism. In other words, what fortune or misfortune befell either community on the historical stage was seen as a visible sign of divine pleasure or displeasure. Consequently, in responding to *the* central historical-theological debacle of the second destruction of the Jerusalem Temple, the Christian community, for its part, had several options in confronting the Jewish claim of chosenness. They could simply have ignored the Jewish contention, treating it as an unimportant part of a defeated rival's immature thinking. Or, at the other end of the spectrum, Christendom could have ridiculed the claim, pointing to the Temple's destruction and the surrender of Jerusalem.

There was a third option. This consisted of contesting the Jewish claim of chosenness. In effect saying, the Jews are not chosen, *we* are. The early church chose this option.[3] From this decision there emerged several deadly consequences: The *Adversus Judaeos* tradition of the early Church Fathers which, among other things, contended that Jews did not know how properly to read their own Bible; the Theology of Supersession which stated that Judaism has been superseded by Christianity, and its corollary the Teaching of Contempt for Jews and Judaism; and the charge of deicide. Richard Rubenstein describes the relationship between Jews and Christians as one of Disconfirming Others, e.g., for one to be true the other must be false.[4] When Christianity became the official religion of the Roman Empire in the fourth century, church law became civil policy. Further, in medieval Europe, the diabolization of Judaism equated Jews with the Devil. While the Catholic Church never officially sanctioned the physical murder of the Jews, it did, in the words of Gary Wills, heap obloquy on the Jews, especially in the writings of the early Fathers of the Church. Wills also speaks of a less harsh "countertradition," which ameliorated rather than canceled the main tradition. One of the Church's great theologians, St. Augustine, in the *City of God*, contended that the Jewish people in exile was a blessing, "since they bore witness to the authenticity of the ancient scriptures on which Christians relied." Wills notes that the idea of Jews as unwilling witnesses to the truth was condescending but at least it discouraged the attempt to get rid of the Jews.[5] Moreover, the Crusades signaled a major turning point in the nature of Jewish-Christian relations. The murder of entire Jewish communities in the name of the Church fostered very different memories for Jews and Catholics. An anonymous three-stanza rhyme serves to encapsulate the chosenness quarrel and its historical outcome:

> "How odd of God to choose the Jews.
> 'Twas not so odd, the Jews chose God.
> But not as odd as those who Chose
> the Jewish God, but killed the Jews."

## THE TRAP OF MEMORY

Post-Auschwitz memory, on the one hand, it would seem, could serve to unite both Jews and Catholics. Both had suffered great losses at the hands of the Nazis. Memories of this vast evil may possibly redeem humanity. Put in another way, if Auschwitz cannot unite people, what can? Moreover, *Zakhor*, the Hebrew verb "to remember," defines the Jewish historical passion; in Elie Wiesel's poignant phrase, "if we stop remembering, we stop being." But what is being remembered depends on who is doing the remembering. Michael C. Steinlauf terms this issue a problem of "conception," i.e., the meaning of the site varies depending on one's cultural context. The meaning of Auschwitz varies for Poles, Germans, Jews, Gypsies, Armenians, Bosnians, Kurds and Japanese; the latter "bracket the site with Hiroshima."[6] As enunciated in the collection of superb essays that Carol Rittner and John Roth edited as *Memory Offended*, the Poles and the Jews have wounded and offended each other's memory.[7] Auschwitz for the Poles is viewed as the scene of national martyrdom. Polish national pride, observes Rabbi Albert Friedlander, "wanted to turn Auschwitz into the Polish Tomb of the Unknown Soldier."[8] For Jews, Auschwitz is the largest single killing center of the Holocaust, raising questions that are of both historical and theological importance. For example: why were there so many killers and so few helpers? Why the silence of the world? And, the most painful query, what of God's role, if any, in the murder of His chosen people? Consequently, the convent affair emerged as a tangled complex of nationalistic, institutional, and religious motifs whose implications for Jewish-Christian relations are far from being fully articulated.

## LITERARY EVIDENCE

Novels constitute important, if frequently overlooked, data for taking the cultural and theological pulse of a nation. Two Polish novels, one of which has recently been translated into English, yield clues as to how the Holocaust and Jews are remembered in Poland. Andrzej Szczypiorski's *The Beginning* appeared in 1986. This, attests Iwona Irwin-Zarecka, is basically a work of "reassurance." [9] For example, there is a "good German" who helps the Jewish people. And there is a "bad Jew," a Jewish woman who is ungrateful for the help she receives. Further, the Holocaust appears as only one among many genocides; e.g., the Soviets had the Gulag, the Asians Cambodia, and the Africans Biafra. Sadly, we can now add the "ethnic cleansing" undertaken by the Milošević regime in the former Yugoslavia. Further, as Irwin-Zarecka notes, by bringing in contemporary examples of genocide, the author diffuses the Holocaust making it simply part of a tapestry of bestial behavior that humans display toward one other.[10] The Polish people, for their part, are portrayed as co-victims of Nazism. Szczypiorski's novel received national and international attention, becoming a best seller in the former West Germany, where it was translated as *The Beautiful Mrs. Seidemann*. Szczypiorski, who is half-Jewish on the maternal side, presents an ambivalent attitude towards the Jewishness of Auschwitz.

The second novel is titled *The Final Station: Umschlagplatz*. Written by Jarosław Marek Rymkiewicz, the book appeared in 1988, and was translated into English in 1995. Unlike the controversy surrounding Auschwitz, the *Umschlagplatz* is an unmistakably Jewish site. It was here that *Jews* were gathered for special handling [*Sonderbehandlung*] to be sent on their journey to oblivion. This site engenders no rival claims, no disputes, no competition for martyrdom. Furthermore, *Umschlagplatz* involves neither national honor nor defense of church doctrine. At Auschwitz, as we have seen, both Jews and Poles could claim martyrdom. And both are correct.

Auschwitz I, the *Stammlager*, was the main camp in which as many as eighty thousand Polish people were murdered. Indeed, one official at the Auschwitz Museum told me "we lost more people here than at Katyń."[11] Auschwitz II (Auschwitz-Birkenau) was the location where approximately one million two hundred thousand Jews were murdered.

Rymkiewicz recalls his childhood in the summer of 1942, in the resort town of Otwock. He played while the Jews were being processed for murder. Initially, this book received little attention. Why should this have been the case? One possible reason concerns aesthetics; it is not as well written as Szczypiorski's work. Another factor is that the author, although a Christian poet, has a Jewish wife. Consequently, he himself was perceived as being "not one of us." Lech Wałęsa echoed this attitude towards Jews as not being essentially Polish in a speech he gave while in America. The Nobel Peace Prize winner referred to Jews in Poland as another nation.[12] Further, at ceremonies marking the fiftieth anniversary of the end of World War II, Wałęsa prepared a speech for delivery at Auschwitz in which the Jews were not mentioned. This situation only changed after Elie Wiesel spoke to him about his egregious omission. To return to Rymkiewicz's novel, it is important to note that he argues that moral responsibility is universal. Like the author, everybody has an obligation to engage in ethical self-reflection. Yet, as Irwin-Zarecka notes, "the Jewish dimension of [the novel] weakens its potential to engage readers in a self-critical inquiry into the past."[13] This is to say that, on one level, if Auschwitz teaches anything, for one segment of the Polish population, it is that while the Poles suffered undeservedly, the Jewish people as "deiciders" had it coming to them.

## THE DECADE OF THE EIGHTIES

The attitude of the Polish people towards the Jews, argues Rubenstein, was largely effected by an interwar debate between Roman Dmowski and Marshal Józef Piłsudski.[14] The latter wanted something that approached what we might call cultural pluralism, although the Poles would be first among equals. Piłsudski envisioned a Polish society that would accommodate a federation of East European peoples including Jews. Dmowski, on the other hand, advocated a strongly nationalistic stance that excluded non-Poles, i.e., non-Catholics, from national life. Rubenstein observes that Dmowski was "the most important leader of the ultra right-wing, antisemitic party called *Ad Endecja*."[15]  Cardinal Glemp, whose 1989 speech at the holy shrine of Częstochowa was laden with classical antisemitic stereotypes, such as Jews are Communists and Jews control the media, etc., has expressed support for *Ad Endecja*.  At best, the Cardinal's remarks were highly insensitive. To him, the centuries-long sojourn of Jews in Poland stood for nothing. Moses ben Israel Isserles' (sixteenth century) pun on the Hebrew word for Poland (Polin), *poh lin*, "Here he shall rest," was meant in praise of the country and to reassure his fellow Jews that while Poland might not have the material attractions of Western Europe, at least Jews would be welcome there. The twentieth century made a deadly mockery of Isserles' observations. Cardinal Glemp's hateful statement is a twentieth-century version of the Church's second-century *Adversus Judaeos* position.

The immediate background events of the convent controversy and the novels date back to the early nineteen-eighties. Since 1982 much attention has been paid in Poland to things Jewish. The work of the Jewish Historical Society in Warsaw and the philanthropic activity of the Lauder Foundation in restoring Jewish culture sites, especially in Cracow, have fueled this curiosity. Everything from Hasidic tales, to kosher restaurants, to the Yiddish theater in Cracow has drawn interest. The fact that there are no *Jewish* performers in the Yiddish Theater is not typically remarked on. Yet there is a curious split between culture and politics. The words, "suspected of being a Jew," are not uttered as a compliment in Polish political life. In the 1990 presidential campaign, Lech Wałęsa, the favorite of American-liberals for his strong anti-Communist and, presumably pro-Democracy stance, wondered aloud why his main rival, Tadeusz Mazowiecki, "concealed [his] origins," i.e., was of Jewish ancestry. Wałęsa's position is a contemporary illustration of the truth that there is no contradiction between political liberalism and antisemitism. Indeed, one has only to think of Voltaire and the *philosophes* in the eighteenth century and Pierre-Joseph Proudhon in nineteenth century France to see examples of this phenomenon.

Holocaust memorials abound in Poland. A highly respected American Holocaust scholar and child survivor of the *Shoah* informed me that, while on a tour of Poland, she commented on certain of the memorials being erected in memory of the Jews. Her host, a gallant Polish gentleman, kissed her hand and said, "Madam, dead Jews are good for business." Further, the recent assault by the Polish government on the veracity of

Professor Yaffa Eliach's story of how her mother and baby brother were murdered by Poles is not a hopeful sign for dialogue. This attempt at "disinformation" is widespread.[16] At a meeting of a prestigious Holocaust conference, a Polish scholar responded to Professor Eliach's presentation with the claim that it "angered" him to hear that members of the Polish Home Army murdered Eliach's mother and baby brother. If the cause of his anger was shame, then perhaps the road to reconciliation might be opened somewhat. Unfortunately, as the professor's subsequent comments revealed, he was not angry at the fact of the murder, but rather that his justification of it — the Home Army had been looking for high ranking communists — was viewed as morally shabby.[17] Unless the past, however painful, can be confronted honestly, there is little hope for the future.

## THE CONVENT CONTROVERSY

Polish discourse on Holocaust responsibility is generally subsumed under the category of what happened during the war. Facts and figures are recited, statistics are brought forth and Polish suffering is highlighted. Historically, this suffering seemed a reification of the nineteenth-century poet Adam Mickiewicz's identification of Poland as the "Christ of Nations."[18] The Jewish claim on Auschwitz, therefore, is viewed by many Poles as an assault on the Catholic religion and its most potent symbol, the cross. This forms a volatile combination of religion and nationalism with the potential for great harm. What is the Church's position in all of this?

Theologically, the Catholic Church, the most important historical actor, is absolved from responsibility. Neither its pre- nor post-War encouragement of violence is discussed. For example, *after* the Holocaust, on July 4, 1946 a pogrom occurred in Kielce; it took the lives of forty-two Jews who were murdered because of a false rumor that Jews had kidnapped and murdered a Christian child. After the pogrom, at a demonstration, the crowd took up the chant: "Down with the Jews; we don't want Jews in Poland."[19] Furthermore, the Church authorities were slow to condemn the violence in Kielce. Irwin-Zarecka insightfully notes that this delayed response was a "clear warning to the Jews: since they were siding with the Communists, Poland's chief enemy, they should accept the consequences."[20] Even after nearly four decades, witnesses to the Kielce pogrom believed that the murder of the Jews seemed "natural," and not at all morally repugnant.[21] Clearly Jews were not viewed as living under what the sociologist Peter Berger terms "The Sacred Canopy." Those outside this canopy are owed no allegiance and are worthy of no human solidarity. Rather, they are stereotyped as eternally *Other*. After the Holocaust, Poland proved that a country does not need Jews to have antisemitic attitudes.

On the Jewish side, there were two types of response to the Carmelite Convent at Auschwitz: negotiations with Church officials, and various protests. Concerning the latter, significant attention was paid to the actions of Rabbi Avraham Weiss who led an American-style sit-in at the convent. Scaling the seven-foot fence surrounding the convent, Weiss and six students, replete with *tallisim* (prayer shawls) studied Torah on the convent porch. Workers inside the convent threw buckets of water mixed with paint on the protestors. Many viewed Weiss's action in storming the gates of the convent as inappropriate and overwrought, showing no respect for the sanctity of the convent. Not to be outdone, however, Cardinal Glemp in his August of 1989 speech in Częstochowa gave thanks that the "squad of seven Jews" was stopped before they had a chance to kill the sisters or to destroy the convent. In fact, even after the convent was moved, one-half of the fourteen Carmelite nuns returned to the mother convent in Poznań, accepting neither the papal decision to move nor the imperative to improve Jewish-Catholic or Jewish-Polish relations. What can be done to achieve more mature Jewish-Catholic, Jewish-Polish, and interfaith relations?

## A POST-AUSCHWITZ PARADIGM

The most critical need for interfaith dialogue after Auschwitz is to recognize the radically new situation of the world. To be an antisemite after the Holocaust is to endorse gas chambers and crematoria. The *Shoah* is now our common text. Learning how to read this text in the form of testimony, written by those who were victims, both those who perished and those who survived, is essential. Further, films and photographs, or visual texts, taken by troops who overran the camps and by the murderers, must be the shared reading for all who engage in interreligious interchange. The question is how ritually to incorporate such testimony into the interfaith effort. This involves nothing less than reconstituting our world. It is perhaps for this reason that the theologian Irving Greenberg admonishes that "no statement, theological or otherwise, should be made that isn't credible in the presence of burning children."

The act of Carmelite nuns praying in Auschwitz fails to recognize the need for a new paradigm of religious behavior. This is so for at least two reasons. On the one hand, it is an attempt to de-Judaize the Holocaust by falsely universalizing the event. Jews and Poles were murdered by the Nazis. Both deserve to be remembered. But also to be remembered is the fact that Jews were murdered because Nazism wanted to create a new, *judenrein* (Jew-free), world. In the insane logic of Hitler and the Third Reich, murder thus assumed a metaphysical dimension. Birth itself was a death sentence. The response of the nuns and of Rabbi Weiss were inappropriate to the situation. They were teetering on the brink of a religious war in which the Devil himself was called upon. Both the nuns and those who opposed the convent were viewed as doing the work of the Devil. Yet Auschwitz is a *novum*. After the Holocaust, it is time to stop blaming the devil and to begin accepting responsibility for human agency in committing acts of evil.

Praying for the souls of the dead is a traditional remedy for evil. Is it too brazen to argue that some in the Church *do not yet understand* that in the face of an unprecedented evil, the old paradigms are inadequate? For instance, although there is a world of difference *(l'havdil)* between Cardinal Glemp and Cardinal O'Connor, the latter announced that Jewish suffering at Auschwitz was the Jewish people's gift to the world. This comment has nothing to do with the reality of the death camps. Suffering is not a gift. Auschwitz was no present, save only to the lord of death.[22] Further, there seems to be insufficient self-criticism on the part of the Church concerning the role its traditional teachings have played in preparing the way for the Holocaust. There is an enormous conceptual remove between, on the one hand, Carmelite nuns praying at Auschwitz and, on the other hand, having the theological and ethical integrity to quarrel with sources, especially biblical sources, that give license to inferiorize and demonize the *Other*. Re-reading classical sources in light of Auschwitz is the only fair criterion of these sources' ability to address those living in the post-Auschwitz universe.

If it is merely theological business as usual, then I think that the Church has missed the point. Auschwitz is about doom, not hope. In 1948, three years after the Holocaust and thirty-six years prior to the eruption of the Auschwitz convent controversy, the German Evangelical Church met in Darmstadt. The Bishops' theological response to the *Shoah* was to term the event divine punishment of the Jewish people and to call on the Jews to cease rejecting and crucifying Jesus Christ. In 1965, *Nostra Aetate* declared the Jewish people was not guilty of deicide. But ambiguity persists in Catholic theological statements concerning the Jewish people and the Holocaust. For example, the document also states that "the Jewish people after the rejection of Jesus... was no longer the church of God as it has previously been." Ambiguity can be creative. It can also be deadly. Paul's earlier noted assertions about the relationship between Jews and Gentiles in Romans 9-11 demonstrate precisely the fatal nature of such ambiguity. If Auschwitz cannot play a clarifying role in teaching the necessity of human compassion and the dangers of triumphalism, then the future of the human condition is in grave peril.

The situation is further muddled by the contradictory statements and deeds of Pope John Paul II. On the one hand, John Paul II's papacy is marked by an unprecedented outreach to the Jewish people. On the other hand, certain of his actions reveal that triumphalism still plays a role in the Church's thought, especially in the doctrine of papal infallibility. Jews, and others, receive mixed signals concerning where the Church stands. Ambiguity seems the best word to describe papal statements concerning the Jews and the Holocaust. For example, on the second of August 1989, the Pope stated that "the Hebrew Bible showed several examples of the Israelites' infidelity to God." Yet, shortly prior to this, Pope John Paul II stated that "The Jewish people are the people of God, the old covenant was never revoked by God." Yet again, and shortly after this, the Pope declared that "God created a new covenant because of Israel's infidelity to its God." Has there been a clearer example of the danger of justifying God at the expense of humanity? In 1987 the Pope visited the death camp of Majdanek and made no reference to Jews who died as Jews. Further, he has also knighted Kurt Waldheim, who served as a *Wehrmacht* officer in the Second World War and subsequently lied about his Nazi affiliation.

On the other side of the ledger, the Pope has also visited the Jewish synagogue in Rome, established diplomatic relations with Israel, gone to Yad Vashem, prayed at the Western Wall, and sponsored a concert in the Vatican in memory of Holocaust victims. He also issued the document *We Remember: A Reflection on the Shoah.* One is perplexed. Where precisely do the Pope and the Church stand? Does Pope John Paul II's groundbreaking *We Remember: A Reflection on the Shoah* represent a beginning or a culmination of the Church's commitment to Catholic-Jewish dialogue? As a point of contrast, it is wholly inconceivable that Pope John XXIII, under whose wise guidance the second Vatican Council was convened, would have endorsed either the theological mixed signals sent by the incumbent, or the morally reprehensible action of the Church in remaining silent in response to the crude anti-Jewish attack of the Syrian President and Minister of Religious Affairs. It is clear that the Church itself is deeply divided between liberal and reactionary elements.

There are other troubling signs that the Pope appears more interested in *exonerating* than in examining the Church's role during the *Shoah*. For example, while denouncing antisemitism, the Pope also beatified Father Maximilian Kolbe, a Polish priest who died for a fellow Polish prisoner at Auschwitz. Kolbe's selfless act notwithstanding, prior to the war he edited an antisemitic journal. Similarly, the beatification of Edith Stein, born Jewish but converted to Christianity, later joining the Carmelite order, appears highly questionable. Stein was murdered because of her Jewishness, not because she was a member of the Carmelite Order. Further, his defense of Pope Pius XII takes account of neither his predecessor's moral failures nor his deadly "politics as usual" response to the Holocaust. The Vatican's refusal to open its archives concerning Pius XII to an independent body of Catholic and Jewish scholars, after initially agreeing to do so, is a severe blow to Catholic-Jewish relations. The recent move to canonize Pius XII is, as Father Stanislaw Musial, S.J., notes, the wrong move. Canonization implies emulation.[23] The Church must ask itself if it wishes future prelates to act in a similar way – placing politics above the priority of saving lives. Pope John Paul II thus appears to perpetuate what Irwin-Zarecka terms Poland's "neutralizing the memory of the morally difficult past." [24] While the *We Remember* document should serve to counter the claim of Holocaust deniers, the Pope's continuing refusal to have a scholarly commission examine Pope Pius XII's historical record during the *Shoah* invites the conclusion that the incumbent does not wish thoroughly to investigate the Vatican's role at that time. John Paul II's vagueness on this point conveys the impression that the Vatican is engaged in a whitewash of the historical record. Further, many will draw the conclusion – warranted or not – that when and if access is granted to such documents, they will have been purged of material damaging to Pius XII.[25]

## LESSONS

What can be learned from the Auschwitz Convent controversy that will help interfaith dialogue? Or, as Robert McAfee Brown asked, "Can Memory be Redeemed?" The first lesson is a need to develop a new language for speaking to each other. Narratives may clash, yet people need to speak. The dialogue needs to be mature enough to accept the position that some differences may be irreconcilable. Yet, dialogue needs to continue. Further, authentic attempts at interfaith must recognize that words may wound, and even kill. When Germany made Nazism's "Word become flesh," two-thirds of the Jewish people in Europe disappeared. Everything depends on the intention of the speaker. A certain segment of Polish society is beginning to develop an awareness of the meaningful role played by Jews in Polish history. Father Stanisław Musiaĺ, a vocal opponent of antisemitism and a professor of the History of Philosophy at the Jesuit Philosophical Faculty in Cracow, is among their leaders. Yet the Polish Church itself is deeply divided. Many parish priests remain antisemitic and refuse to read certain homilies. More of the population needs to learn the Jewish story in Poland.

Jews, for their part, need to learn the names and deeds of the helpers who saved Jewish lives during the Holocaust. Although these individuals constituted about a quarter of one per cent of the Polish population, the result of their efforts is beyond measure. The complexity of goodness is far more mysterious than the persistence of evil. Altruistic behavior in a truly hostile environment merits acknowledgment and exemplifies the fact that an individual can act morally even in the face of an evil system. In fact, Poland, for all its checkered historical relations with its Jewish population, is one of two countries that have the most trees planted in memory of the righteous at Yad Vashem. If Catholics and Jews are interested in working together to seek at least a partial *tikkun olam* (restoration or repair of the world in so far as this is possible after Auschwitz), the dialogue has to deepen. It is encouraging that an interfaith center now stands 500 meters from the location of the former convent in Auschwitz. This is perhaps a step on the path envisioned by Buber's optimism concerning interfaith relations.

A mature Jewish-Christian dialogue can emerge only by recognizing several points. Both Jews and Christians share a spiritual partnership. In order to engage legitimately in post-Holocaust dialogue, there needs to be an acknowledgment of this relationship and of the sanctity of human life. Furthermore, the long tradition of justifying God at the expense of humanity must not continue. Rather, it is necessary to realize the wisdom underlying Wiesel's contention that the road to God leads through humanity. These guidelines can be implemented in a variety of ways. Study groups whose task it is to [re]read scripture non-triumphalistically are important. So, too, are candid discussions of the historical circumstances out of which certain hateful teachings were promulgated. Finally, it is important to listen to each other's stories so as to hear the humanity of the voice of the Other.

It may be one of the abiding paradoxes of the Holocaust that this event of unprecedented evil may serve to bring Catholics and Jews together. As the Baal Shem Tov observed: "Evil can be the footstool of Good." If, I hasten to add, those who are touched by it also seek to learn from the event. Any nationalistic theology after Auschwitz is blasphemy and solidly rooted in the old, pre-*Shoah*, triumphalistic way of thinking. In turn, the triumphalistic paradigm is rooted in fundamentalist Christianity as a whole. Neutralizing memory, i.e., absolving the Church of responsibility, leads neither to sound history nor legitimate theology. If evil can in fact be the footstool of good, it can also be the prelude to further evil. Albert Camus' novel *The Plague* attests to the prevalence of evil. Antisemitism is, like the plague-carrying rats, lying just below the surface waiting to be mobilized whether by resorting to gas chambers or to triumphalistic stereotypes.

## ENDNOTES

1  Martin Buber. Cited by Israel Mowshowitz, "Why Dialogue?" In *Face to Face: A Primer in Dialogue*. Edited   by Lily Edelman. (New York: Crown Publishers, Inc., 1967), p. 12.
2  Amos Oz. *Fima*. Translated by Nicholas DeLange. (New York: Harcourt Brace, 1993), pp. 215-216.
3  In "The Dean and the Chosen People," an essay that has achieved near classic status, Richard Rubenstein reports his post-Auschwitz discussion with Dean Heinrich Gruber who, although a "Righteous Gentile," argued that the Holocaust

was God's punishment of His Chosen People. Rubenstein's theological conclusion is that chosenness leads to stereotypical thinking on the part of both Christians and "...some of this century's leading Orthodox Jewish thinkers: because the Jews are God's Chosen People yet failed to keep God's Law, God sent Hitler to punish them." Consequently, Rubenstein advocates that Jews do away with the notion of election. "The tendency of the Church to regard Jews in magical and theological terms encourages the view that the vicissitudes of Jewish history are God's will." Richard L. Rubenstein. *After Auschwitz: History, Theology, and Contemporary Judaism*, Second Edition. (Baltimore: The Johns Hopkins University Press, 1992), p. 13.

Rubenstein's willingness both to do away with chosenness and to ignore the Christian counterclaim is flawed in several ways: it "blames" the Jews for anti-Jewish attitudes on the part of the Church (a curious modern version of the biblical notion of *mpinei hateinu* – for our sins we are punished); it overlooks the Church's own "magical and theological" self-perception; and it unintentionally tends to make of the Holocaust a monocausal event. Furthermore, it is not the case that a historic religion can simply abolish its central mythic structure and endure. On the other hand, Rubenstein's position has the considerable merit of arguing for seeing human beings *qua* human beings and not as stereotypes.

4   This is one of Rubenstein's central positions and is situated throughout his works. For a succinct summary statement see Richard L. Rubenstein *op. cit.*, pp. 84-95.

5   Gary Wills. *Papal Sin: Structures of Deceit*. (New York: Doubleday, 2000), p. 21.

6   Michael C. Steinlauf. *Bondage to the Dead: Poland and the Memory of the Holocaust*. (Syracuse University Press, 1997), p. 143.

7   Carol Rittner and John K. Roth, Editors. *Memory Offended: The Auschwitz Convent Controversy*. (New York: Praeger, 1991).

8   Albert H. Friedlander. "Jewish and Christian Suffering in the Post-Auschwitz Period," in Rittner and Roth, *op. cit.*, p. 178.

9   Iwona Irwin-Zarecka, "Challenged to Respond: New Polish Novels About the Holocaust," in Alan L. Berger, Editor. *Bearing Witness to the Holocaust: 1939-1989*. (Lewiston: The Edwin Mellen Press, 1991), pp. 275. Hereafter this work is referred to as "Challenged." I am indebted to Professor Irwin-Zarecka's discussion of these two novels.

10   *Ibid.*, p. 278.

11   Author's interview with Teresa Świebocka, Auschwitz Museum, August 1998.

12   See the essay by Professor Harry James Cargas in this volume.

13   Irwin-Zarecka, "Challenged," p. 281.

14   Richard L. Rubenstein, "The Convent at Auschwitz and the Imperatives of Pluralism in the Global Electronic Village" in Rittner and Roth, op. cit., pp. 37-38.

15  *Ibid.* Note on *Ad Endecja*: the party called itself Narodowa Demokracja. The letters N D gave rise to the words *"endek"* and *"Endecja,"* which were sometimes capitalized. I am grateful to Abe Shenitzer for this information.

16  For the Polish assault on the veracity of Eliach's eyewitness account see the New York Times, August 13, 1996.

17  Comments of Professor Piotor Wróbel made at Lessons and Legacies of the Holocaust Conference. University of Notre Dame. November, 1996.

18  Steinlauf, *op. cit.*, p. 9.

19  Bożena Szaynok, "The Pogrom of Jews in Kielce, July 4, 1946," in *Yad Vashem Studies XXII,* Jerusalem, 1992, p. 228.

20  Iwona Irwin-Zarecka, "Poland, After the Holocaust," in *Remembering for the Future: Jews and Christians During and After the Holocaust.* Theme 1. July, 1988, p. 144. Hereafter this work is referred to as "Poland."

21  *Ibid.,* p. 145.

22  More recently, Cardinal O'Connor had deepened his understanding of the necessity of confronting more fully the meaning of Auschwitz. In a full-page ad in the September 8, 1999, issue of the *New York Times,* the Cardinal expressed "abject sorrow" for centuries of antisemitism by members of the Catholic Church. Elie Wiesel calls O'Connor's statement "very strong" and "a great gesture of understanding." H-NET History of Anti-semitism List, AP, New York, 9-20-99. Sadly, Cardinal O'Connor died in May 2000.

23  Stanisław Musiał, J.S., "The Holocaust, Christianity, Poland: Some Reflections of a Polish Christian Fifty Years Later," in From Holocaust to Life. (Cincinnati: Xavier University Division of Spiritual Development, University of Cincinnati Judaic Studies Program, and the American Jewish Committee, 1996), p. 4.

24  Iwona Irwin-Zarecka, "Poland," p. 143.

25  The following works include the wartime role of Pius XII: James Carroll, *Constantine's Sword* (New York: Houghton Mifflin, 2001); Saul Friedländer, *Pius XII and the Third Reich: A Documentation.* Translated by Charles Fullman (New York: Alfred A. Knopf, 1966); John Morley, *Vatican Diplomacy and the Jews During the Holocaust 1939-1943.* (New York: KTAV); John Cornwall, *Hitler's Pope.* (New York: Viking, 1999); Michael Phayer, *The Catholic Church and the Holocaust, 1930-1965.* (Bloomington: Indiana University Press, 2000); Gary Wills, *Papal Sin: Studies of Deceit.* (New York: Doubleday, 2000); Susan Zuccotti, *Under His Very Windows: The Vatican and the Holocaust in Italy.* (New Haven: Yale University Press, 2000).

It is important to note that a Catholic-Jewish Commission was established in October 1999 to study Pope Pius XII's response to the Holocaust. The Commission – composed of Catholic and Jewish Scholars – suspended its inquiry some eighteen months later after being denied unfettered access to the Vatican's

World War II archives. The mutual recriminations that followed cast a pall over Catholic-Jewish dialogue.

# THE LARGE CROSS IN THE GARDEN OF THE FORMER CARMELITE CONVENT AT AUSCHWITZ

## (Facts and Comments)

### Stanislaw Krajewski
### (March 29, 1998)

---

**1979:**

The Auschwitz-Birkenau camp was put on the UNESCO list of World Heritage sites in response to the request of the Polish government. One of the rules for objects on the list is that their character should remain unchanged. According to the map given to UNESCO, the so-called "theater building" (*Theatregebäude*), with the garden around it, located just outside the barbed wire fence of Auschwitz I, is part of the camp. According to the law within which the Auschwitz Museum operates, the building and the garden DO NOT belong to the museum. They were property of the town (Oświęcim).

**1984 - 1992:**

The abandoned "theater building" was given to the Carmelite nuns who had asked for it for years. In response to Jewish protests, some of the nuns, but not all, moved to a new building specially built half a mile from the camp; a direct intervention of the pope was needed to persuade them to move.

**COMMENT 1:**

The nuns intended to pray in the *Theatregebäude*-turned-convent. They did not understand that it could be offensive. Criticisms suggesting that their intentions were somehow against Jews were offensive to them. For me, this remains true even though I know that some of them held antisemitic views. The atmosphere concerning Auschwitz has been spoiled by this

21

controversy. The Geneva Agreements of 1986-87 were signed, on the Polish side, by Cardinal Macharski, who became quite passive later during the controversy, and Jerzy Turowicz, who is highly respected among intellectuals and liberals, but has limited influence on rank and file Catholics.

## 1989:

On 26 July 1989, during the peak of the Carmelite controversy, a group led by a local priest, Stanisław Gomy, put a large 22 foot cross in the garden of the convent (the theater building). This was done without the consent of Church leaders, who, in point of fact, had not been informed about the action. In 1979 this cross had been a focal point of a mass conducted by Pope John Paul II at Birkenau, after which it was kept in storage for ten years. It is located about 40 yards from the barbed wire. Why was it put there? According to the inscription at the bottom of the cross, it commemorates 150 Polish Christians murdered there in 1941.

## COMMENT 2:

It is clear to me that the cross was put there as a step in the religious war over the convent. Normally much smaller crosses are put in places of executions.

On the other hand, almost nobody in Poland understands why Jews are offended by a cross. The sympathetic ones say that if it is so offensive to Jews, it should be removed as a gesture of good will. To others this argument actually confirms the idea that only Jewish sensitivities are taken into account and that Polish-Catholic sensitivities are ignored. The cross does bother me because it dominates the space there, NOT because I see Auschwitz as an exclusively Jewish site. It is also worth stressing that in Communist Poland placing crosses or building whole chapels secretly, with no permission, was a standard way of proceeding. Popular support was so strong that usually the authorities did not dare to demolish the illegally placed religious symbols. For most Poles, in the matter of religion, the policy of *"faits accomplis"* may still seem natural, and the association of the struggle for crosses against an anti-religious government comes automatically. This is why the possibilities of action by the president or government officials are limited.

## 1992-1998:

On the last day that the Carmelite nuns lived in the "theater building," their prioress signed a rental agreement with an obscure nationalistic, antisemitic "Association of Poles - Victims of World War II." The lease was for 30 years. The organization later sublet it to the Maja company that wanted to build a supermarket nearby. (This is the subject of another controversy, completely mistaken according to my understanding.) The Carmelites had legal rights to the place, so they could sign the agreement. Very soon, however, the town authorities sued the Carmelites, arguing that the nuns had gotten the place for their own use only, and not in order to sublet it. The trial lasted until March 1998 when the nuns agreed to transfer their rights to the "theater building" to the Polish state in exchange for reimbursement of the money they had spent for the renovation of the building. The new convent, as well as the Dialogue center that stands together with it, was built with Church money. Yet we are told that the lease is valid until it is legally broken. For some time the building has been empty.

## FEBRUARY 1998:

The controversy over the large cross has been raging in Poland since February 1998, when an interview was given to the French Catholic paper, *La Croix*, by Ambassador Krzysztof Śliwiński, the Foreign Minister plenipotentiary for contacts with the Jewish Diaspora (as distinct from the state of Israel). Based on the knowledge that the building and garden would finally be re-appropriated by the town of Oświęcim, Śliwiński said that the cross would be relocated – according to the previous agreements.

## COMMENT 3:

He was right; a quiet process leading up to the relocation of the cross was under way. Yet, it is a pity that it was the Ambassador, rather than a bishop, who announced it. Ambassador Śliwiński was right in many ways. I spoke with Bishop Tadeusz Rakoczy in 1994 and it was obvious to him that the cross would be relocated in the wake of the controversy. The understanding was that the cross belonged to the convent and not to the museum. The same understanding was expressed to me in private by another bishop of a higher rank. Further, a monument bearing the symbol of a cross as well as an inscription commemorating the mass execution was to be erected at the new location. It is not clear to me when the idea was first raised, but there were some responsible figures in the Vatican who wanted the relocation.

No plan of this kind, however, was presented or explained to the Polish public.

## MARCH 1998:

The reaction to the news that the cross would be removed has been exceptionally strong: articles; meetings; intensification of the guards at the cross by local defenders; committees have been formed; 130 parliamentarians signed an appeal to defend the cross; Lech Wałęsa made an announcement in defense of the cross. Local politicians plan to use this theme during the electoral campaign for the approaching elections. Some Catholics were expressing the fear that Jews, if successful, would also require the removal of crosses from other places. Various paranoid figures have become active, and very few Poles dare to counter the wave of defense of the cross, understood as a defense of the sign of the cross. (I always stress the difference between reference to the cross in general and this particular cross in my interviews, but how many accept this? Rabbi Menachem Joskowicz has expressed an opposite opinion - see below). Early in March Bishop Pieronek said that Śliwiński had expressed his own opinion without consulting either Bishop Rakoczy or the Vatican. Among others who criticized Śliwiński was Rev. Prof. Waldemar Chrostowski from the Episcopate Commission for Interreligious Dialogue; he demanded Śliwiński's dismissal.

## COMMENT 4:

This criticism of Śliwiński's remark was misleading. As mentioned above, Bishop Rakoczy did prepare for the relocation. What Śliwiński said was true. It was not, however, diplomatic and, indeed, has proved damaging. How damaging? Some people seem to believe that if not for Śliwiński's remark, things would have been resolved smoothly. This is not my understanding of the situation; probably the protests would have arisen anyway. It is not right to compare the case of this cross with the crosses and stars of David placed in the field of ashes at Birkenau, and finally removed quietly in December 1997 after secret negotiations. The differences are as follows: (a) the cross is in a busy place with heavy traffic, while the field of ashes is located in a place where almost no one goes; (b) the field of ashes was under the sole jurisdiction of the Museum, so the Minister of Culture had decision-making authority, while the legal status of the area where the cross stands is complicated, and certainly only the bishop could dare to remove the "papal cross;" (c) the committee defending the cross has been active for a long time, while no active group has been directly connected to the other crosses and stars of David; (d) the bishop would never take the cross away suddenly, during the night, let alone physically threaten "the guardians." A publicly achieved consensus would have been needed; most probably quiet diplomacy could not have sufficed. Incidentally, despite its success, the handling of the crosses and stars of David has provoked criticism from the members of the Auschwitz International Committee who were not involved. Rev. Chrostowski has been critical of the move, asserting the right of Christians to erect crosses at the camp as this is the Christian way to honor the dead. His general message is: "let us defend the cross and Star of David" — Auschwitz is a proper place for both. He accuses secular Jews, similarly to Communists, of wanting to ban religion from the camp. Dr. Jonathan Webber has expressed a similar point. In an interview for a Polish newspaper he said that the religious dimension must be present at Auschwitz. That is why he was against the removal of religious symbols. I happen to agree with him concerning the need for the presence of the religious dimension(s). The problem is how to accommodate this presence. It is clearly not possible to accept every sign erected, even if it is done so with pure intentions. What is needed is a general, widely accepted policy establishing what, how, and where a religious symbol can be put. Perhaps the easiest compromise would be to have no symbols at all, but this is a pity and would be a concession due to the variety and complexity of expectations, not an ideal in itself. Various ideas on the possible ways of erecting signs at the camp exist. I believe that it would be good to have a closed space at Auschwitz, such as inside a building, so that each person would have to decide whether to enter it or not, and yet, every person would have the right to add their plaques and religious signs. People deserve it. Also, I have proposed an idea, which has never been well received, that we prepare a field within the camp (or outside of it but directly connected to it) for the purpose of commemorating each victim and place stones with religious symbols — symbolic gravestones, one for each victim. This would amount to over a million stars of David and over a hundred thousand crosses, etc.

## MARCH 1998, CONTINUED:

In a move against the current, Bishop Gadecki, head of the Episcopate's Commission for Religious Dialogue, invoked an earlier idea and proposed replacing the cross with a monument bearing the sign of a cross. On March 22, Cardinal Glemp said in a homily that he and the Polish people liked the cross, be it in Gdańsk, Warsaw or Oświęcim. He said that "the cross should stay" and thereby disavowed Gadecki. Bishop Rakoczy, the only person besides the Pope who can decide the fate of the cross, is reportedly frightened to do anything now. He claims to understand the feelings of all sides and has not made any decision yet.

## COMMENTS:

Polish Jews have felt that they have been waging a war in which they seemed to fight Catholic symbols. Hearing that, for example, a group of several hundred persons from Oświęcim wrote that the attempt to remove the meant a fight "against their dignity and their faith," irritated some of the Polish Jews and frightened many others. Even those Jews who were bothered by the cross felt that the fight against it had already brought more harm than could be gained by its relocation.

## LAST WEEK:

A statement of the Union of Jewish Religious Communities had been planned for some time as the atmosphere had become unbearable. It became especially urgent after newspaper articles reported the inflammatory statement by Rabbi Menachem Joskowicz of Warsaw, who is an Israeli citizen as well as an ultra-Orthodox survivor of Auschwitz. In a radio interview on March 25 he said: "(I don't) care what Glemp says," the cross must be removed "because we Jews cannot pray where there is a cross, as we can't pray in the presence of idols." He also said that Auschwitz is the holiest ground for which the crematorium chimney is the best symbol. To all, his words sounded as if he was fighting a religious war. The Jewish statement was released on March 27, the same day a conciliatory statement was made by the Council on Relations with Jews of the Episcopate's Commission for Religious Dialogue, following a meeting of Jews and Catholics in the Vatican. The coincidence was very fortunate (and, let me add, not quite coincidental). All of the statements were quoted in the March 28-29 weekend editions of newspapers. *Gazeta Wyborcza* published the whole Jewish statement and expressed the hope that the two official voices might show the beginning of the end of the conflict. The Catholic-Jewish voice from the Vatican maintained that "common, persistent work" is needed to find the proper place and form for the relocation of the cross. The Catholic statement expressed "the understanding for the sensibilities of Jews" and the hope that through a brotherly conversation a solution would be found.

## THE POLISH-JEWISH STATEMENT:

"It is painful and sad" that noisy conflicts appear in such a place; Awe respect all the victims" and we know well that Auschwitz is not only the symbol of the *Shoah* but also of the Polish suffering under German occupation. Polish Jews understand how important the symbol of the cross is for Christians. We are not the ones who will decide the fate of the large cross at Auschwitz. We believe, however, that the last Vatican document states that the *Shoah* is of special relevance to the Church. This means that Auschwitz, the symbol of the *Shoah*, should be treated as a special place, requiring a special policy. While it is not possible to satisfy everyone, the compromise of "no religious symbols" seems to respect the largest possible number of victims and their families. It is conceivable, though, that other solutions are possible. Whatever is decided, it is difficult to neutralize the evil that has been done by extremists. What we need is a coalition of reason and good will in order to eliminate the conflict over the ashes of the martyrs.

## FINAL COMMENT:

I am afraid that during the March of the Living there will be some Jewish protests, acts of defense, or provoked incidents that may lead to a disaster. In general, the noisy conflict is completely inappropriate in the camps. To me, it feels sacrilegious. We all bear the responsibility not to let Hitler triumph.

Can we devise a policy so that we can have a clear position with respect to the remark from an article by Rev. Chrostowski? "It is a public secret that even if this cross is relocated, other similar demands will follow."  I hope that this paper will be helpful.

# THE TRUTH ABOUT THE OŚWIĘCIM CROSS

## FATHER STANISŁAW MUSIAŁ

### OPINIONS FROM
### *GAZETA WYBORCZA,* 22 APRIL 1998

The cross at the Oświęcim camp was put up in 1989 at the gravel pit, close to the building of the so-called Old Theater. In the first phase of the existence of the Oświęcim camp most of the people executed here were Poles, but some were Jews who were Polish citizens. This was the so-called Polish phase of the camp. Later, in 1942, the death factory proper was activated in nearby Brzeżinka, primarily for killing Jews. For forty-four years after the end of the war, the gravel pit area was empty and overgrown with grass.

Who initiated the erecting of the cross? Was it the Church authorities or, more specifically, the Cracow Metropolitan, Father Cardinal Franciszek Machavski, who had jurisdiction over Oświęcim at that time? No. The management of the Oświęcim Museum? No. The organization of former Oświęcim inmates? Again no. Combatant organizations or other social organizations? Again no.

At least, was the Cracow metropolitan asked to give Church approval for erecting a cross in this place? He was not. At least, was there consultation with the museum authorities and social organizations who had some say in these matters? No one asked for their opinions.

Finally, after the cross was erected, was there a ceremony inaugurating the new "monument to memory" with the participation of the clergy, museum officials, representatives of interested organizations, representatives of town officials and the faithful? There was neither a celebration nor a ceremony.

The cross was set up "on the quiet," not in daytime, in a great hurry, by the classical conspiratorial and partisan method. Public opinion was presented with an accomplished fact.

# THE CROSS AT THE GRAVEL PIT AT THE OŚWIĘCIM CAMP

## DO WE CHRISTIANS NEED A CROSS AT THE OŚWIĘCIM CAMP OTHER THAN THE CROSS IN THE DEATH CELL OF FATHER KOLBE?

### ASKS
### FATHER STANISŁAW MUSIAŁ

---

Why was the cross erected at the gravel pit? Some might think that the main reason was honoring the memory of the people murdered here. But if this was the aim of the initiators of the enterprise, why did they not consult the organizations that cultivate the memory of the victims? Why was thought given just to Poles and not to Jews as well?

Some might think that the cross was erected to celebrate Christ, who, according to us Christians, is present in a special way in every suffering person. If so, why were the Church authorities, the only authorities who can say in a binding way whether or not God is pleased by such an initiative or not, ignored?

The names of the people who, on their own initiative, decided to erect a cross at the gravel pit at the Oświęcim camp are known – above all, in the local Church milieu. It is not my task to mention them here. What I *will* say is that the people involved belong to the so-called defenders of the cloister of the Carmelite sisters who made various efforts to prevent the move of the Sisters to the new cloister that was to be set up some 500 meters from the Old Theater formerly occupied by the Sisters. The move was decided upon by the Catholic and Jewish sides at a meeting in Geneva in the Spring of 1987.

Since I was a participant in the meeting, I want to challenge some incorrect opinions about it. In Geneva in 1987 there were neither victors nor vanquished. The Jewish side accepted the existence of the cloister of the Carmelite sisters in the immediate vicinity of the camp (albeit outside the reserved zone) as well as the creation of a Dialogue Center in the immediate vicinity of the cloister (according to the Catholic side, Carmel was to be the "spiritual lung" of the Center). The Catholic side agreed to

31

the Sisters moving to the new cloister. These decisions were difficult for both sides. Coming at the close of this millennium, the Geneva agreement was a rare instance of the triumph of reasonableness, tolerance, and dialogue involving seemingly unsolvable matters; such apparent unsolvability often occurs when dealing with a "collision" of symbols as well as of religious and spiritual values.

Those who initiated and realized the erecting of the cross at the gravel pit at the Oświęcim camp wanted to give this piece of land and the adjoining cloister the status of sacred immunity. During the years of communist rule, this method was used to protect Church properties. On the whole, the communists respected places so "designated," sometimes out of respect for the religious convictions of believers and sometimes even out of a superstitious fear inspired by the sacrum. But, for the most part, they did it for the sake of peace.

Where did the cross come from? The cross now at the gravel pit is the one from the Eucharist the Holy Father, John Paul II, conducted at the Brzeżinka camp during his first pilgrimage to the country in 1979. The monumental nature of the cross was justified by the demands of the moment. Untold numbers of people flocked to the ceremony at Brzeżinka and the cross was the only orientation point that enabled the participants to localize the altar and the presence of the Holy Father. Of course, the cross as "content" provided the best "commentary" for the place and the liturgical celebration. After the ceremony, it was removed and deposited in one of the Oświęcim parishes.

In some publications the cross is referred to as the "papal cross." This is an incorrect definition. One could speak of the papal cross if the Holy Father had specially consecrated it and designated it to be erected at the gravel pit (note that the text says "designated it for the gravel pit," which sounds a bit funny). But this was not the case. One should also correct the misleading information in the press which states that the Holy Father said holy Mass at the cross at the gravel pit. John Paul II never said holy Mass at the gravel pit.

For many weeks there has been a proliferation of initiatives to defend the Oświęcim cross. One must categorically condemn all manifestations of hatred, intolerance, and antisemitism which surface on such occasions. But one must also try to understand the protesters. They mean well. They are absolutely convinced that they are defending the cross against profanation as well as protecting the memory of the murdered people. They protest not out of fanaticism, but out of a sense of threat aimed at what must be most precious for them and for all believers: the love of Christ and the respect for dear ones whose lives were taken in a brutal manner.

These protests are based on ignorance and on unfamiliarity with realities. Thus, the problem of the Oświęcim cross is not the problem of the protesters. It is the problem of all those who should enlighten the protesters and fail to do so. There are three categories of these people.

The first category is people who do not know a great deal about the Oświęcim cross. They are poorly informed but express their opinions. They speak in lofty strains involving theology and fatherland, fidelity to Christ, patriotism, and respect for victims. They move the noblest responses in the souls of the faithful but also call forth demons in the hearts of some of them.

The second category is people who know the full truth about the cross but distort it. They know but disinform. It is not for me to decide whether they do this consciously or unwittingly. If they do this consciously, then they should be reminded of the words of Christ about "corrupting simple people".

Finally, there is the third category of people who know everything but keep silent. They do not react, and defend themselves by using the argument that it is none of their business. They are wrong, for protests come from all of Poland and not only from some of its territories. People in the last two categories must be faulted for failure to assist people in need. In this case, help would consist in enlightening minds by telling the truth about the Oświęcim cross and in molding consciences by proper moral and theological information.

Transfer of the cross from the gravel pit to another worthy place – in this case to the church area next to the new Carmel – would most definitely not be a profanation of this religious symbol or lack of respect for Christ. During the pilgrimage to Poland, the Holy Father conducted the Eucharist at many crosses. None of them remained in the original place. Some were moved and others were taken apart. And no one spoke of profanation of the cross.

It is thus clear that the cross erected at the cloister should accompany the cloister in its new location.

Transfer of the cross would not mean that the gravel pit would again be covered by a heavy layer of oblivion similar to that of the years 1945-1989. All agree that the martyrdom of the people murdered here should be suitably commemorated. The particular form of this commemoration should be decided upon in consultation with all sides, including the Jews. If even a single Jew was murdered here, the Jews must not be left out of such consultation.

In principle, the Jewish reservation about the present form of commemoration of the place of martyrdom is not so much the cross (which they accept), but its monumentality. There were ironic references to this topic in the press. The irony was quite improper. The cross is visible from inside the camp, from in front of the death block. And this can really disturb the peace of mind of Jews who visit the camp. One need not be a psychologist to understand the feelings of others. It is enough to be kindhearted.

Will the escalation of Catholic protests keep on growing and will the suffering of the Jews last forever? At this moment, at this stage of the dispute, the only thing that can solve the present Oświęcim problem, which divides some Catholics in Poland and the Jews, is a small room at the Oświęcim camp: the death cell of Father Kolbe (to us, Catholics, St. Maximilian).

Do we Christians, and with us — I dare humbly say — people of good will, need a different monument at the Oświęcim camp? Those who have need of material religious symbols will find plenty of them in Father Kolbe's cell (block X, the so-called death block). Father Kolbe's cell points the way for all of us. It tells us to build a world without death cells, without hatred, in the spirit of love and dialogue, in the spirit of humility, in the face of the prodigious task of interpretation of the world (here all must be humble: the believers and the nonbelievers), in the face of suffering that oppresses mankind, and of the oft rampant evil. Let us leave aside arguments about monuments. For at least 150 years after Christ's death the first Christians had no crosses, no holy pictures, no temples, gravestones, or monuments. The one thing they knew was that they were new creatures in Christ, and this was enough for them to love God and fellow men.

Christianity has no need of monuments. They are pagan by nature. They serve to shock, depress, and humiliate others. Christ did not, and does not, have a liking for "monumentalities." He was born in a stable and died the death of Roman slaves on a wooden cross. Do we, Christians, want to be better than our Master?

# CROSSES IN AUSCHWITZ: CRISIS AND TURNING

## JACOB NEUSNER

## I. COMPETING FOR THE SAME LAND

The competition between Poles and Jews for the possession of Poland does not begin in Auschwitz. Each people laid claim to the same territory and look upon the other as outsider and other.

For the Jews Poland is a vale of tears. Whatever Jewish Poland was, was. Abraham Heschel told me that when in the mid-1930s he would take a train from Warsaw to Berlin, crossing the German border brought a sigh of relief — he was out of Poland. And that was en route to Nazi Germany. The installation of a forest of crosses at Auschwitz carries forward a long tradition of brutal hostility on the part of an indeterminate, but clearly sizable, sector of Polish Catholicism against the Jews and Judaism.

But Poles bear their grievances as well. They look back upon centuries of co-existence with Jews, among other groups on all sides, who spoke their own languages, pursued their own callings, conducted their own cultural and educational life, in complete isolation from the Poles. Jews and Poles, Ukrainians and Poles, Lithuanians and Poles, Belorussians and Poles – all found themselves in competition for the same land. To take a small instance of the isolation from Polish Poland that Jews took for granted, Heschel's knowledge of Polish was limited. So when he was submitting his doctoral dissertation for publication by the Polish Academy, he had to study Polish in order to go through the required procedures in the language of the country whose passport he carried.

## II. THE PRESENT CRISIS

Poland now sustains antisemitism without Jews, having driven out the last sizable Jewish population three decades ago. All that is left, apart from a trivial population, is the holy places of the Jews' martyrdom. For two generations now, we have tried to convey to the Polish custodians of humanity's memory what difference the dignified, austere preservation of the place makes to us. But just as, when three million Jews formed ten per cent of the Polish population, Catholic Poland humiliated Jewish Poland, which responded in its way as well, so today, with scarcely a Jewish Poland left to torment, Catholic Poland plants its crosses on Jewish graves. Few Jews are left alive, on the spot, to respond.

The truth is, no one knows, any longer, how to respond, or can tell what may make a difference. No act of fraternity, no gesture of comity serves to conciliate. A while back Rabbi Weiss climbed the wall of the convent; Professor Dershowitz prepared to sue Cardinal Glemp. I took a different path, one of trying to open a dialogue through Vatican sources. Whether the road they took led to the destination they sought to reach, I cannot say. Mine did not lead anywhere.

The cross stands to humiliate, to express hatred, to serve God by acts of hatred and contempt. After half a generation of negotiation and vigorous efforts to maintain Auschwitz as a place accessible to faithful Israel too, Catholic Poland reserves for itself and its sensibility what belongs to many peoples and faiths, to all who died there, starting with us.

That is one face of Christianity, and not in Poland alone. But Christianity has many faces, and if Roman Catholic Poland shows the world an ugly face of spiteful hatred and spit, Roman Catholic New York and Boston and Chicago and Baltimore show another, nicer face. It is for Catholics themselves to determine the face they will show to the rest of the world. It is for them to explain to themselves why they want to undertake religious dialogue with others, including us: what is God's stake in all this?

Catholic Christianity and Judaism know one another well. We have lived side by side for two thousand years. From Vatican II, much has happened. Have times changed? No Pope, not even John XXIII, has so reached out to the Jewish people and to Judaism, as has John Paul II. And none has received a more trusting response. But in the end, in his powerful and profound work, *Threshold of Hope,* the Pope—certainly a principal religious intellectual of our day—could find no way of affirming the revelation of God to Moses at Sinai except as a promise of what was fulfilled in Christ. He has no Catholic theology of Judaism that Judaism can comprehend. So it is hardly surprising that even Pope John Paul's choice of the saint to form the bridge between the Jewish People and the Catholic faith in the aftermath of the Shoah is none other than a Jewish apostate, who derided and dismissed the Torah that is Judaism. And if after a pontificate devoted to realizing the promise of *Nostra Aetate* ends with Edith Stein, why should the crosses at Auschwitz surprise?

So let them plant their crosses at Auschwitz—especially on Christmas: we know what the crosses stand for, which is the crucifixion of the Jewish People.

## III.   CRISIS AND TURNING

It is clear that no religious dialogue between Judaism and Christianity has yet made a mark on Poland. Political dialogue has progressed, and Israeli-Polish relations exhibit none of the profound animosity that poisons Judaeo-Christian interchange in Poland. Episodic, social relationships prove exemplary; no one imagines that the cross-planters stand for the entire population. But when it comes to the religions, Christianity and Judaism, it is clear people have made remarkably little progress. How do we know whether or not dialogue takes place? Three criteria dictate the answer: (1) each party proposes to take seriously the position of the other; (2) each party concedes the integrity of the other; (3) each party accepts responsibility for the outcome of discussion, that is, remains open to the possibility of conceding the legitimacy of the other's viewpoint. These criteria have only rarely been met in the entire history of Christian theologians' address to Judaism, and Judaism's theologians' address to Christianity. In point of fact, when the representatives of the two religions wrote as though to the other, they turn out to have been speaking to their own communities, respectively, letters written to the outsiders, but sent home in self-addressed, stamped envelopes. Whether or not writers expected the outsider to read and even respond to what was said in the letter, hardly matters; only rarely did theologians write in such a way as to show they knew (or cared) what the outsider would grasp. Judaeo-Christian dialogue (or disputation, the word-choice hardly matters) formed an exercise in inner-facing apologetics.

In this regard, Poland in no way differs from the European norm. On the Judaic side, long centuries of sedulous indifference have left their mark: there is nothing to discuss. On the Christian side, those same centuries have left a burden of frustration and anger. Judaic contributions to dialogue have served only to resist Christianity's insistence that the sole point worth discussing is why the Jews do not convert to Christianity; no Judaic participant in inter-religious dialogue before modern times conceded that Christianity bore a legitimate relationship to God's revealed Torah;

none imagined lending credence to anything the other said. So far as dialogue rests upon shared principles of reason and logic and a mutually accepted corpus of facts, Judaism has only episodically found itself a participant to dialogue. And the same applies to Christianity, to nearly our own day. All Christianity has asked Judaism is, "Why have you not accepted Jesus Christ and so gone out of business?" That Judaism sustained a distinctive covenant with God never, before this time, has entered the mind of Christianity; that Jews sincerely and honestly believe in and practice Judaism lies beyond the imagination of Christianity, which sees Jews as stubborn and perverse; and never did a Christian participant in dialogue suppose that the outcome of debate and discussion might encompass a change in attitude or viewpoint.

In the special case of Poland, a dialogue between the two religious traditions faces special problems. The first is, to be Polish, for Poles, is the same thing as to be Catholic. It has been and is exceedingly difficult for Polish nationalists to find a place in their theory of Poland, in their thinking about "Polishness," for non-Catholics. In this regard, the cross-planters carry forward the attitudes of German nationalism. When the National Socialists came to power, German Christianity found nothing to say to the Jews or to Judaism other than that despite the loathsome character of "the Jewish race," the Jews could still hope to experience the love and grace (and protection) of Christianity, if only they would convert. That no dialogue had ever taken place is best shown, therefore, by the final dialogue that did take place between Judaism and Christianity in Germany, before the destruction of the Jews and Judaism in Germany between 1933 and 1945. On January14, 1933, the eve of the National Socialists' rise of power, Karl Ludwig Schmidt, meeting Martin Buber for the last disputation between German Judaism and German Christianity, extended to Israel the invitation to brotherhood with Christians—"but only as sons of a Germany united through the Christian conception of the Church as the spiritual Israel."

The final voice of Christianity addressed to German, and European Jewry, repeated the first and only message that Christianity ever delivered to Judaism: "God has willed all this; Jesus the Messiah rejected by his people, prophesied the destruction of Jerusalem. Jerusalem has been destroyed, so that it will never again come under Jewish rule." A precursor of the contemporary Christian judgment on Zionism, Schmidt proceeds, "The modern world reacts to Zionism, which is national or even racist." He warns the Jews standing on the brink of destruction: "the Church of Jesus Christ has again and again shown her want of this Jewry, demonstrating her patience by waiting in hope that finally the Jews also...will be able to perceive that only the Church of the Messiah, Jesus of Nazareth, is the people of God, chosen by God, and that the Jews should become incorporated in it, if they indeed feel themselves as Israel." So much for German Christianity, fully aware of the coming triumph of National Socialism in their country. For his part, Martin Buber answered in these words:

> "I live not far from the city of Worms, to which I am bound by tradition of my forefathers; and from time to time I go there, when I go, I first go to the cathedral. It is a visible harmony of members, a totality in which no part deviates from perfection. I walk about the cathedral with consummate joy, gazing at it. Then I go over to the Jewish cemetery, consisting of crooked, cracked, shapeless, random stones. I station myself there, gaze upward from the jumble of a cemetery to that glorious harmony, and seem to be looking up from Israel to the Church. Below, there is no jot of form; there are only the stones and the dust lying beneath the stones. The dust is there, no matter how thinly scattered. There lies the corporeality of man, which has turned to this. There is. There it is for me. There it is for me, not as corporeality within the space of this planet, but as corporeality in my own memory, far into the depths of history, as far back as Sinai...."
>
> "I have stood there and have experienced everything myself; with all this death has confronted me, all the dust, all the ruin, all the world's misery is mine; but the covenant has not been withdrawn from me. I lie on the ground, like these stones. But it has not been withdrawn from me. The cathedral is as it is; the cemetery is as it is. But nothing has been withdrawn from us."

No reasonable person, however sympathetic with Buber's situation, can find in these remarks a serious address to Christianity; all Buber finds to say is that, it is true, Christianity owns the world, but we are what we are: "nothing has been withdrawn from us." A dialogue should have required an address to the proposition, evidence, and argument of the other.

No wonder that, at the end, Karl Ludwig Schmidt found no moral resources whatsoever upon which to draw a message appropriate to an ancient partner in argument. Even after World War II, when what Germany had done to the Jews was well known, German Christian theologians announced to the Jews that the murder of European Jewry constituted

God's punishment of the Jews for not accepting Christ. That response, seen by many as despicable, represented the perfectly reasonable conclusion for the Christian party to the dialogue to draw. For, through time, the Judaeo-Christian dialogue provided Christians with the opportunity to express to Jews their loathing of Judaism and their contempt for Jews; the Jewish partner then found ready access to the high road. The partners to dialogue passed in the dark, going each in his own direction, scarcely aware of the other's presence, except in fantasy: a Jew who would find persuasive arguments in favor of Christianity in a parade of racist bigotry, a Christian who would find compelling a Judaic response framed in terms of God's mystery. So degraded a Jew, so disingenuous a Christian, never lived.

I myself heard the German theologian, Wolfhart Pannenberg, at a Judaeo-Christian dialogue at Harvard Divinity School in 1966, deliver precisely the same message that Rosenzweig heard from Rosenstock-Huessy, and that Buber heard from Karl Ludwig Schmidt. The only question worth discussing, he maintained, is why Jews continue not to accept Jesus Christ, this under the auspices of the Harvard Divinity School and the American Jewish Committee. The death of nearly six million Jews had made no difference; what Schmidt said at the outset of the National Socialist period, Pannenberg said at the end. Nor is this only memory; he wrote the same: "With the message of the resurrection...the foundations of the Jewish religion collapsed."

Some dialogue! It was not even a disputation. Christian aggression, Judaic dissimulation – nothing more. Not only has there been no dialogue, there has not been even a moment of reflection on the requirements of dialogue, beginning, after all, with the condescension of courtesy—the condition of discourse, let along dialogue, if anyone really wants to talk. What we shall now see is that neither Judaic nor Christian parties to dialogue have had any such intention. For each, dialogue provided the occasion of a monologue in affirmation of the faith. That is what I mean by "conspiracy of hypocrites," the hypocrisy being the pretense that one wished to conduct dialogue, the conspiracy being the agreement to pretend at stake were matters of concern to the other party at all. Then what was at stake? The only open question is why either party should have taken the trouble to pretend to wish to talk with the other. Dialogue turns out to have served the quite autonomous requirements of theological apologetics.

## IV.    THE PARTICULAR OPPORTUNITY OF THE HOUR

There was a time at which people interested in Judaeo-Christian dialogue would have dismissed Poland as impossible. No one imagined that in Catholic Christianity in Poland could be found Christian participants. But the advent of John Paul II has shown otherwise. The Polish Pope also has made himself the Pope more devoted than any other Pope in 2,000 years to dialogue with the Jewish People and with Judaism, more responsive to the memory of the Holocaust, more committed to honoring and respecting Jewish sensibilities and Judaic convictions. Not only so, but in the Polish hierarchy are archbishops and bishops who carry forward in the very heart and soul of Polish Christianity John Paul's convictions concerning the unique tasks of Judaeo-Christian dialogue. So the crisis of the crosses at Auschwitz represents an opportunity for a turning as well. And, I propose, the particular situation of Polish Christianity, embodied in Pope John Paul II and in much of the Polish hierarchy today, presents a particularly promising occasion for Judaeo-Christian dialogue: the interchange between faiths, not merely private persons of good will, about matters of deep concern to the respective faiths.

## V.    THE POSSIBILITIES OF DIALOGUE

Let me propose, for Christianity in general, and for Judaism wherever the faith thrives, a program of dialogue.

Since Judaism and Christianity form quite different religions with little in common, it is time for each religion to try to make sense of the other — but to make sense of the stranger wholly in one's own terms. Can I, as a Jew and a believer in Judaism, understand in my context, in my terms of faith, the religion of the Christian? Can I frame a Judaic religious understanding of the religion of Christianity? What it means to understand another religion demands a definition. Up to now, I already have noted some rather unsuccessful efforts as theologies, each of the other, have shown us what not to attempt: a Christian theology of Judaism proves, if not condescending, then unchristian, conceding more than Christianity has ever conceded in the past, and a Judaic theology of Christianity gives no less — and no more authentically. Judaism cannot concede that Jesus Christ is what the Christians say, and any other judgment upon Jesus Christ is simply beside the point. Christianity may concede that we retain our covenanted relationship with God, but it cannot then admit that converts to Judaism have taken the right route to salvation. So all that Christianity concedes is that Judaism is all right for the Jews, a concession to be sure, but not of vast consequence. But if not a theological understanding of one another, then what other understanding can we seek?

My answer commences with a necessary recognition: the commonplace fact that, after all, we really do worship one God, who is the same God, and who is the only God, we and the Muslims with us. So dialogue is required among the three faiths that claim to worship one and the same God, the only God. Within that common ground of being, a human task before us emerges. It is to seek in the religious experience of the other, the stranger and outsider, that with which we, within our own world, can identify. That is to say, I cannot ask the Christian to deny Jesus Christ as Incarnate God, and I also cannot ask myself to believe that Jesus Christ was and is God Incarnate. But I must try to understand the incarnation of God: precisely what is the other side saying? If I am able to locate, in my religious resources, something that will help me to grasp what, within the other's religious resources, the other party is saying, then the other, while remaining other and different, no longer stands beyond the range of understanding. To begin with, can I sympathize, that is, feel how the other feels, the other remaining other? The answer is, yes I can, if I find in my own world analogies that permit me in some measure to feel and so understand what the other feels and affirms in the world of that other. So the critical challenge as the two extraordinarily complex and diverse religions seek to communicate begins with not the negotiation of theological difference, with its intellectual tasks, but with the pathos of alien feeling: can I, in my life, feel what the other feels in the other's life?

In simple words, when I say, "Yes, my heart goes out to you," then I begin to be able to enter into the realm of feeling, thence attitude, thence even thought, of that "you." But so long as I do now know how the other feels, I will listen in sheer incredulity to the attitudes, and various religions, different theologies, joy or sorrow or love or hope or despair – with these feelings, and the experiences that provoke them, God has endowed us all. When, therefore, I know how the other feels, because I have felt the same way, then I may talk with the other, even, about other things.

What moves me, as distinct from what persuades me, is the story the other person tells. Then I can identify with someone in the story, or the storyteller; then, in the present context, I can find among my stories a story that matches the story of the other. To take a homely example, when I read, particularly in the Gospel of John, how Jesus tries to prepare his disciples for the lives that they are going to lead, how he warns them but also strengthens them, I found it easy, as a person who has undertaken to educate young people to change the world, to identify with Jesus, his message, his disciples, and their situation. Here was no doctrine, only an implicit story, and how readily did that story make sense to me, not because it was my story (I never sent out my students as apostles), but because in my story I could find resonance in his story: the pain, the anguish. Why the medium of a story, my story, to help me understand a story, the other's story? First, because stories touch the heart; they are immediate, direct, unmediated. Second, because stories that touch the heart elicit sympathy; I can feel for the other, reach out beyond myself.

This brings me to the search for a story, out of the canon of Judaism, that permits me to grasp, within Judaism, what the other means by God incarnate. A subdivision of anthropomorphism, the incarnation of God in general entails the representation of God as consubstantial with the human person in, first, corporeal form, second, traits of emotions and other virtues, and, third, action. God is represented in incarnate form when God looks like a human being (ordinarily, in the case of Judaism, a man), exhibits virtues and expresses emotions like those of mortals, and does concrete deeds in a corporeal manner, pretty much as do human beings. The representation of God incarnate will not have surprised the authors of a variety of Judaic documents, beginning with the compilers of the Pentateuch, beginning with Gen. 1:9: "let us make man in our image and likeness." Some speaking explicitly, others in subtle allusions, prophets and apocalyptic writers, exegetes and sages, mystics and legists, all maintained that notion.

Here is how Gen. 1:9 is read so as to give explicit notion to the conception of the incarnation of God:

1. A.   Said R. Hoshaiah, "When the Holy One, blessed be he, came to create the first man, the ministering angels mistook him (for God, since man was in God's image,) and wanted to say before him, 'Holy, (holy, holy is the Lord of hosts).'

   B.   "To what may the matter be compared? To the case of a king and a governor who were set in a chariot, and the provincials wanted to greet the king, 'Sovereign!' But they did not know which one of them was which. What did the king do? He turned the governor out and put him

away from the chariot, so that people would know who
was king.

C.   "So too when the Holy One, blessed be he, created the
first man, the angels mistook him (for God). What did
the Holy One, blessed be he, do? He put him to sleep, so
everyone knew that he was a mere man.

D.   "That is in line with the following verse of Scripture:
'Cease you from man, in whose nostrils is a breath, for
how little is he to be accounted' (Is. 2:22).'"

                                        Genesis Rabbah VIII: X.

In light of this reading of Gen. 1:9, we may hardly find surprising
the power of diverse heirs of Scripture, framers of various Judaic religious
systems, to present portraits of the incarnation of God, corporeal, in affects
and virtues consubstantial with humanity, doing things human beings do in
the ways in which they do them.

As a matter of fact, in the final stage in the formation of the canon
of the Judaism of the dual Torah, the incarnation of God forms a principal
aspect of the character of divinity. Prior to that time, the character of
divinity extended to portraits of God as (1) premise, e.g., the one who
created the world and gave the Torah; (2) presence, e.g., supernatural being
resident in the Temple and present where two or more persons engaged in
discourse concerning the Torah; and (3) person, e.g., the one to whom
prayer is addressed. But at the end we find important allusions to the
incarnation of God as well as narratives that realize in concrete terms the
incarnation of God. What is important to us is that when God is incarnate
for Judaism, it is through stories about what God is and does that
knowledge of God reaches us. When I pointed to sharing our stories with
one another as a means of gaining sympathy for what is alien about one
another, I had in mind Talmudic stories about the incarnate God. These we
tell ourselves. When we hear Christians' stories, we hear different stories,
but can respond to our stories in ways that accord with their response to
their stories: a different kind of dialogue, but one that I think is plausible.
How then is the Incarnate God represented by the oral Torah? This story
treats the incarnation of God:

A.   Said R. Judah said Rab, "When Moses went up to the
height, he found the Holy One, blessed be he, sitting and
typing crowns to the letters (of the Torah).

B.     "He said to him, 'Lord of the universe, why is this necessary?'

C.     "He said to him, 'There is a certain man who is going to come into being at the end of some generations, by the name of Aqiba b. Joseph. He is going to find expositions to attach mounds and mounds of laws to each point (of a crown).'

D.     "He said to him, 'Lord of the universe, show him to me.'

E.     "He said to him, 'Turn around.'

F.     "(Moses) went and took his seat at the end of eight rows, but he could not understand what the people were saying. He felt weak. When discourse came to a certain matter, one of (Aqiba's) disciples said to him, 'My lord, how do you know this?'

G.     "He said to him, 'It is a law revealed by God to Moses at Mount Sinai.'

H.     "Moses' spirits were restored.

I.     "He turned back and returned to the Holy One, blessed be he. He said to him, 'Lord of the universe, now if you have such a man available, how can you give the Torah through me?'

J.     "He said to him, 'Be silent. That is how I have decided matters.'

K.     "He said to him, 'Lord of the universe, you have now shown me his mastery of the Torah. Now show me his reward.'

L.     "He said to him, 'Turn around."

M.     "He turned around and saw people weighing out his flesh in the butcher-shop.

N.     "He said to him, 'Lord of the universe, such is his mastery of Torah, and such is his reward?'

O.     "He said to him, 'Be silent. That is how I have decided matters.'"

B.    Men. 29b

The story is open-ended: Be silent. That is how I have decided matters. That statement hardly marks a happy ending, and it assuredly does not answer the question with which the passage commences. The story merely restates the question in a more profound way. In this story the sage is like God, but, like all other human beings, subject to God's ultimate decree. This I take to be the final statement of the incarnation of God of the Judaism of the dual Torah. God incarnate remains God ineffable. When the Judaism of the dual Torah wishes to portray the character of divinity, it invokes in the end the matter of relationship and not tactile quality and character. If we wish to know God, it is through our relationship to God, not through our (entirely legitimate and welcome) act of the incarnation of God in heart and mind and soul, deliberation and deed. And the way to engage with, relate to, God, in the face of (in the suggestive instance at hand) the Torah and torture of Aqiba, is silence.

## VI.    THE COUNTERPARTS: ISRAEL AND CHRIST
## ISRAEL AT AUSCHWITZ, CHRIST ON THE CROSS

So, for the faithful Jew, is the conception of God incarnate beyond all reason? ridiculous? absurd? Not at all. When I tell my stories, in which I learn how the Torah reveals God, both the stories of the prophets and what God said to them, and the stories of our sages of blessed memory and how they knew God in incarnate form, I can understand how someone else may tell stories about God like us, and about how we can become like God. Can I then listen with sympathy to the Christian story of Jesus Christ God Incarnate? Without doubt: I can listen with sympathy, because Torah teaches me how. Do I have to listen to such stories? If I want to know how to understand my stories better, that is to say, to think deeply about what it means for us to be like God, about what it means for humanity to incarnate God – for "to incarnate" is a transitive verb – then, to open my heart and soul to all the ways people can imagine God incarnate, I do. That is, to know what it means to be human "like God," I do well to listen to the stories other people tell, too, about what it means to be "in our image, after our likeness," as their hearts and minds have told the story to them.

If the Incarnation of God in Jesus Christ is critical to Christianity, then for Judaism, the word "Israel" bears the counterpart position. It is exceedingly difficult for outsiders to grasp, a mark of its importance within. When Christians hear the word "Israel," they think first of the State of Israel, then of the people of Israel in biblical times. Identifying with ancient Israel through the Old Testament, Christians inherit another conception of Israel as well, one that makes a sympathetic response to the State of Israel parlous. It is the notion that the destruction of the Temple and the end of the Jewish state in 70 C.E. punished Israel "after the flesh," and until the Jews today repent and accept Christ, they should have no state. The creation of the State of Israel in 1948, in the aftermath of the murder of the Jews in Christian Europe, called into question a long-held conviction. The

State further formed an embarrassment to Christian Arabs, on the one side, and to Christian missions and institutions in Muslim countries, on the other.

When, therefore, Judaic participants in the Judaeo-Christian dialogue raise the question of Christian hostility to the State of Israel, the Christian partners find very difficult the intrusion of a political question into a religious dialogue; what, after all, can be "religious" about a secular state? And that objection underlines yet another on-going Christian difficulty in making sense of the Jews, which is the Jews' intense sense of "being Jewish," whether or not a professed religious conviction about "being holy Israel" infuses that "being Jewish" with religious content. The fusion of the ethnic, the religious, the cultural, and the political, to the Christian partners presents woeful confusion. But there is no dialogue with Israel, the Jewish people, without a clear, Christian understanding of what, in Judaism, "Israel" stands for, and why, for nearly all Jews, there is no sorting out the religious, ethnic, and cultural categories – not to mention, after all, the genealogical as well. For Jews the given of our existence, "Israel" in all its dimensions, involving the State, the land, the people there and everywhere, stands as an obstacle to dialogue for Christians.

Not a Christian, I am hardly to be expected to explain for Christians, out of the resources of Christianity, the Judaic theory of Israel. What I can attempt is to explain to Christians in Judaic terms what "Israel" stands for, in the hope that Christians may find sympathy for our "Israel" by appeal to three profoundly Christian concepts. These, then, must be specified to begin with. First, comes the theory that from the fall of Adam, humanity arose from the dregs of sin through Christ. In Romans 1-3 Paul explains how no human being escapes the domination of sin. The human condition is defined by the first sin, Adam's and Eve's, so sin is natural to the human condition. Then Paul contrasts the first Adam, source of death, to Christ, the second Adam, source of life:

> For as by a man came death, by a man has come also the resurrection of the dead. For as in Adam all die, so also in Christ, shall all be made alive. But each in his own order: Christ the first fruits, then at his coming those who belong to Christ (1 Cor. 15:21-22).
>
> The first man Adam became a living being, the last Adam became a life-giving spirit (1 Cor. 15:45).
>
> The first man was from the earth, a man of dust; the second man is from heaven; as was the man of dust, so are those who

are of the dust, and as is the man of heaven, so are those who are of heaven. Just as we have borne the image of the man of dust, we shall also bear the image of the man of heaven (1 Cor. 15:49).

In the Judaism of the dual Torah, "Israel" serves precisely in the same way, that is, marking the rise of humanity from the fall of Adam to the pinnacle – of Sinai.

The second and third points come together. On the one side, as Hebrews says in so many words, this atonement for sin was achieved through Christ's suffering. And, on the other side, Christ stands for the suffering servant of Isaiah:

> He was oppressed, and he was afflicted, yet he opened not his mouth; like a lamb that is led to the slaughter, and like a sheep that before its shearers is dumb, so he opened not his mouth.
>
> By oppression and judgment he was taken away; and as for his generation, who considered that he was cut off out of the land of the living, stricken for the transgression of my people (Is. 54:7-8)

Christians will not find Judaism's — and the Jews' — conception of "Israel" so absurd, if, in sympathy, they can understand a simple fact. There is scarcely a Jew in the world who reads these words without understanding, beyond all doubt, that when Isaiah spoke, he told us about the Holocaust.

Do I mean, then, to suggest that Christianity now contemplates substituting "Israel" for "Christ"? Of course not, any more than I should want Judaism to make sense of nonsense and therefore consider Jesus Christ God Incarnate to stand for what God meant when God spoke of us "in our image, after our likeness." Just as I seek in the resources of Judaism to find foundations for sympathy for a profoundly alien conception of the other, so I hope that, out of the resources of Christianity — not merely out of sentimentality or a sense of shame or (misplaced) guilt for the Christian contribution to the murder of Jewry in Christendom — Christians may gain some sense of what they see as the Judaic nonsense about this "Israel."

For, in the theory of "Israel" put forward by Judaism, we shall now see, our "Israel" serves like the Christian Christ – the antidote to Adam:

2. A.  "And they heard the sound of the Lord God walking in the cool of the day" (Gen. 3:8). Said R. Abba bar Kahana, "The word is not written, 'move,' but rather, 'walk,' bearing the sense that (the Presence of God) leapt about and jumped upward.

B.  "(The point is that God's presence leapt upward from the earth on account of the events in the garden, as will now be explained:) The principal location of the Presence of God was (meant to be) among the creatures down here. When the first man sinned, the Presence of God moved up to the first firmament. When Cain sinned, it went up to the second firmament. When the generation of Enosh sinned, it went up to the third firmament. When the generation of the Flood sinned, it went up to the fourth firmament. When the generation of the dispersion (at the tower of Babel) sinned, it went up to the fifth. On account of the Sodomites, it went up to the sixth, and on account of the Egyptians in the time of Abraham, it went up to the seventh.

C.  "But, as a counterpart, there were seven righteous men who rose up: Abraham, Isaac, Jacob, Levi, Kahath, Amram, and Moses. They brought the Presence of God (by stages) down to earth.

D.  "Abraham brought it from the seventh to the sixth, Isaac brought it from the sixth to the fifth, Jacob brought it from the fifth to the fourth, Levi brought it down from the forth to the third, Kahath brought it down from the third to the second, Amram brought it down from the second to the first. Moses brought it down to earth."

Genesis Rabbah to Genesis 3:1-13. XIX:VII.

God left the world with Adam's sin; Abraham, Isaac, Jacob, and onward to Moses at Sinai, brought God back to the world. More to the point, as we shall now see, the life of Israel in the Land of Israel forms a counterpoint and opposite to the life of Adam in the Garden of Eden. Israel is the successor to Adam, what God brought about in opposition to Adam:

3. A.  R. Abbahu in the name of R. Yose bar Haninah: "It is written, 'But they are like a man (Adam), they have transgressed the covenant'" (Hos. 6:7).

B.   "'They are like a man,' specifically, like the first man. (We shall now compare the story of the first man in Eden with the story of Israel in its land.)

C.   "In the case of the first man, I brought him into the Garden of Eden, I commanded him, he violated my commandment, I judged him to be sent away and driven out, but I mourned for him, saying 'How...' (which begins the book of Lamentations, hence stands for a lament, but which, as we just saw, also is written with the consonants that also yield, 'Where are you?')

D.   "'I brought him into the garden of Eden,' as it is written, 'And the Lord God took the man and put him into the Garden of Eden' (Gen. 2:15)."

E.   "I commanded him, as it is written, 'And the Lord God commanded...' (Gen. 2:16).

F.   "'And he violated my commandment,' as it is written, 'Did you eat from the tree concerning which I commanded you?' (Gen. 3:11).

G.   "'I judged him to be sent away,' as it is written, 'And the Lord God sent him from the Garden of Eden' (Gen. 3:23).

H.   "'And I judged him to be driven out.' 'And he drove out the man' (Gen. 3:24).

I.   "But I mourned for him, saying, 'How...' And he said to him, 'Where are you?' (Gen. 3:9), and the word for 'where are you' is written, 'How...'

J.   "'So too in the case of his descendants, (God continues to speak,) I brought them into the Land of Israel, I commanded them, they violated my commandment, I judged them to be sent out and driven away but I mourned for them, saying, "How..."'

K.   "'I brought them into the Land of Israel.' 'And I brought you into the land of Carmel' (Jer. 2:7).

L.   "'I commanded them.' 'And you, command the children of Israel' (Ex. 27:20). 'Command the children of Israel' (Lev. 24:2).

M.   "'They violated my commandment.' 'And all Israel have violated your Torah' (Dan. 9:11).

N.   "'I judged them to be sent out.' 'Send them away, out of my sight and let them go forth' (Jer. 15:1).

O.   "'...and driven away.' 'From my house I shall drive them' (Hos. 9:15).

P.    "'But I mourned for them, saying, "How…" 'How has
the city sat solitary, that was full of people?'(Lam. 1:1)."
Genesis Rabbah to Gen. 3:8 XIX:IX.

I find deeply moving the comparison of the story of man in the Garden of
Eden with the tale of Israel in its Land. Every detail is in place, the
articulation is perfect, and the result completely convinces as an essay in
interpretation. All of this rests on the simple fact that the word for "where
are you" may be expressed as "How…," which, as is clear, invokes the
opening words of the book of Lamentations. What is important to us is the
representation of Israel: Israel's history serves as a paradigm for human
history, and vice versa. Then Israel stands at the center of humanity.
"Israel" forms a theological category, like "Christ," in this context, for Paul.

The scandal to the Jews—God Incarnate indeed—is now joined by
the stumbling block to the other side—Israel? indeed! What is critical to
the one side finds its counterpart in what is critical to the other, and, we
now realize, we have found our way to the heart of the matter of whether
or not dialogue is at all possible; by that, I mean, a dialogue formed by an
exchange of stories.

Now I do not know the story that within Christianity will elicit
sympathy for what "Israel" means to me. The correspondence of
Christianity's Christ, or mystical body of Christ, or Church, to Judaism's
Israel explains why, for so long, Christianity has found incomprehensible
Judaism's understanding of Israel. By claiming that "Israel" constituted
"Israel after the flesh," the actual, living, present family of Abraham and
Sarah, Isaac and Rebecca, Jacob and Leah and Rachel, sages met head-on
the Christian claim that there was – or could ever be – some other "Israel,"
of a lineage not defined by the family connected at all, and that the existing
Jews no longer constituted "Israel." By representing "Israel" as *sui generis*,
sages moreover focused upon the systemic teleology, with its definition of
salvation, in response to the Christian claim that salvation is not of Israel
but of the Church, now enthroned in this world as in heaven. The sage,
model for Israel, in the model of Moses, our rabbi, on earth represented the
Torah that had come from heaven. Like Christ, in earth as in heaven, like
the Church, the body of Christ, ruler of earth (through the emperor) as of
heaven, the sage embodied what Israel was and was to be. So Israel as
family in the model of the sage, like Moses our rabbi, corresponded in its
social definition to the Church of Jesus Christ, the New Israel, the source of
salvation of the savior of humanity.

Why do I think Christians should address this issue of "Israel" at all? Obviously, for the same reason that Christians themselves have asked about a dialogue with Judaism. In the aftermath of the Holocaust, Christians examined Christianity's doctrine of Israel, the Jews and Judaism. Not responsible for the National Socialists — themselves anti-Christian, Christianity has come to recognize that Christians were National Socialists. While not the source of racist antisemitism, Christianity made its massive contribution to the racist antisemitism that formed the policy of mass murder of men, women, and children, in the name of the "purification" of humanity; Christianity has come to recognize that its has been a teaching of contempt. But, prepared to enter into dialogue with Judaism, Christians have found the State of Israel an obstacle, and, I believe I have shown, that is for quite profound theological reasons. First of all, though long experienced in governing, with a long history of a politically empowered Church and preference for Christian states, Christianity finds the notion of a Jewish state somehow egregious; religions do not have, or form, states (except, of course, when they do) so what can be Judaic about the State of Israel, so that Christianity, in addressing Judaism, should have to take notice, also, of the State of Israel? Second, the advent of the State of Israel really did call into question the theological convictions of many centuries. And third, when we speak of "Israel," Judaic and Christian faithful really cannot concur that they speak of one and the same thing.

So much for the question. Can there be an answer? To me, the words of Isaiah speak of us:

> He was oppressed, and he was afflicted, yet he opened not his mouth; like a lamb that is led to the slaughter, and like a sheep that before its shearers is dumb, so he opened not his mouth.

To me, Isaiah describes my life and the life of my people; it is with me when I wake up in the morning and when I go to sleep at night. Can Christians tell our story in their way, so that they may find sympathy for us? Clearly, they can, and many do. That is why I do not doubt that Christians can find in the story of Christ resources for telling themselves, also, the story of Israel in our times. And in reading the suffering servant as we do, they will discover in that conviction of ours that we are Israel, after the flesh, after the spirit, alike, the resources not for assent, but only for sympathetic hearing. Then, but only then, dialogue with Judaism as it is, with us as we are, and not with a fabrication of Christianity, can commence. We do our best with the Incarnate God; now I hope Christians for their part may try to do their best with Israel – and no quotation marks this time.

Then the cross will no longer stand for the crucifixion of the Jewish People, but for what Christian faithful aspire that it stand. Auschwitz is where our paths cross. Poland is the place for dialogue.

# CROSS PURPOSES:
# THE CONFLICT OVER
# SYMBOLIC TERRITORY
# BETWEEN POLES AND
# JEWS AT AUSCHWITZ

### MARVIN PROSONO

---

> The central Jewish character in Wacław Koszcyc's *W ogniu wolności* (In the blaze of freedom), who introduces himself as "a Pole and a Jew at the same time," recalls how he carried the cross, sang *"Boże coś Polskę"* ("God who hast Poland") and was shot at by Cossacks in Warsaw in the spring of 1861: (Opalski and Bartal, 1992:42).

Although the work from which this fascinating scene is taken is fictionalized history, it demonstrates the enormous distance that has been traveled in Polish-Jewish relations. The scene purports to represent the harmony that emerged between the Christian and Jewish communities during the period leading up to the insurrection of 1863 in Poland. That moment has been noted as the high watermark in relations between those two communities as they both struggled to throw off the yoke of Russian imperial domination.[1]

In a way, that valiant struggle has succeeded. The Russian yoke has been lifted from Poland, but in the intervening years Poland has suffered the devastation of two world wars, has been the victim of both Nazis and Stalinist imperialism, has experienced the terrible impact of the Holocaust, and for over forty years has had to endure the ruinous domination of a Communist regime. The relations between Poles and Jews are now leavened with the ingredients of this somber history. Those relations are again taking their character from the symbol of the cross, only now that symbol provides a serious point of contention.

In 1994, I published a paper that attempted to analyze the then ongoing controversy over the presence of a Carmelite convent at

Auschwitz, the largest and most notorious among the death camps established by the Nazi occupiers of Poland during the period of the Second World War. That controversy ended when the nuns transferred to a new convent at a short distance from the first. Out of my attempt to analyze the complexities generated by the convent controversy, especially between Poles and Jews (but also between Jews and Catholics generally), the concept of *symbolic territoriality* emerged. This concept permitted the dispute to be analyzed not so much as one over actual, physical territory but over symbols and the symbolic nature of that territory.[2] Here we are, several years after the convent controversy seemed to have been resolved, only to find that another, possibly more polarizing controversy, has arisen in its place — a conflict over the presence of crosses at Auschwitz.

The earlier analysis has been applied and extended to this new situation. Again, reliance has been placed on the perspectives and techniques of the symbolic interactionist tradition. In particular, ethnomethodology and phenomenology provide useful tools. First, it is necessary to review briefly the nature of the controversy and the methods used for studying it. Second, a hypothetical question is generated which is used in the nature of a "breaching experiment." Third, the core elements of this dispute are discussed in terms of the differential reactions to the hypothetical question and the dilemmas of the two major communities involved are described.

## PERSPECTIVE AND METHOD

In all sociological research, method becomes a central issue. In this case, the matter of methods is further complicated by a conflict involving very powerful emotions. Here we speak of the cross and the grave, Christianity and the Holocaust, relations between Christians and Jews, and Poles and Jews. In my view, one of the advantages of the phenomenological approach is that it permits us to penetrate the symbolic depths of the controversy, while at the same time taking into account the taken-for-granted life world of those involved. In this respect, the phrase "province of meaning" (Schutz and Luckmann, 1973, pp. 22-25) is felicitous.[3] The former extermination camp, Auschwitz, which is now a Polish state museum, would seem to function as a "province of meaning" within which communities composed of the living and the dead contend over meaning and memory. The first thing that needs to be established in making any sense out of this controversy is simply to ask what the controversy is about.

On its face it is rather simple. Over 250 crosses have been installed in an area sometimes called the "gravel pit," adjacent to the death camp at Auschwitz. These crosses are located near a larger cross which memorializes the first visit of Pope John Paul II to Auschwitz in 1979 and had been situated near what had been the Carmelite convent. Complicating this situation, however, is the fact that this site is not formally within the Auschwitz complex. It is a privately held plot out of the direct jurisdiction of the Polish government or the Authority of the State Museum.

After the convent was moved, agitation began on the part of various Jewish groups and individuals to have the so-called "papal cross" removed.* In response to this agitation, a Polish World War II veteran, Kazimierz Świtoń,[4] pitched a tent near the "papal cross" and in protest called for the placement of the smaller crosses. His actions have fomented a social movement within which are found conservative Catholics, Lefebvrists, and others, often characterized as "extremists" by their opponents and some in the media (see Gruber, 1998b), and who receive support from a radio station, Radio Maryja, identified as fiercely nationalist and Catholic. The placement of these smaller crosses outraged some Jewish groups and counter-protests ensued for the removal of all the crosses.

The Polish Catholic episcopacy, the Polish government, and the Israeli government have been brought into the dispute, all of whom are seeking to have the smaller crosses removed. The issue of removing the larger "papal cross" remains a matter of contention.[5] At the site itself, Polish Catholics maintain a vigil to prevent the removal of any of the crosses, although public opinion in Poland is divided over the issue (Gruber, 1998c). This entire episode must be seen against the backdrop of recent Polish history. Poland has recently been admitted to membership in NATO (March, 1999) and for the last ten years has been working diligently to establish a market economy that is beginning to flourish. Therefore, the problem of the crosses creates embarrassment as well as real international pressure for a resolution of this matter.

Like the convent controversy before it (and probably an extension of it), this conflict over the symbols permitted at Auschwitz (and over how

---

* Editors note. The cross, erected in 1979 was not a papal cross. See the comments of Father Stanisław Musiał in Chapter 4.

Auschwitz may be permitted as a symbol) is further evidence of the process of *symbolic territoriality*. However, the issues have been streamlined. We now face an elemental dispute over the symbol of the cross itself and all it represents. Antagonists often tend to deflect dealing with central or core issues by attacking the accounts and the motives of the *Other*. In order to avoid the distractions created by these attacks, the ethnomethodological perspective has been employed to finesse the rules by which these interactants are engaging (Coulon, 1995).[6]

The "breaching experiment"[7] of Harold Garfinkel proves the basis for the pursuit of answers to a challenging hypothetical question. That question is: What would have happened if those Catholic Poles wishing to commemorate their fellows who had been massacred by the Nazis had planted small Polish flags at Auschwitz instead of crosses? It is my belief that this question splits open the controversy and allows us to see within, to appreciate the logic and the motives of those involved.

Thus, within temporal and logistic constraints, all major actors in this controversy have been interviewed (by telephone). These include the following: the governments of Israel and Poland (through their American embassies); authorities at the Polish State Museum, Auschwitz; the government of the United States (the State Department); the Vatican (through the papal nuncio in Washington, D.C.): Jewish organizations (the American Jewish Committee; AMCHA — Coalition for Jewish Concerns); Polish organizations (Polish-American Congress); individuals (Chester Grabowski, journalist; Michael Preisler — Polish Catholic survivor of Auschwitz). In discussing the issue of the crosses at Auschwitz with these groups and individuals, all were asked (1) to describe what the controversy is about, and (2) to respond to the hypothetical question described

In addition to the data gathered through these interviews, newspapers, magazines, and other printed and electronic sources were scoured for any story that related to the controversy. Over a fairly short period of time a rather large file has accumulated filled with articles describing relevant events or opining on them. Additional information has come off the Internet and from my own visit to the site itself in June of 1998.

A word must be said about objectivity. The academic study of the Holocaust is not without its critics. There are those who condemn any approach to the study of the Holocaust that does not admit of certain "truths." Although I reject this attempt to pre-empt what can be said about the Holocaust (see Prosono, 1994b), I also believe no one is capable of looking into this abyss with Olympian (or even Weberian) objectivity. I have done my best to avoid weighing the equities embedded in this controversy, but in good conscience I cannot pretend that the set of facts we are presented with in this dismal spectacle have left me unaffected. The very questions I, myself, ask seem to have an acrid quality

Likewise, I believe that there are limits to what sociology can achieve in exploring this problem. I make no pretense that all that is said herein remains within the sociological universe of discourse. Sometimes one must resort to philosophical (or even theological) phrases in order to do justice to the nature of this cheerless conflict.

## MORALS AND MOTIVES

How does one make an approach to such a controversy? Here are two victim peoples desperately trying to come to terms with that historical outrage known as the Holocaust in a radically changed context. More than fifty years have elapsed since the capture of Auschwitz and the end of World War II. Those directly involved in the actual events are fast passing from our midst, leaving historical memory and symbolic commemoration in the hands of a generation which only knows those events second-hand.

Let us now consider the answers received to the hypothetical question. Although there were some variations in the responses given by the Jewish groups and individuals to the question, most responded that it would not have made any difference if, instead of crosses, flags had been used. There was some diffidence expressed because a flag does not evoke religious imagery. In some cases, the individual first responded that a flag would not represent the same kind of problem and then, having thought better of it, shifted ground and stayed with the more consistent position that Auschwitz should be a symbol-free zone.

This facet of the Jewish position was recognized by the spokespersons for Polish groups and organizations. They also acknowledged that had flags been planted instead of crosses, the result would have been pretty much the same; however, for Poles a different problem presents itself when suggesting that flags might have been used.

A flag is a national and political symbol. When one regards the use of a flag in this context from an American perspective, inappropriate assumptions may be employed in understanding what such flags might mean. Americans hold their flag, the "Stars and Stripes," in very high regard (although flag burning has been upheld by the U.S. Supreme Court as a form of permitted expression). Does an equivalent regard exist in Poland for its flag?

Apart from the regard in which the Polish flag is held generally (and that regard is complicated by the fact that the same flag has flown over Poland during Communist and non-Communist regimes alike), what would the display of Polish flags at Auschwitz communicate? By employing flags to commemorate the death of their countrymen, Poles would be emphasizing the national element in their tragic loss, albeit something they are apparently attempting to achieve; however, the use of a national flag would tend to render such a commemoration somewhat parochial. It is not only the *Polish* nature of those murdered by the Nazis that those planting crosses at Auschwitz desire to signify. The cross as a symbol bears a significance that cannot fail to be appreciated. It is the significance of the cross to Poles in particular and the world in general that lies at the very center of this controversy.

## THE POLISH DILEMMA

The positions taken in the controversy are emphatic statements intended to provide unmistakable signals to various targeted audiences. These signals are framed in the language of claims, claims that are made to symbolic territory through the manipulation of physical sites. The Polish claims, although couched in religious or patriotic terms, are interpreted by their (unintended?) Jewish audience as having a tacit agenda. That agenda includes two important elements: (1) the generalized promotion of what is considered endemic Polish antisemitism; and (2) the more specific attempt to Christianize the Holocaust, betraying the memory of its bona-fide victims. Let us briefly consider the first of these elements; the second shall be dealt with more fully in the discussion of the Jewish dilemma.

As Poland evolves into a regularized member of the European community, accusations of antisemitism are particularly aggravating to Polish sensibilities. It is not possible here to review the long and complex history of Jews in Poland. That antisemitism is a component of this history is undeniable, but so is it a component of the history of all societies in which Jews have appeared, including the United States.[8] Whether Poland should be specially singled out on this score is a question of considerable debate. Considering that before the Holocaust, Poland had the largest Jewish population in Europe (approximately ten percent of its pre-war population was Jewish) and that historically Jews were given a large measure of religious freedom and even self-rule, it is not easy to reconcile the present relations between these two people with those of the past. Is it the Holocaust that makes the difference or is the present controversy the culmination of a longer history of antagonism and oppression extending back to the late 19th century?

The death camps in Poland were established by the occupying Nazi regime. Poles suffered enormous brutalization at the hands of the Nazis - 3,000,000 non-Jewish Poles killed during Nazi occupation (see Lukas, 1986). KZ Auschwitz, located at the Polish village of Oświęcim, was chosen as the site for the largest extermination center because of logistics - for one, numerous rail connections with the rest of Europe and for another the largest Jewish population in Europe was situated in Poland. Oświęcim itself was emptied of its Polish population and resettled by a reliable German population. Poles who attempted to assist their Jewish neighbors did so at the risk of death, not only to themselves but also to their entire families.

Is the accusation of Polish antisemitism under this set of facts a cruel canard? Must the display of the cross at Auschwitz be interpreted as a deliberate antisemitic provocation? Even assuming good faith on the part of those Polish Christians who have planted crosses at Auschwitz, i.e., their desire to protect the "papal cross" and commemorate the tens of thousands of Poles who died there, are they lacking in appreciation of Jewish sensibilities? Or are their motives mixed in that they are attempting to send a wider message within the context of Polish society to the effect (1) that Poland should remain free of Jewish influence, or (2) that Poland should hearken to a more traditional understanding of the place that the Church has within society; or (3) both?

The problem for Poles who honestly wish to commemorate their martyred dead is that whatever form such commemoration takes they are more than likely to find themselves chafing Jewish sensibilities. It is not the inappropriate *placement* of the crosses at Auschwitz that is the problem. There is nothing implied in the objections to the presence of the crosses that if they were moved to an alternative site at the camp, they would no longer offend. It is their presence at the camp altogether that makes the difference.

There is probably not a more potent religious symbol in the Western world than the cross. In those Catholic nations of Eastern Europe, the cross bears with it a complex of associations that those living in other nations, especially nations of the Western Hemisphere, do not immediately appreciate.[9] As evidenced by the quote which began this paper, the cross even more than the flag evokes for Poles the sense of nationhood and peoplehood. In more current terms, the Catholic Church has been instrumental in ending Communist oppression. Communist regimes are notoriously unfriendly to religion, and the Church, although itself a victim of this anti-religious posture, preserved not only spiritual values, but also national identities.

It is also necessary to refer to the sinister episode of the Nazi occupation of Poland in order to get a complete understanding of the meaning of the cross in the context of Auschwitz, where thousands of Polish intellectuals and religious were put to death. St. Maximilian Kolbe, canonized by the Catholic Church in 1981, is now widely known both inside and outside of Poland. In the cell in which he died at Auschwitz is a stone memorial around which candles burn. His canonization caused (and still causes) much displeasure within world Jewry because of his characterization as having been antisemitic. That characterization has been hotly debated; in Polish and Catholic eyes it is seen as unfair at the least and possibly even cruel. [10]

There is yet another problem that confronts us when attempting to understand the meaning of the crosses at Auschwitz: the problem of the sacred and the secular. Poland is a nation which is intensely Catholic (95% of its population is Roman Catholic); thus, the visitor to Poland discovers the omnipresence of the cross and ubiquitous Christian religious symbolization. Shrines exist at crossroads; religious figures are found within the niches of buildings; crucifixes may appear in restaurants or commercial establishments. Again, those coming from an American context might find this overwhelming evidence of religious symbolization a violation of the role that religion ought to play in the modern social order (see Cuddihy, 1978 and Epstein, 1996). Religion is relegated to backstage (Goffman, 1959) except for carefully defined occasions; public displays of religious symbols (apart from those found on structures dedicated to a religious purpose and on privately held property) are exceptional (see Neuhaus, 1984).

To illustrate this point, a short digression is necessary. In the United States, challenges to the presence of religious symbols on public property are commonplace. A particularly provocative and apropos example of this phenomenon is to be found in the ongoing struggle of certain individuals and groups to have the 103 foot Latin cross removed from the summit of Mt. Davidson in San Francisco, California. Although the tranquility of the park in which this cross resides can in no way compare to an emotion-shattering death camp, arguments similar to those made in the Auschwitz case are made in the discussion over the removal of this cross. The following are excerpts from the decision of Judge O'Scannlain in the lawsuit brought against the City and County of San Francisco to have the cross removed.[11]

> First, the Mount Davidson Cross is a Latin cross. The Latin cross "is the preeminent symbol of many Christian religions and represents with relative clarity and simplicity the Christian message of the crucifixion and resurrection of Jesus Christ, a doctrine at the heart of Christianity."  Quoting from Okrand, 254Cal. Rptr. At 922. (At p. 4)
>
> San Francisco attempts to borrow the history of Mount Davidson and attribute it to the Cross. However, the cross does not become imbued with the mountain's history merely because it was erected upon it. Mount Davidson will retain its historical significance with or without a cross atop it. (At p. 7) 93 F.3d 627 (Ninth Circuit) 1996

What is interesting in these remarks is Judge O'Scannlain's understanding that there is a relationship between symbol and site and that the meanings attached to either are arbitrary and socially constructed.

What seems implicit within the controversy at Auschwitz is that the site of the death camp should be governed by rules similar to those fashioned by American courts in their approach to the display of religious symbols. This is not a result of a particularly American involvement in the controversy, although Americans such as Rabbi Avraham Weiss, Rabbi James Rudin, and Edward Moskal (President of the Polish-American Congress) are deeply involved. Rather, this approach comes out of a desire on the part of certain Jewish organizations and individuals to have the site at Auschwitz maintained free of any religious, cultural or political symbols. (Is it also possible that one of the effects of globalization is the diffusion of this particularly American (or "Western") taste for relegating religion backstage?)

In fact, there are few other sites in the world which have been the subject of such international attention. On July 2, 1947, the Polish government simultaneously established the Council for the Protection of Memory of Combat and Martyrdom (hereafter, the "Council") and the State Museum of Auschwitz (Council, 1998). That Council's responsibilities were further refined in 1988 to include assessment and protection of the site. The Council credits the Jewish community with having called world attention to the Auschwitz site, but it also recognizes the emergence of a "global Auschwitz-Birkenau syndrome" (Council, 1998, p. 5). During Communist rule, no memorialization of the special nature of Jewish martyrdom existed at the camp. With the collapse of the Communist regime in Poland and the establishment of an International Auschwitz Council by the Minister of Art and Culture in 1989, the original Council's role changed radically. The International Council has now become the decision-making body with respect to the management of the Auschwitz complex.

In 1979, the Auschwitz complex was added to the World Heritage list of sites. Such sites are given attention under the United Nations convention concerning the protection of world cultural heritage.[12] During the convent controversy, two agreements were reached by various Jewish and Catholic authorities: (1) designating Auschwitz as a special place of Jewish grief and as a symbol of the entire Final Solution — July 22, 1986 and (2) planning for the construction of an interfaith center — February 27, 1987. In a 1997 UNESCO report, the World Heritage Committee commended Polish authorities for the adoption of the Oświęcim Strategic Program. This program was described as:

> ...aiming at a long-term and comprehensive development and management of the site while fully recognizing the need to protect and preserve the physical integrity and dignity of the site and abstaining from any commercial development which could compromise the site's symbolic values (UNESCO(b), 1997, IV.52).

The signatories to the agreement establishing the "Oświęcim Program" are the Government of Poland, the United States Holocaust Memorial Council, the International Council of the State Museum of Auschwitz-Birkenau, and the City of Oświęcim.

The "Oświęcim Program" was referenced by Rabbi James Rudin during our conversation as providing for a "green zone" around the camp complex which will assist in avoiding any further disturbances along the lines of the cross plantings. This agreement is significant here because it ratifies the principle that Auschwitz should be free of all commercial development or religious symbols; however, it also creates additional complexity and yet another basis for claims of "violation." Jewish groups have argued with each other over the impact of this "Program" on the status of the crosses already planted (Salpeter, 1998), and the residents of Oświęcim have protested the consequences of this arrangement for those living near the perimeter of the camp ("Residents Protest Poland's Auschwitz Zone," 1999).

## THE JEWISH DILEMMA

On the surface, Jewish motives in this controversy are not difficult to understand. Ostensibly, those motives include a desire to control the transmission of knowledge as that knowledge pertains to the Holocaust, its inspiration, its victims, its lessons. The presence of the crosses at Auschwitz, it is argued, interferes with the transmission of a version of the Holocaust that is believed to have protective power. In what way does such interference manifest itself?

The argument goes that the cross (and not only the cross, but any kind of Christian symbol, shrine, chapel, church, etc.) creates the impression that the Holocaust was something other than principally the attempt to exterminate the Jews.[13] In fact, the cross might lead future observers to believe that Christians were the victims, while at the same time obscuring the antisemitic background within Christendom that provided the inspiration for the Holocaust. Thus, the lessons of the Holocaust might be lost; it is the pedagogic nature of Holocaust remembrance that makes it so desperately important that nothing be allowed to tamper with this line.

But are these the only lessons of the Holocaust? Controversies abound over precisely the origins of the murderous hatred that motivated Nazi Germany to attempt the mass extermination of the Jews (see Goldhagen, 1996). Rather than getting into a debate over those origins, which would need a lengthy digression, let it suffice to say that a definitive answer to the question has been adopted, as witness the fourteen-minute video that begins the tour at the United States Holocaust Memorial

Museum in Washington, D.C. That video is in essence a history of Christian/Jewish relations, which purports to describe the Holocaust as heir to and a direct manifestation of old-fashioned Christian antisemitism. Not surprisingly, that video has provoked criticism and a call for its removal since its major theme, although certainly plausible, cannot be asserted as an empirical fact. It can only operate on the level of polemic. In a way, the presence of the crosses implicitly calls the legitimacy of that video and the *Weltanschauung* behind it into question. Even if one were to grant, for the sake of argument, that this thesis concerning origins was the most worthy among its competitors, removing the crosses at Auschwitz does not guarantee that the Holocaust will be universally interpreted along these lines. Two points will further clarify this dilemma.

First, the number of people who visit Auschwitz each year, although substantial and growing, is still limited. Most people who learn about the Holocaust and its meaning do so far from the sites of the extermination camps; thus, what they understand this calamity to mean is not affected by the presence of crosses at Auschwitz (or by any shape that the physical extermination camps may take). Except for professional historians and archeologists, history is not taught through the handling of relics; it is an intellectual exercise made real through oral and written sources, or in modern times through film.

Understanding this, it must be asked: why create this great scandal over the presence of crosses (and it must remembered the controversy began over the presence of one cross) at Auschwitz? Why call attention to what for most people would be obscured by distance or for others rendered a small detail lost in the enormity of the "Auschwitz kingdom" (Friedrich, 1994)?

The answers to these questions contain the basis for understanding why the Jewish position with respect to the crosses is so adamant. It is imagined that controlling the Auschwitz site also means controlling the direction that memory of the Holocaust will travel. As I mentioned in my prior work on symbolic territoriality (Prosono, 1994a), there is something talismanic in this preoccupation over the symbolic purity of the site. Control the site, control memory, control how history is understood; therefore, the proper lessons will be drawn from the Holocaust and the tragedy itself will provide for the security of the Jewish people in the future.

Here we can take up the second point of the dilemma of remembrance. Once having accepted the logical connection between the symbolic purity of Auschwitz and the survival of the Jewish people, one other problem must be faced. In my discussion with Rabbi Avraham Weiss, one of the leading protagonists in this controversy, I asked him how he could be sure that in time, even if the crosses were removed today, another generation might not forget the urgency of keeping the sites symbol-free and duplicate the present problem. His response was very revealing in that it demonstrates the extent to which at least he is willing to guarantee the nature of the Auschwitz site.

What he suggests is that the entire site be placed under the jurisdiction of the State of Israel. For him, this would be the ultimate solution of the problem inasmuch as he assumes that were Israel to administer the site there would not be any possibility of symbolic encroachments. This is the ultimate in rezoning, an example of symbolic territoriality of a particularly unusual kind. In order to secure the symbolic nature of this location, Rabbi Weiss suggests it become extra-territorial in the same sense as an embassy. Poland would then have to cede part of its territory to the State of Israel. What possible motivation would a sovereign nation have to make such a radical concession?

Although not explicitly stated, its motivation would evidently come out of its recognition that it has a moral obligation to transfer symbolic rights, to grant a symbolic easement, for and to the Jewish people. Such a concession would also further ratify the line that many Jews take toward the Holocaust. According to this view, not only was Christian antisemitism responsible for the tragedy, Polish antisemitism should be singled out for particular condemnation. It is argued that so many Jews died during the Holocaust in Poland because of the potent nature of Polish antisemitism. That it meant death for a Pole to assist a Jew, that the Nazis also murdered many hundreds of thousand of Christian Poles, that an organization, Żegota (Tomaszewski and Werbowski, 1994), existed in Poland for the sole purpose of rescuing Jews, are not determinative in this version of events.

Of course, such territorial arrangements are not unheard of and the State of Israel itself provides many examples. The Dome of the Rock has been placed under Islamic authority; various Christian shrines, such as the Church of the Nativity in Bethlehem and the Church of the Holy Sepulcher in Jerusalem, are maintained by a number of religious confessions, each with its own very heavily circumscribed areas of responsibility. The Temple Mount has been the subject of an Israel Supreme Court decision guaranteeing all religious faiths access to their holy sites ("Supreme Court

Rules on Temple Mount," 1996, p. 5). Israel itself might even be defined as one large holy site shared by a number of religious and ethnic groups. Yet, the final history of Israel has not been written and we witness there how difficult it is for groups with very different ways of symbolizing the same territory to accommodate one another.

The symbolic territory known as Auschwitz is going into foreclosure, forcing the various claimants to implore the highest political and religious authorities for assistance in sorting through who will fall heir to the remaining symbolic assets. Mutual accommodation does not seem a likely resolution of this case. Revealingly, the hypothetical question concerning the Polish flag evokes the same response among Jews as suggestions that Stars of David be permitted at Auschwitz. Absolutely no symbols! If even one is allowed, then no good argument could be made for restricting any.

It is necessary to understand two other elements that work to form the Jewish reaction. The first is the basic aniconic nature of Judaism, i.e., the very rigorous strictures against image-making and worship before images. Even if the representation of the Holocaust were not an issue, a cross placed within the Auschwitz precinct would seem a cruel distortion to many Jews because of the more than one million Jews who perished there. The question arises: should all other victims who died at the camp be denied the remembrance they would expect out of delicacy for Jewish sensibilities? Can no middle way be found such that parts of the camp are designated as a place for Jewish as opposed to Christian commemoration? I believe the answer to this question is bound up with the second of the two elements mentioned at the beginning of the paragraph.

The entire Auschwitz complex is defined as a cemetery. The phrase commonly used is that Auschwitz is the largest Jewish cemetery in the world. Rabbi Weiss made such a statement and in almost all arguments made by Jews for the removal of the crosses, the idea that the site is a graveyard is certain to appear. In our conversation, I reminded Rabbi Weiss that Auschwitz is not, in fact, a cemetery. Cemeteries or graveyards are places where those who have died have been formally interred, usually after elaborate ceremony.

Even if it had the status of cemetery, would that forbid all Christian symbols? Jewish cemeteries all over the world are often adjacent to or actually share grounds with Christian cemeteries. As the Steven Spielberg film *Saving Private Ryan* opens, we are in a military cemetery in France where the camera pans over the thousands of graves marked either by crosses or the Star of David. Obviously, the presence of the cross does not always desecrate a site for Jewish people. Consider, however, the following:

> Poland's chief rabbi Pinchas Menachem Joskowicz, rejected the bishops' stand (The Polish bishops who advocated the removal of the smaller crosses but the maintenance of the larger papal cross), reiterating that all crosses, including the papal cross, must go. The presence of any cross prevents Jews from praying at Auschwitz, he said (Gruber, 1998, p. 2).

Here we have a definition of the situation that would seem to render all of Auschwitz a sacred precinct, defiled if any cross is found within it. Would that extend to Catholic religious who wear easily visible crosses and who visit the camp? Or any Christian who wears a cross that can be seen (or even unseen?). Not all Jews in or out of Poland agree with these sentiments. Stanisław Krajewski, board member of the Union of Jewish Communities in Poland, has recognized that such a statement is perceived as a "war against Christianity" and that Poles have a legitimate need to commemorate the Poles murdered at Auschwitz.

> "Poles do have real, justified rights," he said. "If Jewish leaders publicly expressed this, it could help improve the situation" (Gruber, 1998b).

Auschwitz resembles more a killing field or a crime scene. Birkenau is the name of Auschwitz II (after the name of a nearby village) which was built expressly for reception of deported Jews on their way to the gas chambers. There are no headstones, no markers of any kind in that place. One wonders how the site will speak of the crime to future generations. It is obvious that in order for the silence of Auschwitz to communicate its ghastly historical burden those who would contemplate it will have to do so with prior knowledge. What comes to mind is the Latin phrase *res ipsa loquitur*, in this case, however, the thing cannot speak for itself. Unless individuals come to Auschwitz with prior knowledge of its horror, it stands mute. Of course, if they come to Auschwitz with this knowledge, how is the camp assisting in or capable of preserving its own memory? Is Auschwitz supposed to be the lesson or the illustration? Ironically, this insistence on a symbol-free zone creates a mirror of that medieval social arrangement in which Jews could live with a minimum of Christian symbols, i.e., the ghetto. In this case, we might speak of the ghettoization of the dead, Auschwitz itself turning into one large icon.[14]

## CONCLUSION - A PROVINCE OF MEANING INHABITED BY A COMMUNITY OF THE DEAD

The ethnomethodological and phenomenological perspectives provide insights into the nature of this controversy. The Jewish position has emerged from the imperative to define the taken-for-granted life world within which the Holocaust is appreciated. The presence of the crosses at Auschwitz creates an impediment to this project. The "Oświęcim Program," which is that remarkable agreement to rezone Auschwitz, makes no exception in its vision of an absolutely symbol-free site. We have already discussed the arguments made for instituting this policy. Any attempts to interfere with the achievement of this end are met by active opposition, either quiet behind-the-scene diplomacy or strident action.

On the other hand, the activity of those Poles who have erected and keep a vigil over the crosses suggests very much a kind of "breaching experiment" (See footnote 5). By setting up these crosses as and where they have, they must know they will be evoking a negative response from world Jewry. Thus, the planting of these crosses has a triple effect. For one, it does evoke the sought-after response, and by doing so almost insures the reconfirmation of each (in/out) group's stereotype of the other. It also provides the provocation necessary to ventilate issues that would otherwise go unremarked. Why should the "Oświęcim Program" be implemented without a full airing of all points of view, even from those sectors of opinion that may otherwise be unempowered?

Yet, there is a third effect of the cross plantings. They have provided us as social analysts with a means of understanding the standpoints of the various participants to the controversy. In this respect, the cross plantings are what an ethnomethodologist might design as a way of getting at these standpoints — a kind of breaching experiment, but surely this is not a conscious motive on the part of those involved.

Those who have placed the crosses at the gravel pit claim they are engaged in legitimate commemoration; that is their motive. Is it only the "where" of their activity which is being called into question, and not also the "why"? But Auschwitz *is* a site of Polish martyrdom. "Where" and "why" are so intimately bound up with one another, they cannot be separated. It would seem that those who have designed the "Oświęcim Program" have thought ahead to this point of the dilemma and provided for a solution, albeit a Draconian one.

What is the solution? It is to allow the entire Auschwitz complex to become *the* symbol by preventing interference from any competing symbolization.

From this point, analysis becomes speculation. We are left only with questions, some of which have already been asked. How can a symbol-free zone be maintained indefinitely? What is a mute Auschwitz supposed to communicate? Will there be informational materials available at a reconstituted information center? If so, how will those materials define the situation and who will take charge of this social construction? How will the Jewish nature of the tragedy at Auschwitz be specifically communicated since it is feared that it is this aspect of the story that may be lost? Who will provide for a comprehensive retelling of the tragedy, one that includes all victims? If this comprehensive retelling involves good faith on the part of all parties concerned, why is it that such good faith cannot be read into the present situation? If such good faith does not exist in the present, why should we expect that it will in the future? If not now, when?

> We pray that our sorrow for the tragedy which the Jewish people has suffered in our century will lead to a new relationship with the Jewish people. We wish to turn awareness of past sins into a firm resolve to build a new future in which there will be no more anti-Judaism among Christians or anti-Christian sentiment among Jews, but rather a shared mutual respect as befits those who adore the one Creator and Lord and have a common father in faith, Abraham (National Conference of Catholic Bishops, 1998, p. 54).
>
> From *We Remember: A Reflection on the Shoah,* Holy See's Commission for Religious Relations with the Jews

## ENDNOTES

1. "Actually, it must be said that a relatively large number of Jews took part in the Polish fight for independence. This was principally the case at the time of the January Rising and somewhat earlier. A part of the religious leadership was also

involved as symbolized by the head rabbi of Warsaw at the time, Ber Meisels" (Krajewski in *Więź*, 1998:66).

And, "Pictures of Meisels were distributed all over Warsaw by Polish patriots after the rabbi's (Meisels') arrest in late 1861. When Meisels was released from jail on February 13, 1862, the money raised by selling the picture (some 20,000 rubles) was presented to him as a gift from the Polish nation" (Opalski and Bartal, 1992:86).

But compare these accounts with the rather less enthusiastic coverage given by Simon Dubnow (1916), the renowned Jewish historian, who himself was murdered in his old age when the Germans occupied Riga, Latvia.

2. "The central conception of this paper is that territoriality involves more of a symbolic component than has been heretofore widely recognized and that some forms of territoriality may, in fact, involve only symbolic objects, the boundaries to be drawn around symbols or the ownership of symbols. An essential element in the utilization of symbols may be that symbols are not only created but may be borrowed, stolen, trespassed upon or even rezoned. A symbol may provide the ground upon which the action of territoriality proceeds..." (Prosono, 1994, p. 182).

3. "The finite character of a province of meaning (of the everyday life-world, of the world of dreams, of the world of science, of the world of religious experience) rests upon the character of the unity of its own peculiar lived experience - viz., its cognitive style. Harmony and compatibility, with regard to this style, are consequently restricted to a given province of meaning. In no case is that which is compatible within the finite province of meaning P also compatible within the finite province of meaning Q" (Schutz and Luckmann, 1973, pp. 23-24).

4. More recently, see, "Catholic Radical Petitions for Churches, Synagogue at Auschwitz," 1999.

5. "Polish Prime Minister Jerzy Buzek promised Jewish leaders that the government would remove all "new" crosses erected by Catholics at the former Nazi death camp Auschwitz...Buzek's reference to the removal of "new" crosses may mean that the government would let the large, original cross remain. Poland's bishops have called for the removal of the new crosses while keeping the original cross in place" ("Polish Prime Minister Promises to Remove Auschwitz Crosses," 1998).

6. "My and my fellow-man's biographically determined situations, and therewith our respective purposes at hand and our respective systems of relevances originating in such purposes, must differ, at least to a certain extent" (Schutz in Natanson, 1963, p. 311).

7. '...he (Garfinkel) made use of the analysis of experimental breachings in games to show, through the breaching, the moral background of common activities' (Coulon, 1995, p. 43).

8. See Lindemann (1997) for a provocative discussion of this theme.

9. There is an interesting example of cross planting in Lithuania, which like its neighbor Poland, was occupied by the Soviet Union during World War II. It is the "Hill of Crosses" near Siauliai, three and a half hour drive north of the capital, Vilnius. "The Hill of Crosses is a moving monument to the tenacity of religious belief. It is a small hill filled with thousands of different-sized crosses, placed there by Lithuanians and people from over the world. The Soviets bulldozed the hill three times, but the faithful kept building the memorial back up" ("Outside Vilnius," 1998).

10. See, Ready and Rose, 1996, which references other works reviewing this case.

11. The U.S. Court; Appeals for the Ninth Circuit simultaneously on the day of this decision but in a separate opinion decided the fate of a cross displayed in similar circumstances in a park in Eugene, Oregon. 93 F.3d 617 (Ninth Circuit) 1996.

12. Thus, the Secretary-General of UNESCO, Frederico Mayer, made remarks upon the celebration of the 50th anniversary of the liberation of Auschwitz (1995).

13. Auschwitz is not the only former extermination camp at which one finds crosses or chapels. The problem is seen as widespread and found in many of the former camps both in Poland and in Germany. Dachau has a large Carmelite convent just outside it walls and within the camp are four religious edifices (three chapels and a memorial).

14. My colleague, Gary Brock, and I are in the process of preparing a manuscript which takes for its theme the sacralization of the Holocaust and its becoming the basis for a new religious movement. See, especially, Brock and Prosono, 1995.

## REFERENCES

Boys, Marcy C. 1994. "The Cross: Should a Symbol Betrayed be Reclaimed?" *Cross Currents*, 44(1): 5-31 (Spring)

Brock, Gary and Marvin Prosono. 1995. "Holocaustism: The Emergence of a New Religious Movement?" *Perspectives on Social Problems*, 7:223-248.

"Catholic Radical Petitions for Churches, Synagogue at Auschwitz." 1999. *Central Europe Online*, March 15. (Found at http://www.centraleurope.com/ceo/news/1999031505.htm>)

Coulon, Alain. 1995. *Ethnomethodology*. Thousand Oaks: Sage University Press.

Council for the Protection of Memory of Combat and Martrydom. 1998. Report on the Current Condition of Memorial Sites Located on the Premises of the Former Nazi Concentration Camps and Exterminations Camps for Jews. Conclusions and Proposals for New Solutions. Warsaw: August.

Cuddihy, John Murray. 1978. *No Offense: Civil Religion and Protestant Taste*. New York: Seabury Press.

Diner, Dan. 1997. "On Guilt Discourse and Other Narratives: Epistemological Observations Regarding the Holocaust" *History and Memory*, 9(2): 301-320, Fall.

Dubnow, Simon. 1916. *History of the Jews in Russia and Poland: from the Eearliest Times until the Present Day*. Tr. from the Russian by I. Friedländer, 3v. Philadelphia: The Jewish Publication Society of America.

Epstein, Steven. 1996, "Rethinking the Constitutionality of Ceremonial Deism" Columbia Law Review, 96: 2083-2174 (December).

Friedrich, Otto. 1994. *The Kingdom of Auschwitz*. New York: Harper Perennial.

Goffman, Erving. 1959. *The Presentation of Self in Everyday Life*. Garden City, New York, Doubleday Anchor Books.

Goldhagen, Daniel. 1996. Hitler's Willing Executioners: Ordinary Germans and the Holocaust. New York: Knopf.

Gruber, Ruth E. 1998a. "Vatican Remains Silent Amid Auschwitz Cross Crisis" *Jewish Bulletin of Northern California* (Jewish Telegraphic Agency), September 4. (Found at <http://shamash.org/jb/bk980904/isilent. htm>)

_____. 1998b. "Polish Extremists Seize Control of Debate over Auschwitz Crosses."

*Online JTA* (Jewish Telegraphic Agency), September 7.
(Found at <http://www.jta.org/sep98/07-cros.htm>

_____. 1998c. Survey: "Most Poles Oppose Crosses at Auschwitz" *Jewish Bulletin of Northern California* (Jewish Telegraphic Agency), October 9. (Found at http://www.jewishf.com/bk981009/isurvey.htm>)

Gutman, Yisrael and Michael Berenbaum. 1998 (first paperback edition). *Anatomy of the Auschwitz Death Camp*. Bloomington: Indiana University Press in association with the United States Holocaust Memorial Museum.

Lindemann, Albert S. 1997. *Esau's Tears. Modern Antisemitism and the Rise of the Jews*. Cambridge: Cambridge University Press.

Lukas, Richard. 1986, *Forgotten Holocaust. The Poles under German Occupation, 1939-1945*, Lexington, Kentucky: University of Kentucky Press.

Natanson, Maurice. 1963. *Philosophy of the Social Sciences*. New York: Random House.

National Conference of Catholic Bishops, 1998. *Catholics Remember the Holocaust*. Washington, D.C.: United States Catholic Conference.

Neuhaus, Richard John. 1984. *The Naked Public Square: Religion and Democracy in America*. Grand Rapids, Mich.: W.B. Eerdmans Pub. Co.

Opalski, Magdalena and Israel Bartal. 1992. *Poles and Jews. A Failed Brotherhood*. Hanover and London: Brandeis University Press, published by University Press of New England.

"Outside Vilnius." 1998
<http://www.balticsww.com/ tourist/lithuania/guide/outside.htm>3/22/99)

"Polish Prime Minister Promises to Remove Auschwitz Crosses." 1998. *EWTN News*, December 2.
(Found at <http://www.ewtn.com/ewtn/news/getstory.asp?number=11380.)

Prosono, Marvin, 1994a. "Symbolic Territoriality and the Holocaust: The Controversy over the Carmelite Convent at Auschwitz." *Perspectives on Social Problems*, 5, 173-193.

_____. 1994b. "Towards a Sociology and a Science of the Holocaust" *Perspectives on Social Problems*, 6, 233-256.

Ready, Becky and Margaret-Marcy Rose. 1996. "Patron of Our Difficult Century." *Immaculata Magazine*, May/June.

(Found at http://www.ewtn.com/libraryANSERS/ KOLANTI.TXT)

"Residents Protest Auschwitz Zone." 1999. *Central Europe Online* (Reuters), March 8.

(Found at <http@//www. centraleurope.com/ceo/news/1999030803.html>)

Salpeter. Eliahu. 1998. "The Battle for Auschwitz." *Ha'aretz*, August 12.

(Found at,

http://www3.haaretz./co.il/eng/scripts/article.asp?id=26101&mador=5& datee=8/12/98>)

Schutz, Alfred. 1963. "Common-Sense and Scientific Interpretation of Human Action." In Natanson, Maurice. *Philosophy of the Social Sciences*. New York: Random House. [Paper originally appeared 1953.]

_____. 1970. *On Phenomenology and Social Relations. Selected Writings*. Edited and with an introduction by Helmut R. Wagner. Chicago: The University of Chicago Press.

"Supreme Court Rules on the Status of Temple Mount" 1996. *Christians and Israel.* V(3): 5 Summer.

Tomaszewski, Irene and Tecia Werbowski. 1994. *The Rescue of Jews in Wartime Poland.* Montreal: Price-Patterson, Ltd.

UNESCO(a). 1995. "Address by Frederico Mayer on the occasion of the celebration of the 50th anniversary of the liberation of Auschwitz." January 25. [DG/95/3]

UNESCO(b). Convention Concerning the Protection of the World Cultural and Natural Heritage. Bureau of the World Heritage Committee. 1997. *Report of the Rapporteur.* Paris: UNESCO, September 3, [WHC-97/CONF.204/11]

*WIĘŹ:Under One Heaven: Poles and Jews.* Warsaw Monthly Special Issue 1998. Warsaw: published with the financial support of the Irena Kozłowska-Fiszel and Edmund Kon Foundation and the Stefan Batory Foundation. Cezary Gawrys, editor-in-chief.

# CROSSES AT AUSCHWITZ
## A FIST AGAINST

### FATHER STANISŁAW MUSIAŁ, SJ.
### *Tygodnik Powszechny*
### 9 AUGUST 1998

A few days ago, near the former Auschwitz camp, a second three-meter cross was erected at the gravel pit. It was placed next to the seven-meter cross put there ten years ago by "unknown" perpetrators under cover of night. The second cross was erected by known perpetrators in broad daylight, and they themselves provided notoriety for their exploit by using the media. Certain people predict that the gravel pit will soon become a forest of crosses. In this way it will presumably become a "valley of crosses."

The shameful game of crosses at Auschwitz continues. Of course, what is involved here is neither God nor the honoring of the memory of the victims murdered at Auschwitz. For close to 45 years after the war neither Catholics nor patriots took an interest in the place. It was overgrown with tall grass.

Who should interrupt this game? There is an Institution in the country which, in view of its calling, should put an end to this duel with crosses at Auschwitz. But all signs indicate that this Institution hid its head in the sand, and worse still, wants public opinion in the country and in the world to recognize this gesture of silence as an indication of the virtue of caution and of civic discretion.

There was a time in Poland when the Church knew how to defend religion. It could react quickly, precisely, and assertively against dangers, both external and internal, that the faith was then threatened by. This was especially so in the case of profanation of religious symbols and in the case of attempts to exploit religion for political purposes. Now, in the changed political and social reality, the Church seems unable to defend religion. It seems deaf and blind to dangers to the faith coming from the extreme right. Actually, a direct attack on the faith is less harmful to religion than instrumentalization of religion for nonreligious purposes or for purposes contrary to religion (I have in mind, for example, hatred between national

77

or religious groups). The first of these forms of war with religion mobilizes the faithful while the second dilutes religiosity and promotes its secularization.

It is high time for the Church in Poland to wake up and speak about the abuse of religious symbols for nonreligious purposes. It is not true that in this it is doomed to helplessness. The Church has at its disposal an instrument that is the envy of all secular authorities. This instrument is neither a police force, which the Church does not have, nor courts, nor parliament, nor regional councils. This instrument is the word, a clear statement as to when a symbol commonly regarded as a religious symbol is actually a religious symbol, that is, when it fulfills a religious function, and when this symbol does not fulfill such a function because it has been "profaned," that is, has been used for nonreligious purposes. Such a declaration either deprives the symbol — recognized as a religious symbol — of its sacredness or confirms it. Contrary to what some say, the Church need not own the terrain where the "disputed" religious symbols are located. In such cases, the removal of symbols which do not fulfill the conditions of "religiosity" is a matter to be handled by the secular authorities and not by the Church.

A declaration by the Church in Poland in this matter would be extremely important for two reasons:

First, the Church must reaffirm the inalienable rights which it alone has in this matter. For it seems that in recent years the Church has not only failed to affirm this right but appears to have relinquished it in favor of groups which adopt the patriotic or Catholic label. It cannot be that, whoever wants to puts in public places Christian religious symbols and demands that the community of the faithful, or even the Church, should defend these marks as Christian sacred objects. This is inadmissible because it boosts the use of religious symbols for political battles. Moreover, we witness with increasing frequency the exploitation of these symbols by advertising.

Second, a declaration by the Church that it alone can decide whether a certain religious symbol actually fulfills a religious function would be important if, whenever the need arises for such symbols — declared as not fulfilling a religious function or even being contrary to it — to be removed or moved (for it can happen that, if moved, the symbol in question does have a religious significance). In addition to other reasons, such a declaration would avoid unnecessary conflicts of conscience in the case of people carrying out such functions, people who might otherwise feel that they are doing something contrary to religion or God.

Incidentally, one is surprised that the local bishop is left to deal with the decision concerning the Auschwitz crosses by himself. The Holy Father constantly emphasizes that bishops are responsible not only for their dioceses but for the whole Church as well. In this concrete case one does not see the collegiality of Polish bishops. The opposite is true. Not only is the Bielsko-Żywiec bishop not helped in his effort to solve the problem, but, to the contrary, the proverbial monkey wrench is thrown in his plans. For how else should one describe the profuse and general appeals "Defend the cross!" recently delivered by certain Polish clergymen? Do these clergymen not realize that these appeals cut both ways? Today one can "defend" the cross while actually profaning it. To tell the truth, it is not those people who demand that the crosses at the gravel pit near the Auschwitz camp be transferred or removed who are against the Cross of Christ, but those who put them there and are for leaving them there. The Cross of Christ is not a fist. And this is what the crosses at the gravel pit at Auschwitz are. They are this because of the will of those who built them and their allies. They are fists against.

It is the Church that must settle this dispute.

# STATEMENT OF THE GOVERNMENT
## on the Matter of Crosses at the
## Former Hitler Death Camp at Auschwitz

The Polish Government watches with concern the escalating dispute connected with the memorial at Oświęcim - Brzeżinka. The former Hitler death camp is a symbol of worldwide significance. This place especially memorializes the horrible crime of the Holocaust. The world's biggest Jewish graveyard calls for special sensitivity and special respect. Polish citizens and representatives of the Polish government are aware of this. But it must be borne in mind that the victims of Hitler's death factory were also Gypsies, Poles, Russians and members of scores of other nationalities.

The conflict centers on the area of the former Gravel Pit, where initially those executed were almost exclusively Poles. We are disturbed to see that the cross, the most precious Christian symbol, became there the subject and tool of a contest in which one discerns political motivations.

We wish to remind people that this place is a subject of a legal dispute between the State Treasury and the private owner who actually administers this terrain. Thus the state authorities cannot effectively interfere in the management of the area of the former Gravel Pit.

The Concordat between the Polish Republic and the Apostolic See assigns the care of Catholic religious symbols to the Church. Thus it seems that demands connected with the merits of the dispute should not be addressed to the Government of the Polish Republic.

Of course, the Government will make every effort to insure that a place as important as Auschwitz should not divide nations, both of which were victims of Nazism. We are aware of the role of the Cross for Poles and of the significance of Auschwitz-Birkenau for Jews in the whole world. But we are convinced that the only way for solving disputes is the search for a solution that respects the sensitivity of all who bow their heads before the victims of Oświęcim and Brzeżinka.


The Chancellery of the Prime Minister
The Government Information Center
Warsaw, 5 August 1998

# THE CROSS AS THE SYMBOL OF THE HIGHEST LOVE OF MAN

## Archbishop Muszyński about the situation at Auschwitz

### KAI (Catholic Information Agency)

I am deeply concerned about the development of events connected with the "action of the crosses" at the gravel pit near the death camp at Oświęcim, I wish to state the following.

From the beginning of Christianity the cross of Christ has been, like Christ himself, a mark of salvation, as well as a mark of resistance. For St. Paul, who met the Resurrected One, the cross became *glory* (Gal. 6,14); for those *Jews and pagans alike*, who, like St. Paul, believed in the Resurrected One, the cross became *God's power* (I Cor. 1,18) and highest *wisdom* (see I Cor. 1,24). The same Christ crucified who was the core and fullness of the gospel proclaimed by St. Paul *became an outrage for the Jews and nonsense for the pagans* (I Cor. 1, 23).

The sharp controversy surrounding the crosses recently erected at the Gravel Pit in the immediate vicinity of the death camp at Auschwitz makes us painfully aware that the outrage of the cross continues to this day.

For us Christians the cross will always be the most sacred thing, the mark of salvation and symbol of greatest love accepted voluntarily for the salvation of the world. From the beginning of Polish history it has been deeply inscribed in the land of our fathers, so that it is impossible to understand Poles and the Polish nation without Christ, without the cross and the resurrection, of which the cross is a symbol, condition, and mark (John Paul II in Warsaw, 2. VI 1979, and when addressing the Poles in Kurytyba, 5 VII 1980).

The cross so conceived deserves to be defended at all times everywhere, for it is the fullest symbol and mark of all Christianity. We know of people who, in the not so distant past, sacrificed their lives for the cross as Christians, and this imposes on us, disciples of Christ and believers in the Crucified One, a greater obligation than on anyone else.

We expect respect for our Christian identity into which it is intrinsically inscribed. For there is no Christianity without Christ, and this means also (that there is no Christianity) without the cross on which — we believe — the salvation of the world was consummated.

But we must not forget that our Brothers the Jews who are not Christians associate completely different contents with the cross. They expect the same respect for their convictions as we Christians (expect for our convictions). There is no common denominator for these convictions. But instrumentally, the exploitation of the symbol of the cross and of its Christian content for battling anybody is a denial of Christianity and the cross.

The cross is a mark of love. The defense of the cross must find its extension and reflection in the attitude of the disciples, in accordance with Christ's summons: *"If anyone wants to be a follower of mine, let him renounce himself and take up his cross and follow me."* (Matt. 16, 24) One's cross is expressed in the dying in us — disciples of Christ — of (individual and collective) selfishness and hatred, and in the imitation of Christ's love for brothers. It is only in this way, by our own example, that we can demonstrate to the world the *power and wisdom of the cross* to which we have been summoned as disciples of the Crucified One. For those who use the cross as a tool for fighting anybody, act, in fact, *as the enemies of the cross of Christ* (Phil. 3, 18).

Quoting the words of the Pope, who said in *Zakopane*, "Defend the cross," to justify the "action of the crosses" at the gravel pit is an abuse and obvious distortion of the Pope's intention, as is the instrumentalization of the cross which is turned into a tool for furthering one's own murky affairs which seriously hurt the welfare of the Church, of our Fatherland, and the Christian-Jewish dialogue.

When he said, "Defend the cross, do not allow the NAME OF GOD to be insulted," the Pope clearly points to the cross as a symbol of highest love of man "which found its deepest expression in the cross" (John Paul II, *Zakopane*, 6 VI 1997).

To think that the Holy Father wants to use the defense of the cross to fight anybody is to be completely bereft of a sense of realism. If anyone is not persuaded by the Pope's words, let him imitate his life, and his attitude full of openness, humility, and love towards Jews.

It is only through such testimony that the cross can be a mark of power and victory over weakness, sin, hatred, and all those things that are the negation of full love and true Christianity.

Henryk Muszyński

Archbishop and Metropolitan of Griezno

# BULLETIN

## No. 32 (335, Tuesday, 11 August 1998)

### KAI (CATHOLIC INFORMATION AGENCY)

---

*The cross is not the property of the Catholic Church.*
**The Primate of Poland on the Auschwitz Conflict**

1. I wish to declare that the Polish Episcopate and the Polish Catholic Church are anxious to have a dialogue and to achieve Judaic-Catholic as well as Polish-Jewish reconciliation. We support the earlier declarations based on documents of ecumenical councils, on the creation of institutions for mutual recognition and understanding, of which a persuasive indication is the moving of the cloister of the Carmelite Sisters.

The present situation involving the cross at the gravel pit has become not only tense but also very complicated. The complications have increased as a result of the interventionist declaration of the government of Israel which demanded the removal of the crosses. The result of state intervention is that religious dialogue is not sufficient. This great complication of the matter calls not only for calm reflection but also for the revision of concepts used until now. These concepts failed because they were flawed.

First, the concept of the cross. The cross is not the property of the Catholic Church but is connected with Christianity. As a symbol it is understood and recognized in Western Civilization as a mark of the sacrifice of love and suffering. The right to this interpretation of this mark and to its defense belongs not only to the Episcopate but also to all those who, with their faith, accept this cross.

Another issue is defining both sides of the argument. There are too many subjects engaged in fighting the Auschwitz cross as well as in fighting the subjects of defense for their precise delimitation. On the Jewish side, there are those who demand that the cross be liquidated or decreased in size. The Catholic side is also non-uniform. There are determined defenders of the cross as well as proponents of the Jewish option, such as Mr. Śliwiński, a government official, and Father Musiał, editor of *Tygodnik*

*Powszechny.* The one-sided condemnation of the Episcopate for its failure to satisfy the Jewish side cannot be effective, primarily because it lacks basic justifications.

The essence of the argument seems to be to find a justification for the removal of the cross. The Jewish side argues that the cross cannot stand because millions of Jews perished in Auschwitz. The Christian side argues that the cross should stand because thousands of Christians, including Jews-Christians, perished here. This is Polish land, and the imposition of another will is viewed as interference in sovereignty. In other graveyards, such as Monte Casino, next to crosses of killed soldiers are stones with Stars of David.

As a reason for the escalation of tensions some point to Mr. Świtoń and his group, who describe themselves as defenders of the cross, at Auschwitz. In truth, this group came into being not because of a fantasy but because of constant and increasing pestering by the Jewish side for the fastest possible removal of the papal cross. The initiative of Mr. Świtoń and those around him, incommensurable with the dangers, points to far reaching social emotions, which cannot be discharged immediately and in a radical manner.

One has to think how the fact of erecting new crosses can be used in the process of understanding and conciliation. The issue is bound to be positively resolved provided that people in favor of a one-sided solution, such as, for example, Father Musiał, do not exacerbate matters by apodictic judgments.

# APPEAL OF THE PRIMATE

## Gazeta Wyborcza

Cardinal Józef Glemp, primate of Poland, unexpectedly made an appeal in which he asked for an end to the erecting of crosses at the gravel pit next to the Auschwitz extermination camp.

He wrote to the bishops: The wave of emotions is rising, and it is no longer rising on the foundation of the faith.

We recall that, while admittedly stipulating that Kazimierz Świtoń's initiative — who called for the erecting of new crosses — is "incommensurable with the dangers," Glemp wrote that "this group came into being not because of a fantasy but because of constant and increasing pestering by the Jewish side for the fastest possible removal of the papal cross." But yesterday Cardinal Glemp expressed his unease that "the action of erecting crosses is frequently taken over by irresponsible groups."

In the Thursday statement, the primate wrote that "the complication is increased by the interventionist declaration of the Israeli government which demands the removal of the crosses."

He admitted yesterday that "it turns out that the statements of the Israeli side did not have the character initially ascribed to them."

Before yesterday's statement by the primate, the Gdańsk metropolitan, Archbishop Tadeusz Gocławski said on Radio Plus that the "papal cross" should stay at the gravel pit and other, recently erected crosses, should be removed.

Earlier, on Sunday, Deputy Primate Achbishop Henryk Muszyński said that the erecting of new crosses is an abuse that hurts the Church, the fatherland, and dialogue.

The primate's appeal will certainly turn out to be a decisive step towards the solution of the embarrassing argument about crosses at the gravel pit. It is difficult to imagine that groups which stubbornly erect new crosses will not heed the head of the Polish Church. This statement is the voice of a Christian who had the courage to admit that his estimate of the situation was faulty.

Mikołaj Lizut

# TO THE VENERABLE PRIESTS-BISHOPS

## Declaration of the Primate of Poland

---

A few days ago I made a statement concerning the resumption of the dialogue about the presence of a cross at the gravel pit at Auschwitz. In view of the increase of emotion resulting from statements by the Israeli government, I wanted to call attention in order to soothe tensions and to point to the larger plane of the dialogue involving the cross. It turned out that the statements on the Israeli side did not have the character initially attributed to them. But the emotional wave did not subside. On the contrary, it increases, and it does so not on the foundation of the faith.

I see two undesirable phenomena: one is the diminution of the cross-symbol due to the erecting of additional crosses and little crosses; the other is that the action of erecting crosses is often taken over by irresponsible groups. Thereby, the gravel pit loses its solemnity.

I appeal to all those interested in this matter to stop erecting additional crosses at the gravel pit.

I ask all venerable Brothers-Bishops to stop this unchurchlike action.

# PSYCHOLOGICAL AND THEOLOGICAL DYNAMICS

# THE AUSCHWITZ CONVENT CONTROVERSY: A FAILURE OF SYMBOLS

## PROFESSOR HARRY JAMES CARGAS

The Auschwitz Convent controversy is so heavily fraught with misunderstanding, mistrust and misdirected efforts on the parts of both Christians and Jews that it may seem presumptuous for someone not directly involved with resolving the issue to address the subject at this time. On the other hand, it may be precisely from the point-of-view of a non-participant that a clearer picture may be presented. I want to try to understand what has happened/is happening because the problem *as symbol* is of extreme importance and, frankly, has been approached, generally, from a confused perception in two ways.

First, those who criticize the establishment of the Carmelite house of prayer near the Auschwitz ground as well as those who support its existence, somehow, are forgetting that there are two opinions being exerted here, one Polish and one Catholic. The political, nationalistic basis for a feeling about the convent is not the same as the religious basis. People who attack the convent as well as those who defend it sometimes fail to make the distinction.

The second confused perspective which appears to muddle the topic has to do with symbolism. Many backers and critics see a symbol dear to them being attacked, but fail to see that those on the other side of the issue also have a symbol that is being threatened.

On both of these fronts there is right and wrong, I think, to a heartbreaking degree. There are people of good will who disagree; there are also men and women who are very strident, determined to compete, to have their side win, regardless of tactics. The result is shame.

To begin with there has to be a context. This cannot be a caricature of a nation of 600 years of unrelieved antisemitism nor of a minority dedicated to economic control and an international conspiracy to weaken Poland.

When Lech Wałęsa visited the United States in November of 1989 some people were rather surprised to hear him refer to Polish Jewry as a second or other nation. While Wałęsa and his Solidarity movement have been strong in bringing up the nearly buried subject of Polish-ethnic Jewish relations in his country, the designation of Jews living in Poland as "another nation" bespeaks an attitude, which many will have to understand as divisive. This clearly reflects, however, the general situation in Poland today and historically.

It is not necessary here to go back centuries to discuss the experience of Jews in Poland. What is more appropriate is to recall the relationship between Polish people and Jews — and it is very difficult to have to refer to Polish people who are Jewish as Jews and not as Poles, but this distinction is enforced on us — during the time period after the First World War and up to the period leading to the Nazi invasion. David Engel, in his authoritative now half-completed study of the Polish government in exile, titled *In the Shadow of Auschwitz,* reminds us that historian Pawel Korzec observed that "the manner in which Poland treated Polish Jews between the two world wars contributed to making the immense tragedy which was to befall them under the Hitlerite yoke possible."[1] Engel himself observes ironically that while most of the 40,000 Polish Jews who survived the war in hiding owed their lives to Polish non-Jews who aided them, how many more owe their deaths to the "unwillingness of other Poles to do the same thing."[2]

Engel is my major source for a summary of the between wars era. Just previously the highly urbanized Jews were perceived by many Poles to monopolize commerce and manufacturing in their country. This "corresponded to reality only in part" writes Engel.[3] Demographic shifts brought on job competition and, in 1912, an anti-Jewish boycott. Waves of immigration of Jews from Russia raised fears about their loyalties to Poland. Even the preference of Yiddish to Polish by many Jews was considered a sign of hostility to Polish national interests. That Poland was earmarked to become the New Palestine truly frightened many Poles and international pressures on Poland to treat Jews fairly were interpreted as a sign of Jewish power to be feared. Laws were passed severely limiting the civil rights of Jews. Many Jews were removed from the armed forces, while others were forced to work on Saturday, the Jewish Sabbath. Moreover, state support for Jewish education was regularly withheld. By 1936, the government openly condoned the boycott of Jewish businesses. Discrimination was rampant and 1935-38 saw a wave of pogroms resulting in many Jewish deaths and injuries. Antisemitic pamphlet literature targeted Jews as disloyal while a decline in apparent Western concern over all of these happenings caused no decline in the injustices.

Polish authorities demanded that the West aid in Jewish emigration from their country and Jews, even Zionists, split among themselves over how to respond to this policy. When war approached, Jews were portrayed not as loyal Poles but merely as anti-Germans. When the war did come and the Polish government went into exile, Engel says that news of atrocities to Polish Jews was released only when it was helpful to its anti-Nazi strategy. Yet for some of the top government officials, discrimination against Jews was not to be tolerated, although much behind the scenes activity did not bear this out. The historian also indicates, however, that at times "Jewish complaints concerning the behavior of Polish officials were inaccurate or exaggerated, yet Jewish leaders tended for the most part to dismiss the government's refutations of them as contrived and self-serving."[4] He also writes that certain demands made by Jews of the government-in-exile were clearly unrealistic.

Furthermore, we read that the exiled officials had many difficulties in retaining the confidence of the population and "it feared that to allow itself to be perceived as especially solicitous of Jewish interests might critically impair its success."[5] While these words of David Engel are offered by him as mitigating blame for actions not taken, we cannot overlook the fact that they betray the populace's antisemitism, however inadvertently, to a depressing degree.

That antisemitism, of course, carried over to the post-war period. The infamous pogrom at Kielce is one of many examples. About 200 Jews returned to that community. There, on July 4, 1946 they were attacked; 42 were murdered (including two children) and some 50 others were wounded.

In my book, *A Christian Response to the Holocaust,* I tell about an interview I had with two Polish Holocaust survivors, a married couple now living in the United States. They told me of going back to their hometown immediately after the war, but having to flee because returning Jews were being murdered by local Polish citizens. The man said that "We were afraid because the hatred against Jews remained from before the war. We knew it would go on and on, the same thing. It was no use to be over there." When

I asked the woman if she had any wish to visit Poland again, she screamed. "Never. Poland to me is blood."[6]

Iwona Irwin-Zarecka, in a study presented at the Annual Scholars' Conference on the Church Struggle and the Holocaust in 1988, discussed the relationship of "Catholics and Jews in Poland Today."[7] She told of a nun who was excommunicated by her Church for sheltering Jews,[8] of the hostile reaction of a significant number of Poles when a government spokesman reminded people that their new saint, Maximilian Kolbe, has been "an active promoter of antisemitic literature in the 1930s...,"[9] of how many rescuers of Jews preferred anonymity after the war for fear of retaliation by their Polish neighbors, and of at least two Warsaw Catholic parishes freely distributing *Protocols of the Learned Elders of Zion* and other works on the so-called Jewish conspiracy.

The thesis of Professor Irwin-Zarecka's remarks is that there is an absence of moral self-questioning regarding the Church's record in promoting antisemitism. Such reflections, she insists, could lead to a broader acceptance of moral responsibility. The issue at hand has to do with antisemitism rooted in religious tradition as distinct from that which is more nationalistic, outlined earlier. The separation is not, to be certain, a clear one and may even be more obscured when we consider the chapter on Poland in John Morley's book *Vatican Diplomacy and the Jews During the Holocaust 1939-1943*.[10] Nevertheless, I reiterate, there is a difference.

Morley, a Catholic priest who was permitted into the Vatican historical archives, writes in the Introduction to his volume that "The Holy See has loudly and repeatedly proclaimed its uniqueness as a religious and moral power. If the records demonstrated that its diplomatic activity during the Holocaust was parochial and self-serving, it would, of necessity, stand condemned by its own criterion."[11] In this context the three final sentences of Morley's last chapter are particularly telling. He writes, "It must be concluded that Vatican diplomacy failed the Jews during the Holocaust by not doing all that it was possible for it to do on their behalf. It also *failed itself* because in neglecting the needs of Jews, and pursuing a goal of reserve rather than humanitarian concern, it betrayed the ideals that it had set up for itself. The nuncios, the secretary of state, and most of all, the Pope share responsibility for this dual failure."[12]

I add a personal note of clarification here. Anyone familiar with my writing knows that I have long been a critic of Pope Pius XII's failure to intervene decisively on behalf of Jews during the *Shoah*.[13] While I am absolutely convinced of the antisemitism of many Vatican functionaries, I have never labeled the Pope an antisemite even where I have been almost strident about his silence. While perhaps being one who lacked compassion for Jews (rather than, say, hating them), Pius XII may be more justly criticized as one who froze in times of crisis, as a man incapable of making a commitment, a decision to act, when such commitments, such decisions, were required.

While there is undeniable evidence that the Pope knew very early on what the fate of the Jews under Nazi domination was, most are less aware of his reaction to the sufferings of non-Jewish Poles who were struggling under the Hitler yoke. In September 1942, a Polish bishop in exile, Charles Radoński, complained to a Vatican official about the Pope's silence regarding atrocities committed against the non-Jewish Poles.[14] (He also complained about the persecution of Jews, it should be recorded.) Another bishop, Stanisław Adamski, residing in Warsaw, wrote in January of 1943 that many Poles shared the opinion that the Pope had forgotten them.

That same month, the president of Poland, Władysław Raczkiewicz, in a letter to Pius XII, outlined the three years of agony his countrymen and women had experienced. He, too, made specific reference to the particularity of the Jewish terror. President Raczkiewicz very pointedly reminded the Pope of statements made by his predecessors on behalf of Poland and asked him to break his silence in a manner which has been described as begging.

Poles criticized Pius XII's Christmas message of 1942. For example, Kasimir Papee, the Polish ambassador at the Vatican, was instructed to demand a specific condemnation of Germany for its crimes. The Pope's letter of response only dealt with generalities and never once did it refer to Germany or Germans. Later, Vatican diplomats in Washington and Berne, Switzerland, and other locations were instructed on how to defend the Pope against such attacks.

Here is John Morley's conclusion on the Vatican's efforts, or lack of them, in Poland. "Pope Pius XII said little and did nothing on behalf of Polish Catholics, whose political and religious leaders appealed to him for some words or for a gesture of support. It was a silence deeply resented by the Polish Catholics and never adequately broken by the Pope, except for some fairly general words in his June, 1943 address. Pius XII's silence in regard to the suffering Catholics in Poland is a matter of history..."[15]

Morley goes on to say, "The sad conclusion is that the tragic events in Poland were not able to move the pope or his secretary of state to face the reality of a situation whose cruelty was unparalleled in human history. A more sobering conclusion might be that diplomatic relations with Germany were considered such a premium that no word or deed could be permitted that would endanger them."[16]

All this has been by way of establishing a context for the Auschwitz convent controversy.

The Church is nothing if not an institution of symbols. So much of what we Christians do is wrapped up in symbolism. We must recognize, then, that the first saint to be canonized as part of the Holocaust experience is a powerful symbol. There is no doubt in my mind that the Polish priest, Maximilian Kolbe, died heroically and, by whatever measures the Roman church used to judge its great persons, Kolbe qualifies. However, Kolbe was not specifically a Holocaust martyr and should not be passed off as one. Nor was the proposed canonization of Sister Edith Stein a better *symbolic* choice. This convert from Judaism became a nun and was imprisoned and killed by the Nazis. It appears that she died a heroic death. Nevertheless, her martyrdom must not be misunderstood. She was murdered not because she was a Catholic nun, but because she had been born a Jew, and she is even reported to have said that hers was a sacrifice for the Jews who had refused Christ. In my judgment, both she and Kolbe could have been canonized a hundred years from now. (They do not need *our* recognition immediately to gain their eternal rewards, which are independent of our notice.)

Another symbolic act which I find it difficult to comprehend has to do with the *style* of the current Polish Pope's welcome of Austrian chancellor Kurt Waldheim to the papacy. I need not elaborate. We may need a reminder that it is *not only* Jews who reacted to the reception Waldheim received in Rome. It is *not only* Jews who are concerned that Christians hid *Nazis* after the war. It is *not only* Jews who are reacting to the establishment of the Carmelite convent at Auschwitz. Christians too are speaking out and that must be recognized by the media, by Jews *and by Christians.*

It must be remembered that thousands of Catholics expressed dismay over the Carmelite affair. Cardinals from France, Belgium, the

United States and elsewhere vigorously protested the events. *Then* the Vatican intervened.

We must not overlook the fact that Solidarity introduced the problem of Jewish-Catholic relations into the public arena. We have to acknowledge that the issues of the conversion of Jews and of Catholic triumphalism, were imposed on the discussion from outside and do not seem to have been part of the Carmelite plan. I think Rabbi Avraham Weiss used poor judgment in scaling the convent fence (with colleagues) to protest the house of prayer on Auschwitz property, then claiming they were on a study mission. Yitzhak Shamir did not help this situation by saying that in Poland antisemitism is imbibed with mothers' milk. And, personally, I was very disappointed to see that at the groundbreaking ceremony for the new location of the convent, no Jewish officials were present. The boycott not only was unhelpful to what must be an ongoing dialogue, but I think that many of us who did support the Jewish complaints were thereby let down.

Auschwitz, as has been said many times, is more than Auschwitz. Its symbolic value has penetrated our psyches. A Carmelite convent is also a symbol that cannot be ignored. I urge both communities to recognize this. As a Christian I particularly remind my coreligionists that when Jews say that what we are doing is painful to them, we owe them the cosmic courtesy to believe them, to try to understand them, to make every effort to ease that suffering. Failing to do so may be failing as Christians. Dare we risk such failure?

## ENDNOTES

1. Quoted in Engel, David. *In the Shadow of Auschwitz.* Chapel Hill, University of North Carolina Press, 1987, p.3.
2. *Ibid.*, p.5.
3. *Ibid.*, p.13.
4. *Ibid.*, p.206.
5. *Ibid.*
6. Cargas, Harry James, *A Christian Response to the Holocaust.* Denver, Stonehenge Books, 1981, p.9.
7. Irwin-Zarecka, Iwona, "Catholics and Jews in Poland Today" *Holocaust and Genocide Studies,* vol. 4, 1989, pp. 27-40.
8. *Ibid.*, p.39.

9. *Ibid.*, p.40.

10. Morley, John F., Vatican Diplomacy and the Jews During the Holocaust 1939-1943. New York, KTAV, 1980.

11. *Ibid.*, p.5

12. *Ibid.*, p. 209.

13. See for example Cargas, *op.cit.*, *passim.*, and Cargas, Harry James, *Reflections of a Post-Auschwitz Christian* (Detroit, Wayne State University Press, 1989), pp.91-108.

14. For this and what follows, cf. Morley, pp.139-140.

15. *Ibid.*, p.146.

16. *Ibid.*

# THE STRUGGLE FOR MEMORY AND MEMORIALIZATION AT AUSCHWITZ

## JOHN T. PAWLIKOWSKI

As I write this essay, the erection of numerous "small crosses" at the Auschwitz death camp site by Polish nationalists who intertwine politics with Catholic identity continues to create intense controversy. While the issue is now moving through the Polish legal system and eventually will come before the Polish parliament, the situation will continue to impact Polish-Jewish and Catholic-Jewish relations for the foreseeable future. Whatever the eventual legal and political outcome of the present crisis, it has brought to ascendancy militant forces on both sides of that controversy that will not easily be neutralized. And even if the "small crosses" issue is resolved fairly amicably, the much deeper question of the large cross[1] which has stood on the site since the time of the Carmelite convent will continue to present a formidable challenge to Polish-Jewish reconciliation for some time to come. The reality is that while the tensions resulting from the opening of the Carmelite convent were successfully defused, due in large part to the strategic intervention of Pope John Paul II who urged the nuns to relocate, many of the deeper issues connected with memory and memorialization did not vanish once the convent was moved to a location away from the camp itself.

In the following pages I would like to examine briefly some of the principal issues raised by the original Auschwitz convent controversy[2] and now again by the crisis over the "small crosses." Until such time as these questions are put on the table and responsibly debated by all concerned parties there will be no final resolution of the conflict that would bring permanent dignity to the site, and above all, to its many victims. The danger is that we shall put too much stock in the mere removal of the "small crosses" and the original large cross and fail to recognize that a final resolution demands much more from both sides. If Poles and Jews particularly, and Jews and Catholics more generally, have not reached a point of genuine understanding and reconciliation over memory and

103

memorialization at Auschwitz, legal and political victories may turn out to be Pyrrhic with the real possibility of continued flare-ups into the new millennium.

As we look back over the decade of controversy that began with the crisis of late Summer 1989, we see evidence of persistent issues that are far from complete understanding, let alone adjudication. Both the original convent controversy as well as the present impasse over the Cross and crosses show that many people in the Christian community as well as in the Jewish community remain unaffected by the constructive developments that have occurred in Christian-Jewish relations since Vatican II. Cardinal Józef Glemp's remarks at the height of 1989 during the course of the annual national pilgrimage to Jasna Góra (in the presence of Poland's Prime Minister Tadeusz Mazowiecki, who himself was an early lay leader in Catholic-Jewish reconciliation in the immediate aftermath of World War II) accused Jews of offending the Polish nation by their criticism over the Carmelite convent and went on to speak about supposed Jewish power to manipulate the mass media, seeming to many to echo strongly classic Christian stereotypes of Jews. While some prominent Catholics and Jews committed to a negotiated settlement of the Auschwitz-Birkenau controversy have defended Cardinal Glemp against charges of outright antisemitism, his Jasna Góra statement certainly nurtured the views of the overtly antisemitic Polish groups in Poland and abroad. And Cardinal Glemp's initial reaction to the controversy surrounding the emergence of the small crosses (a stance modified after the Polish episcopal leadership called for their removal in an August 1998 meeting in Częstochowa), while it did not have the clearly offensive language of the 1989 address, nonetheless criticized Jews for raising a fuss over the Cross and crosses.

On the Jewish side, it was the remark of Israeli Prime Minister Yitzhak Shamir and the actions and comments of Rabbi Avi Weiss that generated the greatest ire among Poles within and without Poland. Shamir exhibited, in the eyes of most Poles, the use of unnuanced charges of endemic Polish antisemitism, which Polish leaders often term "anti-Polanism," when he spoke of Poles acquiring antisemitism through their mothers' milk. Even though we might attribute the harshness of Shamir's statement to unresolved anger over the death of a brother at the hands of Poles after the end of World War II, they were nevertheless unbecoming a head of state and, more importantly, misrepresented to the world the complex Polish-Jewish relationship.[3] And Rabbi Avi Weiss' remarks during the recent negotiations over Auschwitz-Birkenau, led on the Jewish side by Miles Lerman, Chairman of the United States Holocaust Memorial Council, especially Weiss's statement at the December 1998 meeting of the Council in Washington, are devoid of any sensitivity towards Polish victimization at the camp. If we are to understand and successfully resolve the continuing controversy over the Auschwitz-Birkenau site, which involves more than the removal of the small crosses and the ultimate relocation of the large cross, we need to probe more deeply the historical and contemporary facts that have generated misperceptions and mutual mistrust.

Jewish fears concerning Auschwitz-Birkenau, in the end, seem to boil down to one reality – desecration of the MEMORY of the millions for whom the site constitutes, in the words of Elie Wiesel, "an invisible cemetery." Since the time of the Auschwitz Convent controversy Jewish leaders have expressed concern that an effort was underway by the Vatican and the Polish Catholic Church to clothe Auschwitz-Birkenau in Christian garb. There has been an intensification of such accusations in some quarters of the international Jewish community since the emergence of the new crosses. Associating the large cross, and especially the new crosses, with other concomitant events such as the canonization of Edith Stein, the World Jewish Congress in particular has launched a veritable attack on the Vatican. Recent publications from the Congress have escalated the rhetoric. WJC Policy Dispatch #31, issued from Jerusalem in August 1998, says the following: "At the end of July of this year a new assault on the integrity of Auschwitz was perpetrated: some 50 crosses were erected adjacent to the perimeter of the camp. World Jewry will not tolerate this blatant attempt at "Christianization" of the site."[4] And Policy Dispatch #36, released in November 1998 with the title "A Great Leap Backwards," argues that "dialogue has not prevented a slide in Catholic-Jewish relations over Catholicism's narrative and the symbolization of the *Shoah*." It goes on to add that "While Pope John Paul II has affirmed that the *Shoah* is an instance of moral failure, the Church's choice of saints from the period suggests an effort to 'Christianize' the victims of the *Shoah* and whitewash the Catholic leadership's reticence to aid victims of persecution. Until the Catholic Church makes a frank accounting of its activities during and after the Second World War, such Church decisions chip away at the bridges of dialogue between Jewish and Catholic communities."[5] While not directly related to the "crosses/Cross issue at Auschwitz-Birkenau, Policy Forum #5, which appeared in the Summer of 1998, tries to establish a "conspiracy of silence" regarding Vatican responsibility during the Holocaust and immediately afterwards. The publication argues that "Vatican officials were pivotal in using illicit funds or the Church's own monies to facilitate Nazis escaping Europe,"[6] referring to efforts of *Ustasha* (a Croatian fascist organization) to remove funds from that country which the Croatian College of San Girolamo in Rome aided and abetted. While there is little question that people connected with this college had some connection with this operation, particularly a priest named Krunoslaw Dragonovic, there is no evidence of high-level Vatican involvement as this WJC publication claims. To enhance the argument for direct Vatican involvement, this claim is based on the discovery in 1997 of a memorandum by Emerson Bigelow, an expert in illicit funds, which suggested such a Vatican involvement. Elan Steinberg of the World Jewish Congress is quoted in this publication as insisting that the Bigelow letter "is an extremely significant development that fits into the pattern of the Nazi gold question. It is a pattern that involved not only Switzerland and other neutral countries, but according to US intelligence documents, went into the heart of the Holy See."[7]

Even if all the charges against the College of San Girolamo and against Fr. Dragonovic were to be proven true, this would not establish a conspiracy at the "heart of the Holy See" as Steinberg claims. Such rhetoric is totally inflated. The implication of Vatican involvement in the Bigelow letter was thoroughly researched by the Office of the Deputy Secretary of the Treasury, Stuart Eizenstat, as part of the Nazi gold investigation that he supervised. No concrete evidence was in fact unearthed in this investigation. The June 1998 Report to the U.S. Congress by Deputy Secretary Eizenstat's office indicates that no substantial link existed and that Fr. Dragonovic was his own operation. "He's not the Vatican," according to the report.[8] In fact, Deputy Secretary Eizenstat subsequently apologized to Vatican officials for his staff even including this discredited charge in the final report to Congress. The World Jewish Congress report rejects this section of the Eizenstat report.

This concerted attack on the Vatican by the World Jewish Congress has significantly eroded a basic level of trust within the Vatican and in Polish Church circles. Coupled with a frontal assault on Poland's Primate Józef Glemp as "an unabashed antisemite" in the WJC Policy Dispatch,[9] this attack has made it more difficult to conduct substantive, constructive discussions on the Auschwitz-Birkenau situation, since the World Jewish Congress is a central member of the International Jewish

Negotiating Team. In Europe especially the World Jewish Congress is looked upon as the most important voice of world Jewry. While it is important for non-Jews to recognize that the WJC does not speak for all Jews on Auschwitz-Birkenau issues or any others, its influence is substantial.

I am not suggesting that fault is absent on the part of institutional Catholicism, both at the Vatican and in Poland, for the current climate. I will address this subsequently in this essay. But, since I am quoted favorably in Policy Forum #31, I want to make it clear that whatever criticisms I have of Vatican wartime activities and its present policies regarding those activities, I in no way associate myself with the tone or the inflated charges that are made in these recent WJC documents. We will have great difficulty securing any positive movement on the Auschwitz-Birkenau accord so long as these attacks continue. The Vatican, the Polish Catholic leadership, and the World Jewish Congress are vital players in any final accord. Any poisoning of the relationship among them will only serve to undercut the negotiating process. Jewish groups who do not share the WJC approach to Holocaust-era issues must do more to separate themselves publicly from the stance of the WJC. One of the lessons that emerges from the negotiations over the Auschwitz Convent is that a considerable level of trust remained during the deliberations. We stand on the verge of losing this trust in the current controversy over the crosses/Cross.

The basic fear of the Polish community, within Poland and in the worldwide Polish diaspora, during the period of conflict over the Convent as well as the present controversy, centered on the memory of its victims. Repeatedly, the Polish accusation, warranted or not, in the original Convent dispute was that Jews were trying to take possession of the Auschwitz site. Both the militant Polish nationalists as well as the more responsible elements in present-day Poland have raised similar concerns. They argue that once again Jewish leaders reveal a lack of understanding of Polish victimization under Nazis in general, and specifically the role Auschwitz played in that victimization process. Auschwitz, in fact, served as the premier camp for the extermination of the Polish leadership elite (academics, politicians, artists, clergy) in the Nazi effort to reduce Poland to a permanent state of servitude to the Third Reich, and perhaps even to the point of total annihilation as Nazi leaders such as Himmler, Hitler and Hans Frank (who headed the Nazi "General Government" in Poland) suggested on occasion. Poles often express great dismay at the seeming lack of information on the basic origins of Auschwitz initially as a camp for political prisoners (a short period) and then as the primary center for the liquidation of Polish leaders. Only towards the end of 1942 did Auschwitz become predominantly Jewish, well after the Nazis had totally conquered Poland. This subsequent Jewish majority at Auschwitz must be clearly acknowledged, but not at the expense of an understanding of Polish suffering at the site.

The memory of the Auschwitz camp with its unprecedented human destruction has been unalterably implanted in Jewish consciousness. For many, the name Auschwitz is a synonym for the entirety of the *Shoah*. But this fact does not excuse, even in the mind of those Poles quite prepared to acknowledge the ultimate significance of Auschwitz for the *Shoah*, the narrowness of the remarks made during the Convent crisis by Ady Steg, president of the Alliance Israelite Universelle, at the first Geneva meeting on the Convent situation held in July 1986, which included Catholic leaders from France, Poland, and Belgium and Jewish rabbinic and communal leaders from France, Belgium and Italy. Professor Steg, speaking to these leaders assembled in Geneva, argued that the Jewish people had acquired, through the martyrdom of its children there, "inalienable rights to Auschwitz." He further declared that the memory of the hundreds of thousands of non-Jews who were murdered there should be preserved. But, he noted, "their murder was perpetrated as an 'extra measure'...a matter of subjecting the non-Jews to facilities which were installed for the working out of the Final Solution. In truth, Auschwitz, with its gas chambers and its crematoria, was conceived, constructed, and put to use solely for the extermination of the Jews." [10] Apart from total insensitivity to the crucial role played by Auschwitz in the Nazi onslaught against the Polish nation that constituted an integral part of the overall Nazi plan for "human purification" whose centerpiece was Jewish annihilation, Steg simply had his facts wrong. Poles were the majority of inmates at Auschwitz until 1942, when Jews assumed that dubious role. The first killings by poison gas at Auschwitz, according to historian Richard C. Lucas, involved 300 Poles and 700 Soviet prisoners." [11]

In the context of the current controversy over Auschwitz-Birkenau we have not witnessed any uninformed statements from the Jewish side that parallel those of Professor Steg. But, despite my interventions with the Jewish International Negotiating Team and with Elie Wiesel, and calls from other Christian and Jewish leaders close to the Polish scene, such as

Professor Stefan Shreiner of the Institutum Judaicum at Energard-Karls-Universität in Tübingen, Germany and the respected Dr. Stanisław Krajewski of Warsaw, the international Jewish leadership has so far refrained from any public statement on the Auschwitz-Birkenau issue that would clearly acknowledge the need for memorialization of Polish suffering at the camp. How such memorialization is to be achieved concretely is certainly open to negotiation, but such acknowledgment would go a long way in alleviating Polish fears that a final settlement of the controversy will ignore their history at the site. It would be the kind of confidence-building measure that is essential for successful negotiations of any public dispute of the magnitude and significance of the present one over Auschwitz.

A second Polish fear, rooted both in historical experiences and contemporary reality, is in some ways a corollary to the Jewish fear of looking too weak. The Polish psyche, both in Poland and in the foreign communities of Polonia, has been deeply affected by experience of oppression and prejudice, particularly in this century. Coming out of a long history of occupation and divisions of their nation by foreign powers, Poles in the twentieth century, after a brief interlude of national independence, were subject to the tyranny of the Nazis and subsequently by the Communists. Just when new possibilities for a measure of democracy and national self-respect have appeared, into the picture come the Jews and their claims to the Auschwitz camp which many Poles regard as a national political shrine. While some of the Polish reaction in this area has been interwoven with classical Polish antisemitism and antisemitic Polish nationalism which was rampant in the years prior to World War II,[12] especially in the current crisis with the statements of those who have established themselves at the site and those made by Fr. Henryk Jankowski of Gdańsk, the former chaplain to the Solidarity movement and to President Lech Wałęsa, it is necessary to understand that this other dynamic has been at work as well. So when some Jewish leaders have attempted to threaten Poland's financial stability by urging the U.S. Congress to cut off financial support for the fledgling nation's stabilization as part of the process of its European integration, many Poles and their Polish American supporters reacted with great dismay. In raising quite legitimate concerns about the Auschwitz-Birkenau site, Jewish leaders and their organizations must become more sensitive regarding tactics lest they inadvertently play into Polish fears that Jews are trying not only to shut out Polish memorialization at Auschwitz, but also to undermine as well the country's oncoming democratic development. These Polish fears are real, even if some of the motivation behind them is highly questionable. Calls for an international extraterritorial status for Auschwitz-Birkenau by Kalman Sultanik of the World Jewish Congress and the Chief Rabbi of Poland Menachem Pinkas Joskowicz in the midst of the current discussions over the crosses/Cross further intensify these fears.

But just as elements in the Jewish community must bear some responsibility for the erosion of mutual confidence in the present crisis, so Polish and Polish American political leaders, as well as the Vatican, also must share the blame. Over the last decade or so important efforts have been underway to improve Polish-Jewish understanding and to recapture the sense of Jewish identity with Polish culture. The annual Jewish culture week in Cracow is one such example. And the Polish Episcopal Conference issued important statements in 1991 and 1995. The first, read in all churches throughout Poland on January 20, 1991, acknowledged the specificity of Jewish extermination at Auschwitz as well as some Polish complicity in the Nazi-led effort. And the 1995 document issued along with statements from other Catholic episcopal conferences on the occasion of the fiftieth anniversary of the liberation of Auschwitz reinforced the thrust of the earlier pastoral.[13] While some may regard these statements as incomplete, they nonetheless represent Polish implementation of the vision of chapter four of Vatican II's historic declaration on the Church and the Jewish people. And despite the efforts of leading Polish intellectuals such as Fr. Stanisław Musiał, S.J., who has served as secretary of the Polish Episcopate's Commission for Relations with Jews, the late Jerzy Turowicz, internationally acclaimed editor of *Tygodnik Powszechny,* Professor Ryszard Rubinkiewicz of the Catholic University of Lublin, Archbishop Henryk Muszyński of Gniezno, Bishop Stanisław Gadecki of the Polish Church's Commission for Interreligious Dialogue, Bishop Tadeusz Pieronek, Archbishop Józef Życiński of Lublin, people connected with the Polish Council of Christians and Jews in Warsaw, and the inauguration of an annual Day of Judaism within the Polish church, popular attitudes have not been completely swayed. And Prime Minister Jerzy Buzek, in a speech in Warsaw, insisted that Jewish culture must be seen as an integral part of general Polish culture.

Studies of Polish popular opinion have shown a significant decline in antisemitic attitudes, particularly when compared to the thirties. Overtly antisemitic candidates have generally lost elections for the Polish parliament. Nevertheless, during the height of the Convent crisis and again in the midst of the new controversy, disturbing evidence of significant anti-Jewish feeling regarding the Auschwitz site clearly emerged. Most Poles who responded to the original Convent situation with statements, articles, or letters-to-the-editor strongly criticized Jews for supposedly denying any Polish rights to Auschwitz. Even within the circle of the Solidarity Union, whose daily newspaper *Gazeta Wyborcza* ran a strong editorial against Cardinal Glemp's infamous Częstochowa address, the prevailing response was negative. Respected journalist Konstanty Gebert, writing under the pen name of Dawid Warszawski, has reported on the outraged mail received by the newspaper as a result of its editorial. [14] And, during the crisis over the crosses/Cross, the statements of the militant nationalists have been even more disturbing. Kazimierz Świtoń, a former member of the Solidarity Union political party who has encamped himself at the site of the crosses, proclaims that Jews have no right to tell Poles what to do on Polish soil. He insists that he and his followers will not vacate the area until he has written assurance from Catholic leaders that the crosses/Cross, which, in his words, "pay tribute to the Polish victims of Auschwitz," will remain permanently at Auschwitz. On many of these crosses a slogan has appeared which reads: "Only under this cross, only under this symbol, Poland is Poland and a Pole is a Pole." [15]

Both the leadership of the Polish Episcopal Conference and the Buzek government have called for the removal of the small crosses while saying that the large cross (sometimes called the "papal cross" – a term Archbishop Muszyński has termed misleading) [16] should remain in place. And public opinion seems generally to support the call for the removal of the small crosses. Yet, prominent Polish historian Jerzy Ladlicki, while acknowledging that Świtoń represents a lunatic fringe, argues that residual support for Świtoń may not be as narrow as some imagine. Hence, the actual removal of the crosses may prove far more difficult for the government and the Church and could provoke an outcry not only from Świtoń, but from the independent Catholic Radio Maryja which has considerable following in rural Poland. The fact that over one hundred and fifty members of parliament belonging to Prime Minister Buzek's coalition government have strongly endorsed the continued presence of the large cross at the site adds further pressure on the government. And in Canada and the United States, the largest Polish organizations, the Polish American Congress and the Canadian Polish Congress, have used language in their commentary on the crosses/Cross dispute that further inflames the situation.

Many Poles and Polish Americans have tended to assume that because Auschwitz is on Polish soil, Poland has the exclusive rights to determine what shall be located at the site. In a manner that parallels Professor Steg's claim of the Jewish "inalienable right to Auschwitz," Polish assertions have been equally unbending. And most Poles and Polish Americans assume that Jews have precipitated the crisis in both instances by their failure to acknowledge legitimate Polish sovereignty over the camp and the making of counter claims instead. While in some cases this perception may have a factual basis, what Poles have often not admitted was that the establishment of the Convent, the erection of the large Cross, and the placing of the small crosses were unilateral actions that involved no consultation with the Jewish Community. The fact that this is the largest Jewish cemetery in the world, and the fact that it has been designated a UNESCO World Heritage, site mean that decision-making about Auschwitz cannot be done without the involvement of the world Jewish community. So, in fact, the original Convent crisis and the present dispute were precipitated not by Jewish aggressiveness, but by an inexcusable Polish mistake of excluding Jews from any voice about memorializing of victims at the camp. This "priority of error" must be underlined because Poles overwhelmingly have accused Jews of trying to preempt their rights at Auschwitz. The truth is the reverse of that. Polish Catholics initially failed to recognize the distinctive bonding to Auschwitz-Birkenau that exists within world Jewry.

Another source of contention in both of the disputes over Auschwitz involves significantly different understandings of how to memorialize the dead. Elie Wiesel and others on the Jewish side have called for the removal of all religious symbols from Auschwitz-Birkenau. For many Poles religious symbols are a must, particularly in light of their recent experience of the Communist era when all religious symbols were forcibly removed from public places. For classical Catholicism it is considered honorable, even commendable, to erect monuments and chapels in cemeteries, which in Poland have frequently been associated with a church. To pray for the dead or to arrange for the celebration of Mass in their behalf traditionally has been strongly encouraged by the Church. No doubt this is directly related to a firm belief in purgatory where those who are still required to make amends for past sins must go prior to passage into heaven. Prayer for the dead is viewed as of direct benefit to the dead whose souls may still remain mired in purgatory, in terms of hastening their departure for heaven. In this sense, it remains the most "productive" activity members of the Catholic community can undertake for their immediate and extended family members who are deceased.

In the Jewish community, the attitude toward memorializing victims is virtually the exact opposite of the Catholic position. Traditional Jewry has always been opposed to the erection of worship sites in cemeteries. And, unlike the situation in Catholicism, cemeteries have never been developed adjacent to a synagogue. Jews do pray in cemeteries, both on the day of burial and on the anniversaries of the death of loved ones. But the prayer texts for these occasions do not refer directly to death. In fact, they have been imported from other situations having no connection with the passage from life. Instead they focus first and foremost on the sanctification of God. Again, it is likely that theological understandings of the afterlife play a critical role. As descendants of the Pharisaic/rabbinic tradition of the Second Temple period, classical Jewry today accepts the notion of resurrection of the faithful individual. But this point of belief is emphasized far less than in Catholic theology. And one does not find in Judaism any sense of temporary purgation akin to the Church's view of purgatory. Hence there exists no sense of responsibility on the part of the living community of faith to assist those who have gone before them in finally attaining heaven. Resurrection in Judaism is something that will occur once for all at the end of human history when righteous Jews will enter the new kingdom inaugurated by the coming of the Messiah. Resurrection is entirely the activity of God. Humans can have little, if any, direct impact on its speed. The state of the dead in the interim period is of little concern to Jewish theology, in contrast to classical Catholic thought. Rather, praying in cemeteries is intended to remember the deceased person, but first and foremost to honor the Creator God, Lord both of the living and the dead, whose power continues to energize the People Israel as they move on through history toward the final Messianic age.

These fundamentally different, in some ways even diametrically opposed, perspectives on memorializing the dead will of necessity make the task of achieving harmony between Jews and Catholics over the Auschwitz site an extremely delicate proposition that will require considerable understanding and sensitivity. Both qualities have been in rather short supply among many Poles and Jews who have entered the discussion over

Auschwitz. A final resolution over the issue of symbols will require some compromise. Certainly the small crosses need to be removed. In many cases they represent more of a nationalistic statement than a religious one. Even the Polish bishops acknowledge this. And important persons connected with the original negotiations over the Auschwitz Convent have assured me that there was a verbal agreement that the large Cross should be transferred to the site of the new convent. But the status of this large Cross should not be made a pre-condition for the continuation of the negotiations regarding Auschwitz-Birkenau's final status. A great deal of trust, which does not presently exist, will be required to reach an agreeable compromise on this. In a sense, the large Cross parallels the "Jerusalem" question in the Middle East peace negotiations. It is very likely that some memorial, perhaps with a cross inscribed on it, will need to be erected at the site to commemorate Polish victimization in a manner that will adequately honor Polish religious sensitivities.

On the Polish side there will also need to be an evident willingness to probe the issue of Polish antisemitism, particularly in the period between World War I and World War II, as well as the question whether Poles did enough to save Jews during the Holocaust. Polish antisemitism is certainly not the full story of Polish-Jewish relations and it is regrettable that on occasion Jewish leaders and writers tend to make it such. One blatant example of this is to be found in the often-seen video "The Longest Hatred" where it is argued that such antisemitism has not abated, through an interview with an extreme Polish nationalist whose party went nowhere in Polish parliamentary elections. There is a rich, constructive history of the relationship that needs full airing as well. But some Polish leaders leave the impression that Polish antisemitism has been rather marginal at best. Certainly the evidence brought out by scholars such as Ronald Modras[17] and the controversy engendered by the publication of the article in *Tygodnik Powszechny* in January 1987 by Professor Jan Błoński[18] need to be digested much more fully by Poles and Polish Americans. The Polish Episcopal Conference certainly began this necessary process of national self-examination in its statements of 1991 and 1995, but it has still not reached the depth and extent that the evidence would warrant.

And greater openness is also required on the part of the Vatican. Just as the recent statements of the World Jewish Congress discussed above have created tension in the international Catholic-Jewish relationship, so, to a lesser degree, the unwillingness of the Vatican to be as candid as it might on some issues has also harmed the negotiating atmosphere. There will be no successful resolution of the dispute over Auschwitz-Birkenau without the participation of the international Catholic and Jewish leadership. This is especially true on the Jewish side. Certainly there is need to learn from the Auschwitz Convent controversy where there was a feeling in Poland that outside forces had dictated a settlement without sufficient input from within Poland itself. That feeling was probably overstated. I certainly would be prepared to defend the role played by European and American Jewish leaders as well as Catholic leaders from the Vatican, France, the United States and Belgium in particular. Both sides need to hear the voices of Jews and Catholics in Poland itself. If there is somewhat of a difference between the negotiations over the convent and the current negotiations over the total site, it is in involvement of the Polish government in particular and the Polish Episcopal Conference. Nonetheless, the World Jewish Congress and the Vatican will continue to be important players in the discussion even if, in the case of the Vatican, its role may be more behind the scenes. So if there is lack of harmony between international Jewish organizations such as the World Jewish Congress and the Vatican, as there is now, it definitely impacts in the discussions over Auschwitz-Birkenau.

From the side of the Vatican there must be a greater willingness to state unambiguously that important church leaders and church institutions were directly involved in the promotion of antisemitic teachings through, popular religiosity, and preaching. In post-*We Remember* addresses, Cardinal Cassidy has moved the analysis of Catholic responsibility for antisemitism in that direction and he deserves commendation for doing so.[19] But such a connection is not in the actual text of *We Remember* and may well be missed by those Catholics who read the Vatican document in isolation from Cardinal Cassidy's interpretation of it. And such interpretations, while very important, do not have the same status within the church as *We Remember* itself, which carries the imprimatur of Pope John Paul II himself.

The Vatican will also need to take a less defensive posture about the opening of the Vatican archives from the period of the Holocaust, as well as on the record of Pius XII. I support the calls of the late Cardinal Joseph Bernardin of Chicago and Cardinal John O'Connor* of New York for access to the relevant materials by a select group of scholars. It does not meet the canons of academic scholarship for Vatican spokespersons to

* Editors' Note. This essay was written prior to the death of Cardinal O'Connor

assure us that nothing of relevance remains in the unavailable documents. Gerhart Riegner, for example, has pointed to a key missing document in the released material from the period which the Vatican has not adequately explained. And the effort to promote the canonization of Pius XII should be put on hold until scholars have done far more work on his record. I recognize that the Vatican and many Catholics throughout the world are frustrated with the repeated attacks on Pius XII as "silent" and "uncaring." Such characterizations are patently false based on the evidence we have. But we cannot counter such biased portraits of Pius XII by quoting very selective Jewish leaders and the questionable research of a few Jewish authors as *We Remember* and the writings of Vatican archivist Fr. Pierre Blet, S.J., have unfortunately done.[20] Important questions as to whether the Pope did all he could, and as early as he could, must continue to be pursued. These issues remain important not only for the full understanding of Pius XII's papacy, but also for what they might tell us about the Church's posture in the midst of contemporary situations of possible genocide. In the end, whatever Pius XII's record finally turns out to be, it will remain buried with him. Perhaps, in the end, it will appear both to Catholics and Jews that he deserves sainthood. If that proves to be the case, his canonization would represent a greater mark of glory. In the meantime, the Vatican will have facilitated a climate of trust which will go a long way in promoting reconciliation on such ongoing questions as the status of Auschwitz-Birkenau. [21]

To promote a constructive atmosphere, several other steps need to be taken jointly and individually by the Polish and wider Catholic community as well as by the leadership of the international Jewish community. For one, the current negotiation process needs to be expanded to include a wider group of people. A concerted effort needs to be mounted to extend the conversations to interested parties, at least informally, and to create opportunities for genuine discussion among people on all sides. We may not need as formal a process as has occurred with respect to Northern Ireland and the Middle East. But if any agreement is to gain widespread support there must be a greater consultation than exists presently. This might be accomplished through a series of meetings of key leaders on the Auschwitz-Birkenau issue in some nearby European country under the aegis of a reconciliation group such as the St. Egidio community.

Likewise, it would positively impact the process if the Polish government and the Polish Catholic Church developed a concerted effort to educate the Polish people about the moral and legal dimensions of the controversy and the advantages that would accrue to Poland as a result of a permanent resolution. Thus far both the government and the Church have tended to focus their efforts primarily on responding to the charges of the militants. Prime Minister Jerzy Buzek's strong statement about the fundamental contribution of Jewish culture to general Polish culture mentioned above represents a definite step in the right direction.[22] Jewish leaders involved with the negotiations, besides issuing the public statement on Polish victimization that I spoke of earlier in this essay, should consider launching an educational effort in the Jewish community where this victimization, as well as Polish rescue by a group such as Żegota, are not well understood.[23]    During the original Convent crisis Dr. Stanisław Krajewski, a Polish Jewish leader, wrote that people in the West, including Jews and many Christians committed to improved  Jewish-Christian relations, do not appreciate the depth of Polish suffering at Auschwitz. "The historical fact is that the Nazis tried to crush the Polish nation; they not only introduced bloody terror but began to murder Polish elites and destroy Polish culture. The Auschwitz camp was used for this purpose, and during the first two years of existence, this was its main function."[24]

The conflict that emerged from the original Auschwitz Convent crisis, thus, is not over. In some ways we can say it has had a positive effect, at least to the extent that it brought to the surface issues which were corroding the relationship between Poles and Jews, and between Catholics and Jews generally. The successful negotiations over the Auschwitz Convent did teach us that patience and trust can prevail over hatred and militancy. The current challenge over the fate of the entire site will demand even greater patience and trust. We are at a crossroads. Either we will commit ourselves as Poles and Jews, and as Catholics and Jews, to a long term process that will lead to a mutually acceptable permanent plan for the site or Auschwitz-Birkenau will become an ongoing place of intense hatred and controversy that will serve to give Hitler a posthumous victory.

## ENDNOTES

1. Some refer to the Cross as the "Papal Cross."  Archbishop Henryk Muszyński, the leading Catholic Prelate on Catholic-Jewish Relations in Poland, has argued against using "Papal" in reference to the Cross (cf. National Catholic Register, Nov. 8-14, 1998).

2. Cf. John T. Pawlikowski, "The Auschwitz Convent Controversy: Mutual Misperceptions," in Carol Rittner and John K., Roth (eds.) *Memory Offended; The Auschwitz Convent Controversy.* New York, Westport, CT., London: Praeger, 1991, 63-73

3. The Polish-Jewish relationship is examined in great detail in the annual publication of the Institute for Polish-Jewish Studies (Oxford) and the American Association for Polish-Jewish Studies (Cambridge USA) entitled *POLIN* and now released through the Littman Library of Jewish Civilization in London and Washington. Early volumes were published by Blackwell Publishers of Oxford.

4. Institute of the World Jewish Congress, "The Christian Assault on Auschwitz Renewed," Policy Dispatch #31, August 1998, 1.

5. Institute of the World Jewish Congress, "A Great Leap Backwards?", Policy Dispatch #36, November 1998, 1.

6. Institute of the World Jewish Congress, *The Vatican and the Shoah: Purified Memory or Reincarnated Responsibility* ed. Ariah Doobov, Policy Forum #15, Jerusalem, 1998, 16.

7. The Vatican and the Shoah, 17.

8. "Report Summary" from "US and Allied Wartime and Postwar Relations and Negotiations with Argentina, Portugal, Spain, Sweden, and Turkey on Looted Gold and German External Assets and US Concerns about the Fate of the Wartime *Ustasha* Treasury," US State Department, June 1998, 10 (Internet Edition).

9. Institute of the World Jewish Congress, "The Christian Assault on Auschwitz Renewed," 3.

10. As quoted in the American Jewish Committee Journal (Spring 1987), 6.

11. Richard K. Lukas, *The Forgotten Holocaust; the Poles Under German Occupation 1939-1944.* Lexington, KY: The University Press of Kentucky, 1986, 38.

12. Cf. Ronald Modras, *The Catholic Church and Antisemitism: Poland 1933-1939.* Chur, Switzerland: Harwood Academic Publishers, 1994.

13. The most important of these documents have recently been published by the Secretariat for Ecumenical and Interreligious Affairs of the National Conference of Catholic Bishops. *Catholics Remember the Holocaust.* Washington: United States Catholic Conference, 1998.

14. David Warszawski, "The Convent and Solidarity," *Tikkun* 4 (November/December 1989), 29.

15. Cf. Roger Cohen, "Poles and Jews Feud About Crosses at Auschwitz," The New York Times, December 20, 1998, 12.

16. Cf. *National Catholic Register*, Nov. 8-14, 1998, 3.

17. Cf. Ronald Modras, The Catholic Church and Antisemitism.

18. Cf. Antony Polonsky (ed.) My Brother's Keeper? Recent Polish Debates on the Holocaust. London: Routledge, 1990.

19. Cardinal Edward Idris Cassidy, "Reflections Regarding the Vatican's Statement on the Shoah," in Secretariat for Ecumenical and Interreligious affairs, *Catholics Remember the Holocaust*, 61-77.

20. Cf. Pierre Blet, S.J., "Myth vs. Historical Fact: Response to Accusations Against Pius XII," *L'Osservatore Romano* 17 (29 April 1998), 16-19.

21. For a fuller discussion of my views on Pius XII, cf., my essay, "The Legacy of Pius XII: Issues for Further research," *Catholic International* October 1998, 459-462. On opening the Vatican Archives, cf. Eugene J. Fisher, "Forward," in Harry James Cargas (ed.), *Holocaust Scholars Write to the Vatican*. Westport, CT & London: Greenwood Press, 1998, xiii; and Cardinal Joseph L. Bernardin, *A Blessing to each Other*. Chicago: Liturgy Training Publication, 1996, 158.

22. The monograph on "Polish Victimization" issued by the United States Holocaust Memorial Museum represents a good start in this direction.

23. The Polish Catholic Church's "Day of Judaism" program held in January, is certainly a move in the right direction. But its scope and impact need to be expanded.

24. Stanisław Krajewski, "Carmel at Auschwitz: On the Recent Polish Church Document and Its Background," SIDIC 22 (1989), 16. The Scholarly Exchange Program organized by the American Jewish Committee, which brings Jewish scholars to Poland to teach in seminaries and Polish scholars to lecture in Jewish educational institutions in the United States, represents a positive development in this regard.

# TOWARD A HEALING OF MEMORIES: CATHOLICS, JEWS AND THE *SHOAH*

## EUGENE J. FISHER

## PRELUDE: A MINOR CONFESSION

I must acknowledge at the outset that before I began my own contribution to this volume, I asked Alan Berger if I could see John Pawlikowski's. My motivation was not that I thought I might disagree with him or feel a need to correct any of his points. The times this has happened over the years can be counted on the fingers of one hand. Fr. Pawlikowski's control of the evidence and the scholarly literature, and his sense of balance and fair-mindedness are perduring features of one of the great theoreticians and practitioners of Jewish-Christian dialogue in our time. Rather, I feared that on a good day I might simply be redundant. And there is so much to say on the exceedingly complex set of issues evoked by the editors of this volume that I felt fairness to the reader demanded I not cover ground already thoroughly covered.

The present paper will thus presume the reader's acquaintance with Fr. Pawlikowski's contribution to this volume, though with the exception of this "prelude" it is designed to stand on its own as an analysis not of the Polish Catholic-Jewish dilemmas aptly called "The Continuing Agony" by the editors, but rather of the state of larger Catholic "memory" of the *Shoah* as reflected in the official documents of the Holy See, Pope John Paul II, and local conferences of bishops in Europe and the U.S. Here, I would like briefly to add a few details that might help to fill in a couple of the many salient points made so well by Fr. Pawlikowski.

First, the World Jewish Congress 1998 "policy" pamphlets contained, if anything, even more outlandish material than that adduced by Fr. Pawlikowski. The elaborately published "Policy Forum #15, for example, relied heavily on the long-discredited conspiracy theories of John Loftus and Mark Aarons. Loftus and Aarons first made their mark with a book entitled, sarcastically and offensively, *The Unholy Trinity* (St. Martin's Press, 1990). The "Trinity" (a term Christians, of course, normally reserve to G-d), was, in this instance, the Nazis, the Holy See, and the Stalinist Soviet Union. They would go on to allege in subsequent volumes even more extensive conspiracies between the Dulles brothers, Nazis, and Stalin himself. In popularizing and peddling such fabricated nonsense as truth, the World Jewish Congress, in my opinion, passed beyond the bounds of civil discourse, as I stated at the time in support of Cardinal Cassidy's statement calling the pamphlet series "anti-Catholic." It is to be hoped that by the time this volume is published, that will all be in the past. Already, there are some indications that the path of dialogue of mutual esteem will be chosen over the blind alley of confrontation.

Secondly, while reaffirming my support for Cardinal Bernardin's Baltimore, 1992, suggestion with regard to access by responsible scholars to the Vatican Secretary of State's archives, to which Pawlikowski kindly refers, I would note that Cardinal Edward I. Cassidy, of the Holy See's Commission for Religious Relations with the Jews, in the International Catholic-Jewish Liaison Committee meeting of March, 1998, made the concrete suggestion that a small group of Jewish and Catholic scholars work together on the vast amount of archival literature of the period already released by the Holy See, to see where, in all objectivity, that might lead. Given the spiritual and confessional nature of some of the material gathered by the priests who serve in the Vatican diplomatic corps, such an approach may well be both the most efficient and the most sensitive possible. This suggestion was mutually agreed upon with IJCIC in the joint declaration from the meeting, but has yet to be implemented, though expressions of interest from member agencies of IJCIC indicate that this too remains a real possibility.

## THE HOLY SEE'S *WE REMEMBER* IN CONTEXT

The statement of the Holy See's Commission on Religious Relations with the Jews, *We Remember: A Reflection on the Shoah*, has most often been interpreted in isolation from other statements of the Commission and at times in opposition to statements of local Catholic Churches such as the French, the Dutch and even the American. This isolated view thus judges harshly the more general statements of the Holy See's document as opposed to the more specific and therefore relatively stronger language employed by local churches. The interpretative methodology implicit in such attempts to pull the Holy See's document out of its natural context in the flow of statements from Pope John Paul II, the Commission, and statements of local churches, however, can only lead to an erroneous reading of the document's actual intent, as Cardinal Edward I. Cassidy, who signed the document as President of the Commission, clarified in his address to the plenary session of the American Jewish Committee's 1998 annual meting:

> "It is also important not to take the present document in isolation from those already issued by the episcopal conferences of several European countries or from the numerous statements made by Pope John Paul II in the course of his pontificate. There is no contradiction in these various texts. There is a variety in the tone and in the emphasis placed on certain aspects of the question, due as I have explained to the context in which they were issued and to the audience being addressed."[1]

This is why, when the U.S. bishops' conference came to publish the document for dissemination in this country, the European statements as well as Cardinal Cassidy's clarification were all included.[2] Together, the ten statements make a whole that fills in the gaps in historical reckoning that critics of the Holy See's document perceived. Indeed, this is the way the Holy See's document was intended to be read, and its issuance was postponed precisely to allow the local churches to put their varying (though not contradictory) perspectives on the public record.

Likewise, *We Remember*, to which was appended the Pope's personal letter,[3] can only be read properly within the context of the many papal statements that preceded it, a number of which are cited or alluded to in the text itself.[4] This principle of interpretation within the larger context of magisterial teachings is especially important, I believe, when interpreting the Vatican text on the three crucial issues that have received the most criticism. These are the relationship between historical Christian anti-Judaism and modern racial antisemitism, the degree of culpability of the Church as an institution because of the former in the development of the latter, and what the Church, again as an institution, not just the acknowledged heroics of a relatively few individual Catholics on all levels, did and did not do for the Jews during the *Shoah* itself. The first two questions, in my mind, have been to a considerable extent resolved by contemporary historical scholarship. The third involves judgment calls that may render a "final" historical verdict (i.e., one acceptable to both Catholic and Jewish memories of World War II) well out of reach for the foreseeable future.

The Holy See's document, it should be noted, itself commendably raises all three of these issues, calling for further, open-ended discussion on them between Catholic and Jewish scholars. Far from presenting itself as the "last word" on these incredibly complex and sensitive issues, then, *We Remember* intends to launch a dialogue commensurate with the two thousand years of history and the immensity of World War II that provide the wider historical and global context for their deliberations. As Cardinal William Keeler, Episcopal Moderator for Catholic-Jewish Relations for the U.S. National Conference of Catholic Bishops, and I commented in welcoming the Holy See's document in a statement issued from Rome on the day after it was promulgated:

> "The document directs us (Catholics) to contemplate what was done and was not done by Christians in those terrible years and over the centuries leading up to them. It properly expresses the Church's sense of repentance for the failures of that long and complex history. It presents us as well with the record of the righteous who did try to save Jews against all odds and at risk of their lives. This twin focus, repentance for the past and hope for the future, challenges Catholics in the United States in many ways. First, we must commit our resources, our historians, sociologist, theologians, and other scholars, as the document mandates, to study together with Jewish counterparts all the evidence with a view to a healing of memories, a reconciliation of history."[5]

This was a "maximalist" interpretation of the document, of course, but one made inevitable for knowledgeable Catholics by our awareness of the other magisterial, especially papal, statements that formed the matrix within which the Holy See's document is properly to be understood. While our statement was welcomed, it should be noted that the document's critics nonetheless stuck to their "minimalist" interpretation of the document, preferring, I suppose, to see it as intending to close the doors that we (who based our understanding on a dialogue with Cardinal Cassidy concerning it which had taken place that very morning[6]) saw as an opening to further dialogue.

## DOCUMENTS OF THE HOLY SEE

In effect, four documents constitute virtually the entire corpus of universal Roman Catholic teaching on Jews and Judaism since the close of the apostolic period.[7] While much was said about these subjects by popes and councils over the centuries (some of it negative, some, albeit less, positive), those statements were disciplinary in character, not doctrinal. Cardinal Johannes Willebrands, who worked on *Nostra Aetate* with his predecessor Cardinal Bea during the Council, frequently cited the uniqueness of *Nostra Aetate* no. 4 as the only text of the Second Vatican Council devoid of any reference to earlier councils, or to patristic or papal teaching. *Nostra Aetate*, Willebrands asserted, represented the first systematic, doctrinally relevant statement on the Church's relationship with the Jewish people in Catholic history.[8]

It is, sadly, most likely that the reason that neither popes nor councils in earlier centuries felt called upon to debate and decree officially on the Church's doctrinal position with regard to Judaism was that the negative portrait of Judaism painted by the early church fathers was so widely presumed by later Christians that no one thought to question what in our time has aptly been called "the teaching of contempt."[9] The four statements are *Nostra Aetate* itself (1965), *Guidelines and Suggestions for Implementing Nostra Aetate* (1974), *Notes on the Correct Way to Present the Jews and Judaism in Preaching and Catechesis* (1985), and *We Remember: A Reflection on the Shoah* (1998).[10]

While these statements have no true doctrinal precedent in Catholic tradition, however, they do have a wider magisterial context today in the statements of the popes[11] and of local churches since the Second Vatican Council. These can provide most useful insights for interpreting and applying the universal documents.

In 1986, I was invited by the Holy See to give a paper at a meeting of the International Catholic-Jewish Liaison Committee.[12] In it, I attempted to analyze the development of the then three official statements of the Commission for Religious Relations with the Jews: the Conciliar text and the Commission's two implementing documents of 1974 and 1985. The most recent document of the Commission, *We Remember: A Reflection on the Shoah*, like its three predecessors, was greeted with initial skepticism and critiques by Jewish and even Catholic commentators. Great concern was expressed in 1965, for example, that *Nostra Aetate* failed to mention the term, "deicide," and that it "deplored" rather than "condemned" antisemitism. The former term, it was feared, might someday creep back into Christian vocabulary, while the sinfulness of antisemitism might not be clear in the use of the latter.[13]

Yet over time, these understandable concerns and fears have been allayed as it became apparent that the Church has turned itself irrevocably unto a course of replacing the ancient negative attitude toward Jews and Judaism with a positive, even fraternal, one of mutual respect and solidarity with the Jewish people and the even more ancient faith given them by God. In 1974, the Vatican Guidelines summarized the Conciliar text as having "condemned" antisemitism, while in 1986, Pope John Paul II declared antisemitism to be "sinful."[14] It is an interesting irony that when I started working in this field a quarter of a century ago I could not give a talk to a Catholic group without defining what I meant by the word, "Holocaust." Today, "Holocaust" is part of the working vocabulary of our culture, and thanks to the most recent Vatican document, *Shoah* will be. But the term, "deicide," has virtually passed from usage among Catholics, so it, now, is the term I must define.

Such progressive clarifications of the doctrinal and catechetical intent of the Conciliar declaration, *Nostra Aetate*, are what I meant by the term "evolution of a tradition." The dynamic that drives this process of progress toward an ever more positive appreciation of Judaism and its ongoing role in the mystery of salvation, of course, is dialogue. It is a dialogue that has taken place since the Council not only at the top, between the Holy See's Commission and the International Jewish Committee for Interreligious Relations, but on all levels of the life of the Church and the Jewish people. In the U.S. and increasingly elsewhere as well, there have been national dialogues, diocesan-level dialogues, and congregational level dialogues, nurturing and "enfleshing" the teaching documents issued by the Holy See and intended for the guidance of the whole Church.

The documents of the Holy See's Commission over the years thus reflect not only a dialogue between the Church and the Jewish people, but equally a dialogue within the Church as well, since they draw upon, reflect, and in turn affirm statements made at the level of national episcopal conferences and dioceses throughout the world. One may say without exaggeration that the amazing progress in Catholic-Jewish relations since the Second Vatican Council is a classic example of how the Conciliar vision has been received and implemented over time. Catholics, I believe, owe a tremendous debt of gratitude to those Jews who, despite the deep trauma of the *Shoah* (one out of every three Jews in the world and two out of every three in Europe were systematically murdered, mostly by people who, if they cannot be called Christian, at least were baptized as such), have come forward to participate in these sometimes very painful dialogues with us. Indeed, as Pope John Paul II told the tiny remnant of the once thriving Jewish community of Warsaw in 1987, theirs is a "saving warning" and sacred witness to the Church and the world alike.[15]

The 1985 Vatican *Notes* spoke of the ongoing witness of the Jewish people that is theirs alone and not exhausted in Judaism's role of preparing the way for the first coming of Christ: "The history of Israel did not end in 70 A.D. (Cf...*Guidelines*, II). It continued, especially in a numerous Diaspora which allowed Israel to carry to the whole world a witness — often heroic — of its fidelity to the one God and to 'exalt him in the presence of all the living' (Tobit 13:4)." "Heroic witness" is the precise meaning of the term "martyrdom." Over the centuries, we know, many of the persecutors of Jews, who martyred so many of God's people, were active Christians.

On the one hand, the Holy See is here inviting all Catholics to contemplate and repent for crimes against Jews *qua* Jews committed by Christians on all levels of the Church. On the other hand, they are making, in direct continuity with the Second Vatican Council,[16] a doctrinal assertion, the implications of which may take centuries to unfold. The Jewish witness to the world is intrinsic to the ongoing status of the Jewish people as divinely chosen, i.e., as "the people of God of the Old Covenant which has never been revoked."[17] This status has perdured over the centuries and, according to Catholic teaching, will perdure until the end of time.[18] The chosenness and the saving witness of the Jews to the Church and to the world, therefore, was not exhausted in its role of preparing the way for Christ's first coming, but is integral in itself and to be respected by the Church as a proclamation of revealed truth in its own right. This is why the Pope during his 1986 visit to the Great Synagogue of Rome, and the documents included here, speak of the "joint witness" of the Church and the Jewish people to the world based on revelation itself.[19]

The 1985 *Notes*, speaking in the context of the eschatological dimension of our shared proclamation, urges us to "a greater awareness that the people of God of the Old and the New Testament are tending towards a like end in the future, the coming or the return of the Messiah, even if they start from two different points of view...Attentive to the same God who has spoken, hanging on the same word, we have to witness to one same memory and one common hope in Him who is the master of history. We must also accept our responsibility to prepare the world for the coming of the Messiah by working together for social justice, respect for the rights of persons and nations, and for social and international reconciliation. To this we are driven, Jews and Christians, by the command to love our neighbor, by a common hope for the Kingdom of God and by the great heritage of the prophets."[20]

## *WE REMEMBER* IN THE CONTEXT OF ITS PREDECESSORS

In this context of the predecessor statements, a few remarks can already be said about the 1998 document, *We Remember: A Reflection on the Shoah.* Like the three which preceded it, *We Remember* was greeted cautiously, and by some in the Jewish community negatively. Again, ambiguities in language were noted, and again it was feared that the worst possible interpretation of anything vague would in the long run prevail. But as with the Council itself and the two previous implementing documents of the Holy See in 1974 and 1985, I would suggest that this document's actual impact on Catholic understanding will be positive. What will last is not what the document failed to say (which was the focus of much of the Jewish critique) but what it did say, and say very powerfully.[21]

It is also important to note that the document now has received an official interpretation in the light of Jewish concerns by Cardinal Edward I. Cassidy, who signed it as president of the Pontifical Commission which issued it. Cardinal Cassidy's definitive interpretation,[22] for example, clarifies both the distinction and the causal relationship between ancient Christian anti-Judaism and modern racial antisemitism. The distinction is clear. Christian anti-Judaism was a form of theological triumphalism held in check by its own theoretical foundations as well as the Church's moral restraints (as can be found already in St. Augustine and in the legislation of Pope Gregory the Great which afforded Jews a legal place in Christian society and Judaism alone the right to exist as a non-Christian religion). Modern antisemitism, on the other hand, found its theoretical base in a post-Enlightenment, pseudo-scientific racialism set in an ideology (Nazism) that was every bit as opposed in theory to Christianity and the Church as it was to Judaism, though in practice the chilling decision was made, consciously and with infinite malice, to destroy first the witnesses to God's first covenant, the Jews.

What is admittedly less clear in the document, though clearly implicit in the structure of the relevant sections, is that while Christian anti-Judaism differed profoundly from racial antisemitism in theory and in the practices that flowed from those theories,[23] Christian anti-Judaism did pave the way for the successful spread of antisemitism through a populace that Christian teaching had for centuries pinpointed as an "alien other" in Christian society, and one whose moral failings, beginning with falsely alleged collective guilt for Jesus' death, were many and frightening to the people. Thus, by the twentieth century all too many Christians were ripe to fall into the temptation that Nazi antisemitism offered to blame all of society's ills on "the Jews." The Vatican document thus cites the words of Pope John Paul II: "In the Christian world... erroneous and unjust interpretations of the New Testament regarding the Jewish people and their alleged culpability have circulated for too long, engendering feelings of hostility toward these people." These negative feelings fed by Christian anti-Judaism in turn, the Pope stated, "lulled the consciences" of many Christians so that they did not act toward the Jews "as the world had the right to expect" Christians to act when their time of testing came.[24]

Put another way, Christian anti-Judaism was a necessary cause of the Holocaust, but not a sufficient cause. Without it, the Holocaust would most probably never have happened. But a number of other causes, sociological, economic, historical and ideological are necessary even to approach a "sufficient" explanation for what happened.

Cardinal Cassidy also clarified another vital point in the text. In quoting the Pope in the passage cited above, the Vatican document naturally included a phrase that the Pope had used, "I do not say the Church as such" was guilty. And in making its statement of the need for universal repentance by the Church, the document used the phrase "the failures of her (the Church's) sons and daughters in every age." This led some commentators to conclude that the document intended to exculpate the institutional Church in the former, and the hierarchy in the latter.

This was not at all the intent of the document, Cardinal Cassidy affirmed. Rather, the use of the phrase was meant to distinguish the Church as a human institution (with its need for repentance without reservation) from the Church as a sacrament, the locus of the encounter between Christ and the communion of the baptized, living and dead, past, present and future. "For Catholics the Church is not just the members that belong to it. It is looked upon as the bride of Christ, the heavenly Jerusalem, holy and sinless. We do not speak of the Church as sinful but of the members of the Church as sinful." Likewise, he reminded his audience, "sons and daughters" excludes no one, but, like the term, members, "can include according to circumstances popes, cardinals, bishops, priests, and laity." So one can, according to the Vatican document, indict the Church as a human institution on all levels for its sins of omission and of commission with regard to the Jews over the course of the centuries and during the *Shoah* itself.

Indeed, one must say that such an interpretation is the central point of the entire exercise undertaken in the document, as the document ringingly concludes:

> "At the end of the millennium the Catholic Church desires to express her deep sorrow for the failures of her sons and daughters in every age. This is an act of repentance (*teshuvah*), since as members of the Church we are linked to the sins as well as the merits of all her children...It is not a matter of mere words but of binding commitment...Humanity cannot permit all that (the *Shoah*) to happen again. We pray that our sorrow for the tragedy which the Jewish people has suffered in our century will lead to a new relationship with the Jewish people. We wish to turn awareness of past sins into a firm resolve to build a new future in which there will be no more anti-Judaism among Christians...but rather a shared mutual respect as befits those who adore the one Creator and Lord and have a common father in faith, Abraham."

In a statement on the implications of the document issued from Rome by Cardinal William Keeler and myself the day after its promulgation, we drew out two critical mandates for its implementation in local Churches around the world:

> "First, we must commit our resources, our historians, sociologists, theologians and other scholars, to study together with their Jewish counterparts all the evidence with a view to a healing of memories, a reconciliation of history. Second, we must look at the implications of this document for our

educational programs, its opportunities for rethinking old categories as well as probing the most difficult areas of moral thought. To take the Holocaust seriously is to look back at centuries of Christian misunderstanding both of Judaism and of the New Testament itself, as the text emphasizes, and seek to replace them with more accurate appreciation of both. How shall we embody what this statement calls us to do in our classrooms and from our pulpits?"[25]

## STATEMENTS OF LOCAL CHURCHES ON THE HOLOCAUST

Reading through the statements included in *Catholics Remember*[26] reveals the difficulty of making one, generalized statement about the institutional Church and the Holocaust. The statements of the Polish and the German bishops, while dealing with the same events, are strikingly different. The two conferences had worked for over two years trying to craft a joint statement on the anniversary of the liberation of Auschwitz. They failed. So different were the experiences of those whose grandparents had fought Hitler and those whose grandparents had followed Hitler that it was impossible to craft common language for a common statement. What the German bishops, to their great credit, felt they had to acknowledge in terms of the guilt and responsibility of their predecessors, the Polish bishops, out of the same sense of honest reckoning with the past of their people, simply could not say. It would not be true. Neither Blitzkrieg nor Auschwitz were Polish conceptions. They were German, as the German bishops quite candidly admit: "The crime against the Jews was planned and put into action by the National Socialist rulers in Germany."[27] The German bishops, again to their credit, do not attempt to slide over what made Nazi racialist policies possible in Germany:

> "The commemoration of the fiftieth anniversary of Auschwitz gives German Catholics the opportunity to re-examine their relationship with Jews...Already during earlier centuries, Jews were exposed to persecution, oppression, expulsion, and even to mortal danger. Many looked for and found refuge in Poland... Jews decisively contributed toward the development of German science and culture. Nevertheless, an anti-Jewish attitude remained, also within the Church. This was

one of the reasons why, during the years of the Third Reich, Christians did not offer due resistance to racial antisemitism. Many times there was failure and guilt among Catholics. Not a few of them got involved in the ideology of National Socialism and remained unmoved in the face of crimes committed against Jew(s)...Others paved the way for crimes or even became criminals themselves. Today the fact is weighing heavily on our minds that there were but individual initiatives to help persecuted Jews and that even the pogroms of November 1938 (*Kristallnacht*) were not followed by public and express protest...(T)he heavy burden of history recalls that 'the Church, which we proclaim as holy and which we honor as a mystery, is also a sinful Church and in need of conversion' (statement of the German and Austrian bishops, Nov. 1988)...The failure and guilt of that time have also a church dimension...(W)e were, as a whole, a church community who kept on living our lives while turning our backs too often on the fate of this persecuted Jewish people. We looked too fixedly on the threat to our own institutions and remained silent about the crimes committed against the Jews. The practical sincerity of our will of renewal is linked to the confession of this guilt and the willingness to painfully learn from this history of guilt of our country and of our church."[28]

These are stark, moving and necessary words. Ultimately, such words of sincere repentance for the past are also words pregnant with the hope of healing for the future. Ultimately, too, the Polish bishops had to articulate their sense of repentance within the context of their own history:

"Only a few months into the war, in the spring of 1940, the Nazi Germans created the Auschwitz concentration camp on occupied Polish territory annexed to the Third Reich. At the beginning of its existence, the first prisoners and victims were thousands of Poles, mainly intelligentsia, members of the resistance movement as well as clergy and people representing almost all walks of life. There probably isn't a Polish family that hasn't lost someone close at Auschwitz or another camp."[29]

This, of course, is simple fact. The Polish people stand with the Jews as primary witnesses to the reality of the death camps. Witnesses, indeed, to the *Shoah*, as the document continues:

> "Almost from the beginning, Polish Jews were sent to this camp, as part of Polish society, to be destroyed. From 1942 on, the Auschwitz-Birkenau complex, as well as other camps in occupied Poland, as a result of the Wannsee Conference became extermination camps to realize the criminal ideology of the 'final solution:' in other words, the plan to murder all European Jews." While acknowledging the "heroic courage" of "many Poles" (themselves already victims of Nazi oppression) who attempted to save Jewish lives, the bishops state that "unfortunately there were also those who were capable of actions unworthy of being called Christians. There were those who not only blackmailed but also gave away Jews in hiding into German hands. Nothing can justify such an attitude."

In other words, while in German Catholic memory, the "many" are oppressors and the "few" are victims and rescuers, in Polish Catholic memory the "many" are first of all fellow victims of Nazi persecution, some of them rescuers, and the "few" are victimizers. These, of course, are generalizations, since generalizations, with all their flaws, are inescapable in general, national statements. But I believe they are reasonably accurate ones, historically, and they are certainly in both cases painfully honest.

What generalization that the Holy See could offer, however, could possibly be adequate to both of these statements in all of the particular complexities of each? And these are but two of the many Catholic national and communal experiences that were suffered in World War II. Yes, I agree with my Jewish colleagues who criticized *We Remember* that its few paragraphs summing up history were not adequate to the task. And yes, I agree that much, much more could be said. Indeed, I would argue that *We Remember* probably should have been more diffident about the task it undertook for itself, and not tried to summarize the history of two millennia and of the *Shoah* in a limited space. Rather, "parameters" or guidelines for Catholic-Jewish dialogue on these issues might better have been assayed. In fact, these can be found in the text, which calls for such ongoing dialogue, so on the level of principle *We Remember* has it just right even if it, like the German and Polish bishops conferences which preceded it, could not find just the right words to say all that needed to be said.

One can find a number of other significant parameters well set forth in the various statements of the national bishops' conferences included in *Catholics Remember*. The Hungarian bishops jointly with the Ecumenical Council of Churches in Hungary in 1994, for example, said that "we have to state that not only the perpetrators of this insane crime are responsible for it but all those who, although they declare themselves members of our churches, through fear, cowardice or opportunism, failed to raise their voices against the mass humiliation, deportation, and murder of their Jewish neighbors. Before God we now ask forgiveness for this failure committed in the time of disaster fifty years ago."

The statement of the American bishops on the fiftieth anniversary of the liberation of Auschwitz was similarly specific. "As we join this year with our fellow Americans, especially our Jewish sisters and brothers, in prayerful commemorations of the millions of victims of the Holocaust, American Catholics will recall with profound gratitude the tremendous sacrifices made by the generation which defeated Hitler. But as Americans and as Catholics, we also recall with humility and a sense of regret the opportunities that were lost to save lives." Archbishop Lipscomb goes on to mention the failure to bomb "the railroad lines leading to Auschwitz" and the repulsion of the St. Louis. He concludes, "Having fought the war against Hitler, Americans do not feel personal guilt for what the Nazis did. But American Catholics do acknowledge a real sense of responsibility for what fellow members of the community of the baptized did not do to save lives." This distinction between "personal guilt" and "responsibility" can also be found in the Holy See's *We Remember*, and I believe rightly so. Catholics are well represented among all the categories of the generation of Europeans and Americans that endured the Holocaust. They can be found among both its direct victims and its perpetrators, among its bystanders and among the "righteous" who sought to save Jewish lives at the risk of their own and of their families.

Cardinal William Keeler of Baltimore, speaking as Episcopal Moderator for Catholic-Jewish Relations for the U.S. bishops nationally, reflected for all of us on "The Lessons of the Rescuers" during a ceremony honoring them held at the U.S. Holocaust Memorial Museum in Washington in 1997. The first lesson, Cardinal Keeler reminded those gathered, is that "the Church can only approach the *Shoah* in such a place and on such an occasion in a spirit of repentance (*teshuvah*) for the evil that so many of its baptized members perpetrated and so many others failed to stop...The saving deeds and lives of Catholics that we remember here today represent crucially important moral lights in a period of darkness. Our celebration of the brightness of that light and the preciousness of that witness is at once intensified and muted by the poignant awareness that they were, when all is said and done, relatively few among us, and no one can know how many, because some surely perished with those they tried to save."[30] The righteous are to be contemplated, not as a means of escaping responsibility for the past, but as "our models for the future." These were people who, whatever their station in life, tended to have a secure understanding of the most basic moral values, and "a deep sense that there was ultimate meaning to life beyond the present." Thus, when faced with life and death decisions, which needed to be made immediately, they acted seemingly instinctively, to save.

The 1997 statement of the Swiss bishops reflects the ambiguous nature of their own history. Recalling that Switzerland during the war was "completely encircled by National Socialist and Fascist dictatorships" and thus "forced to make some compromises," the bishops declare that "in particular, Switzerland did not welcome as many refugees as she could have," while "the goods and fortunes of the victims" were allowed to "flow" into the country. While the "massacre (of the Jewish people) was organized by a regime which also persecuted Christians and the churches, we must not lose the perspective that, for centuries, Christians and church teachings were guilty of persecuting and marginalizing Jews, thus giving rise to antisemitic sentiments. Today, we shamefully declare that religious motivations, at that time, played a definite role in this process. It is in reference to these past acts of churches for which we proclaim ourselves culpable and ask pardon of the descendants of the victims."[31]

The Dutch bishops in October of 1995 also issued a nuanced appraisal of their own history: "In the same way that we are filled with gratitude this year when we recall the end of the War, we are also filled with shame and dismay when we recall the *Shoah*... Looking back on the attitude of Dutch Catholics during the war, our thoughts turn to the courageous actions of the episcopacy (which publicly denounced the deportations, with disastrous result in Nazi reprisals)... But could Catholics not have done more? The history of the twenty-century long relationship between Jews and Christians is very complex and has left many traces of its passing. There is no doubt that church institutions have made errors. A tradition of theological and ecclesiastical anti-Judaism contributed to the climate that made the *Shoah* possible. What is known as "the Catechesis of vilification" taught that Jewry after Christ's death was rejected as a people...Partly due to these traditions, Catholics in our country sometimes were reserved toward Jews, and sometimes indifferent or ill-disposed. We reject this tradition of ecclesiastical anti-Judaism and deeply regret its horrible results. With our pope and other episcopal conferences, we condemn every form of antisemitism as a sin against God and humanity."

The Italian bishops in 1998 revealed remarkable candor and succinctness: "It is true, as you (Rabbi Toaff, chief rabbi of Rome to whom the episcopal letter was addressed) have said, that "in Italy we had antisemitism of the state not of the populace.' But this does not take away from the fact that we deal with a dark page in the recent history of our country. Christian clergy had for long centuries cultivated "erroneous and unjust interpretations of scripture" (John Paul II, Nov. 1, 1997). Because of this we did not know how to muster energies capable of denouncing or to oppose with the necessary force and timeliness the iniquity that struck you. Spontaneous human charity and Christian solidarity with the Jewish people...did come to mitigate in some manner the lack of prophetic action when the situation passed from the violence of words to violence against persons. Yet such individual deeds were not sufficient to stop the catastrophe. We recall these events with dismay and also with a profound and conscientious *teshuvah.*"[32]

The fact that Italy, and especially its convents and monasteries, managed to save some eighty-five per cent of its Jews, and the Italian army thousands of others wherever it went, underscores the profound Christian humility of this statement. In a way, for me, it speaks for the whole Church no less than does that of the Statement of the Holy See itself.

Finally, perhaps because it was the most dramatic in its presentation, I would mention the "Declaration of Repentance" of the French bishops. In September of 1997, bishops from all the dioceses from which Jews were taken gathered at the deportation point for the death camps, Drancy, to declare solemnly: "The Church of France questions itself. It, like the other churches, has been called to do so by Pope John Paul II as the third millennium draws near...The time has come for the Church to submit her own history, especially that of this period, to critical examination and to recognize without hesitation the sins committed by members of the Church and to beg forgiveness of God and humankind...For the most part, those in authority in the Church, caught up in a loyalism that went far beyond the obedience traditionally accorded civil authority, remained stuck in conformity, prudence and abstention.[33]  This was dictated in part by their fear of reprisals against the Church's activities and youth movements...We pass no judgment either on the consciences or on the people of that era. We are not ourselves guilty of what took place in the past. But we must be fully aware of the cost of such behavior and such actions. It is our Church, and we are obliged to acknowledge objectively today that ecclesiastical interests, understood in an overly restrictive sense, took priority over the demands of conscience – and we must ask ourselves why...Certainly, at a doctrinal level, the Church was fundamentally opposed to racism for the reasons, both theological and spiritual, which Pius XI expressed so strongly in his encyclical *MIT BRENNENDER SORGE*... (Yet) in the process which led to the *Shoah*, we are obliged to admit the role, indirect if not direct, played by commonly held anti-Jewish prejudices, which Christians were guilty of maintaining...This is not to say that a direct cause-and-effect link can be drawn between these commonly held anti-Jewish feelings and the *Shoah* because the Nazi plan to annihilate the Jewish people has its roots elsewhere. In the judgment of historians, it is a well-proven fact that for centuries, up until the Second Vatican Council, an anti-Jewish tradition stamped its mark in differing ways on Christian doctrine and teaching, in theology, apologetics, preaching and in the liturgy. It was on such ground that the venomous plant of hatred for the Jews was able to flourish. Hence, the heavy inheritance we still bear in our century, with all its consequences which are so difficult to wipe out. Hence our still open wounds...While it may be true that some Christians – priests, religious, and lay people – were not lacking in acts of courage in defense of fellow human beings, we must recognize that indifference won the day over indignation in the face of the persecution of the Jews and that, in particular, silence was the rule in the face of the multifarious laws enacted by the Vichy government, whereas speaking out in favor of the victims was the exception...Today we confess that such a silence was a sin...This failing of the Church of France and of her responsibility toward the Jewish people are part of our history. We confess this sin. We beg God's pardon, and we call upon the Jewish people to hear our words of repentance."[34]

No more fit conclusion can be found to these reflections than the prayerful petition placed in the Western Wall in Jerusalem by the Pope on 26 March 2000.

## Note Placed by His Holiness Pope John Paul II
## in a crevice of the Western Wall

God of our fathers,
you chose Abraham and his descendants
to bring your Name to the Nations:
we are deeply saddened
by the behaviour of those
who in the course of history
have caused these children of yours to suffer,
and asking your forgiveness
we wish to commit ourselves
to genuine brotherhood
with the people of the Covenant.
Jerusalem, 26 March 2000

## ENDNOTES

1. Secretariat for Ecumenical and Interreligious Affairs, National Conference of Catholic Bishops, *Catholics Remember the Holocaust* (Washington, D.C.: U.S. Catholic Conference, 1998) 66-67.
2. *Ibid.* The statements are those of the bishops' conferences of Hungary (1994), Germany (1995), Poland (1995), the U.S. (1995 & 1997), Holland (1995), Switzerland (1997), France (1997), and Italy (1998).
3. It is extremely unusual, of course, for the Pope to issue a letter welcoming and by implication providing a personal introduction to a document of any Curial body. The letter was released by the Holy See along with the document and printed with it in *L'Osservatore Romano*, thus becoming an integral part of the text itself. Again, those who compare the document unfavorably over against the Pope's reflections are missing the point.
4. Papal texts on Jews and Judaism up to 1995 are collected in Eugene Fisher and Leon Klenicki, editors, *Spiritual Pilgrimage: Pope John Paul II: Texts on Jews and Judaism 1979-1995.* (New York: Crossroad, 1995).
5. *Catholics Remember,* 57.
6. The occasion for the dialogue with Cardinal Cassidy on March 17, 1998 was the last leg of a "bishop/rabbi" joint pilgrimage to Israel and Rome headed by Cardinal Keeler and Rabbi Joel Zaiman of the Rabbinical Assembly. As the trip had been memorable and profoundly dialogical, so too was the spirited exchange with the Cardinal Cassidy. Indeed, the first two speakers on the Jewish side, Rabbi Mordecai Waxman and Rabbi A. James Rudin, in succinct and incisive yet respectful style, raised all of the key issues and questions, *panim al panim,* with his Eminence, that

were to be raised subsequently by the document's critics. Cardinal Cassidy, in his turn, quite graciously acknowledged the validity of most and gave, at the time, what turned out to be a foretaste of his definitive interpretation of the text delivered later than spring at the American Jewish Committee meeting. See Footnote 1.

7. The Dogmatic Constitutions of the Church, *Lumen Gentium*, no. 16, and *Dei Verbum*, nos. 15-16 also contain  doctrinally relevant statements affirming central aspects of the teaching of the Declaration, *Nostra Aetate* no. 4.

8. Johannes Cardinal Willebrands, *Church and Jewish People: New Considerations*. (New York/Mahwah, Paulist Press, 1992) p. 40.

9. The term, "teaching of contempt," was coined by the great French Jewish historian, Jules Isaac, to describe the overall effect of Patristic polemics against Jews and Judaism, Isaac's 1960 meeting with Pope John XXIII resulted in the Pope mandating that the Council take up the topic. Cf. Jules Isaac, *The Teaching of Contempt* (1964) and *Jesus and Israel* (1971), both translated and introduced by Claire Huchet Bishop for Holt, Rinehart, Winston.

10. These have recently been published together under the title, *Catholic Jewish Relations: Documents from the Holy See* (London: Catholic Truth Society, 1999). It is distributed in this country by U.S. Catholic Conference Publications (Washington, D.C. no. 062-X). Some of the material from my introduction to the CTS publication has been re-worked for inclusion in this essay.

11. The statements of Pope John Paul II have been collected in *Spiritual Pilgrimage: Texts on Jews and Judaism 1979-1995*, edited by Eugene Fisher and Leon Klenicki (New York: Crossroad, 1995).

12. Eugene Fisher, "The Evolution of a Tradition from *Nostra Aetate* to the Notes", in International Catholic-Jewish Liaison Committee, *Fifteen Years of Catholic-Jewish Dialogue*, 1970-1985. (*Libreria Editrice Vaticana/Libreria Editrice Lanteranense*, 1988) pp. 239-254. An expanded version of the paper is available in E. Fisher and L. Klenicki, *In Our Time: The Flowering of Catholic-Jewish Dialogue*. (N.Y./Mahwah: Paulist Press, 1990).

13. Examples of concerns expressed with regard to the 1974 and 1985 texts are given in Fifteen Years and In Our Time, cf..*supra*.

14. John Paul II, 26 Nov. 1986, *Spiritual Pilgrimage*, p. 83: "For the Jewish people themselves, Catholics should have not only respect but also great fraternal love for it is the teaching of both the Hebrew Scriptures and Christian Scriptures that the Jews are beloved of God, who has called them with an irrevocable calling. No valid theological justification could ever be found for acts of discrimination or persecution against Jews. In fact, such acts must be held to be sinful." The 1998 Vatican document, *We Remember* similarly places antisemitism (and crimes motivated by it) in the category of very serious sins committed over the centuries by members of the Church, not only individually but institutionally as well.

15. John Paul II, *Pastoral Visit to Poland*, June 14, 1987. *We Remember*, p. 99.

16. Cf…not only *Nostra Aetate* no. 4, but also *Lumen Gentium*, no. 16.

17. This phrase, first spoken by Pope John Paul II in his allocation to the Jewish community of Mainz on 17 Nov. 1980, was reaffirmed by the 1985 Vatican *Notes* as a "remarkable theological formula" which establishes the "permanent reality of the Jewish people" as a "living reality closely related to the Church."

18. Cf… the 1985 *Notes*, nos. 2, 3, 10, 11, 25

19. Spiritual Pilgrimage, p. 65.

20. 1985 *Notes*, no. 11.

21. Cardinal Cassidy in his reflection on the document cites a number of Jewish commentators who have made this and similar positive points. See *Catholics Remember*, pp. 68-69.

22. It has been published in *Origins* and *Catholic International,* as well as in the collection of statements on the *Shoah* of the Bishops; Conferences of Hungary, Germany, Poland, the U.S., Holland, Switzerland, France, Italy and the Holy See. See *Catholics Remember the Holocaust* (Washington, D.C.: National Conference of Catholic Bishops, 1998) pp. 61-76.

23. In almost two millennia Christianity never attempted anything like a systematic destruction of the Jewish people as such. The word "genocide" is a modern coinage developed specifically to describe what happened to the Jews of Europe in the 20th Century, a new word never felt to be necessary before, though used in a wide variety of contexts today.

24. John Paul II, Symposium on the Roots of Anti-Judaism, 31 Oct 1997, *L'Osservatore Romano* (1 Nov 1997): no. 1.

25. See *Catholics Remember*, 57.

26. Cf…Fn. 1

27. *Catholics Remember*, 9.

28. *Ibid,* 10-11.

29. *Ibid.* 12.

30. *Ibid.,* 28. Cardinal Keeler mentioned especially Pere Jacques Bunuel of France, Blessed Bernard Lichtenberg of Germany, the Polish Catholic organization, Żegota, and Polish and Italian Catholic nuns, whose deeds have recently been recounted in Ewa Kurek, *Your Life Is Worth Mine: How Polish Nuns Saved Hundreds of Jewish Children in German-Occupied Poland, 1939-1945* (New York: Hippocrene, 1997) and Margherita Marchione, *Yours Is a Precious Witness: Memoirs of Jews and Catholics in Wartime* (New York, Mahwah: Paulist Press, 1997).

31. *Catholics Remember*, 26.

32. *Ibid.,* 39.

33. The document in a footnote does cite the condemnations of the rounding up of Jews by bishops such as Saliege of Toulouse, Theas of Montauban, Gerlier of Lyons, Moussaron of Albi, Daly of Marseilles, and Vansteenberghe of Bayonne, all in 1942. Interestingly, the American bishops' own condemnation of the murder of

innocent Jews in Eastern Europe, issued as a major section of their annual joint statement in 1942, joined its voice with those of these courageous French bishops. The key section of the 1942 American document is quoted by Archbishop Lipscomb in *Catholics Remember*, p. 17. On the historical context of the period, the French bishops recommend Michael R. Marrus and Robert O. Paxton, *Vichy France and the Jews* (New York: Schocken Books, 1983).

34. *Catholics Remember*, 36.

# AN "UNFINISHED BUSINESS": SOME REFLECTIONS ON "JEWISH POLAND" TODAY

## RACHEL FELDHAY BRENNER

My "unfinished business" with Poland emerged upon my arrival at the Okęcie airport in Warsaw in January 1998. "Does Madam have a Polish passport?" asked a pleasant young immigration official with the customary Polish *politesse*. Astonished, I answered: "No, I don't." I am sure my tone was not as polite. "Why not?" was the next question. Caught off guard by this lack of basic historical knowledge, I explained with some impatience that in 1957 Jews leaving the country had their Polish passports invalidated. In my naivete and, no doubt, some arrogance, I thought it was common knowledge that after Gomułka had come to power Jews were "invited" to leave Poland never to return. But once this matter got clarified, no more questions were asked and after paying the requested fee, I was given permission for a short stay in Poland.

Even though the episode was commonplace and the place looked ordinary, to me the whole thing seemed and sounded totally unreal. Now, upon further reflection on the subsequent intense, often bewildering, and always absorbing seven days in Poland, I can view this first encounter with Poland as both instructive and proleptic. It was a harbinger of an experience of reentering a paradoxical reality that, on the surface, seemed definitely foreign, yet on the emotional level felt intimately familiar. Over my entire stay, a sense of intuitive understanding of this reality defied the enormous distance of time, geography, life style, and ideologies that separated me from my childhood.

This intimacy, not so much with the place as with the people, was unexpected despite the fact that I certainly cannot call myself a novice at crossing and recrossing social, cultural and political borderlines. The emotionally complex, never completed process of adjustment to each of my two adopted-adoptive citizenships — Israeli and Canadian — as well as to the estranging category of "Resident Alien" conferred upon me by the

143

United States, traces a rather nomadic life style. And yet, the cumulative experience of the recurring migrations had never led to any reconsideration of my relationship with a country, which, however hesitatingly, I must call my mother/fatherland. My other "lives" in other places among other people seemed to have erased all identification with Poland. That is why the routine question about my Polish citizenship posed at Warsaw airport confronted me with a surprisingly palpable sense of my place of birth, and the consciousness that this place implied more than a geographic location, as I had believed for the past forty years. The indignation with which I responded to the question of the immigration official revealed the "business" with the Polish part of me was far from finished.

Indeed, the initiating episode posed poignant questions about the nature of this trip. What was I doing in this place? Was I *visiting* this country as a Jewish tourist of Polish descent to reconfirm the tragic disappearance of Jewish Poland? If this were the intention, then my visit would only reinforce the categorical dictum that my only remaining aunt, who lives in Israel, pronounced once she heard about my trip: "Polish Jewry came to its end on *Umschlagplatz.*" No further discussion, especially not with my aunt. How sad, also how liberating and simple her solution!

But I had another way of looking at Poland. I was *returning* to a country in which my childhood, however much shaped by and entangled in the tragic history of my family and my people, was emphatically my own. Therefore it was up to me to reckon with it. Of course, return would signify an emotional homage paid to the annihilated history of Polish Jewry and to the grandparents I never knew; of course, it would constitute another failed attempt to understand the horror of the Holocaust. But the notion of a *return,* not just a visit, also signified an acknowledgment that the important formative years of my life had been shaped by this country, that I recognized the rhetoric, the manners, the ways of relating as *so* familiar, and that my Polish sounded so natural that people who did not know me did not even suspect that I did not live here. In other words, the sense of return was bound to engage me in the complex issue of my relationship with my Polish/Jewish identity and the part it had played in my life.

Luckily, the first-hand exposure to the Jewish problematic in Poland today precluded the danger of my sinking into self-centered ruminations which would have focused merely on myself. Rather quickly I realized that, paradoxical as it may sound, nostalgic and sentimental recollections needed to be placed in a secondary place on this journey of re-initiation. It dawned on me that if I truly wanted to understand anything about myself and my ties to Poland, I had better open myself to the reality in which I found myself and connect with as much of an unbiased mind as possible to the people who lived this reality and experienced it as theirs.

Thanks to the Miernowskis, my Polish friends, who told their Jewish friend, Józef Kwaterko, about my arrival, I had the rare and invaluable opportunity to enter, even if only for a short while, the dynamic world of Polish Jewish life. In many ways, Mr. Kwaterko represents this world. A professor of Quebec literature at the University of Warsaw, Mr. Kwaterko inherited thousands of volumes of Yiddish literature and of Yiddish translations of world literature from his late father, a famous Yiddishist and journalist. An intellectual, he is an active participant in the Jewish groups and organizations, most of which emerged in Poland, especially in Warsaw after 1989. Listening to Mr. Kwaterko, I reached an understanding, which was reconfirmed later in other discussions, that the search for a meaningful Polish-Jewish life in Poland had become an intense and even consuming preoccupation of Jewish Polish intelligentsia. The Jewish Polish individuals whom I met seemed to have undertaken the daunting task of reconstructing a viable and vital Polish Jewish community. The building blocks for this enterprise present a paradoxical combination: an identification with an enormously rich Jewish legacy, which was irrevocably lost and which needs to be practically reinvented, interplays with an unequivocal consciousness of an unbroken affinity and identification with Polish culture.

This particular confluence of identifications explains why questions of the Jewish self-image and of the image of the Jew in Polish society at large kept arising at every meeting and in every conversation I witnessed. No wonder. Complex and often painful issues of national, cultural, religious, and political identity permeate, not to say haunt, every aspect of Polish existence. I have intentionally said "Polish" rather than "Jewish Polish." Even though there are so few Jews in Poland now (nobody knows for sure, and it depends, of course, on the definition of Jewish identify, but the numbers range between 5,000 and 15,000), it seems that the lives of Poles and Jews have remained symbiotically entangled. The presence of the Jews, even if in small numbers, continues to play an important role in Poland's everyday life.

That is why the Jewish question (the perennial *jüdische Frage*) cannot be separated from the transformation that Poland has been undergoing since the 1980s. In the 1989 bloodless yet extremely dramatic collapse of the Eastern block, Poland turned into a free country. To gain an insight into the complexity of the Jewish position, we only need to recall that a considerable number of older generation Jews, that is, the survivors of the Holocaust, actively participated in building communist Poland, whereas the generation of their children, most of them born in postwar Poland, actively participated in the struggle of the Solidarity movement against the communist regime. I also need to mention here the third generation coming of age that has started to work on its own definition of Jewishness in free Poland. Jewish existence in the post-liberation era thus seems to have been inextricably connected to the problematic interaction among the major political forces: the communist party and the Solidarity movement. Let us, however, not forget the Church and its crucial role as Solidarity's major proponent and today a major player in Polish politics.

The new era of freedom marked by the advent of a democratic political system and capitalist economy has had a tremendous impact on the position of Polish Jews and on Poles of Jewish descent. This differentiation seems necessary, if only to indicate the extent of the diversity that typifies this community. Distinction should be made between Jews who define themselves as Poles but consider their Jewishness important, and Jews who consider themselves first and foremost Poles, and do not attach much importance to their Jewish origins. Such a distinction offers some insight into the complexity of Jewish identity in Poland. Małgorzata Melchior, a sociologist at the University of Warsaw — I first met Małgorzata at the Jewish Studies Congress in Jerusalem and now we renewed our acquaintance in Warsaw — distinguishes between two groups in the middle-age bracket, that is, in the generation of the children of survivors. There are what she calls "barren" Poles of Jewish origin, who have no sense of Jewish belonging, and "returned" Polish Jews, who have demonstrated acceptance of their Jewishness and willingness to deepen the Jewish aspects of their life.

The newly won political freedom has created a new situation for those Polish Jews who wish to affirm their Jewish roots and rebuild Jewish presence in Poland. I had the opportunity to meet some of them in the home of Ms. Helena Datner, where I was invited to speak at an informal meeting. Ms. Datner is the Director of the Jewish Pedagogical Center, which is sponsored by the Jewish Distribution Committee. She is the daughter of the late Prof. Datner, an eminent Jewish historian, often mentioned with admiration and deep respect. Among the participants in the meeting was Mr. Stanisław Krajewski, a professor of mathematics and philosophy at the University of Warsaw, and the principal promoter of what he calls "dissimilation" of the Polish Jews. Mr. Krajewski, who wrote and published extensively on the subject of Jews in Poland, is one of the founders and chairman of the Jewish Forum Foundation established in 1994. The aim of the Forum is to intensify Jewish life in Poland. Among its other activities, it operates a Jewish help-line for those who are struggling with issues of Jewishness and identity.

What Mr. Krajewski means by "dissimilation" is the search for equilibrium between Polish and Jewish components of the identity of Polish Jews. Whereas Polish identification is an incontestable element, integral to the self-identification of the middle generation of Polish Jews, their identification with Jewish heritage requires a considerable effort. In other words, the identity search of the Polish Jew does not entail rejection of his or her Polishness, but rather raising awareness of the Jewish aspect of this Polishness.

Indeed, all the individuals who gathered that night in Ms. Datner's apartment have been, in one way or another, involved in strengthening the Jewish component of the identity of Polish Jews. It was a highly educated group of people, which included members of the Forum Foundation, an editor of the Jewish magazine *Midrasz*, interviewers for the Spielberg foundation, and a researcher of Jewish life in Poland. I chose to speak about the problematic of Jewish identity in North America. I focused on the impact of the Holocaust on the North American Jew, the changing relationships of North American Jews to Israel, the problem of conversion and the pluralism of North American Jewish life. I talked about the desire to preserve and develop Jewish culture in North America, which no longer seems to ground itself in an unequivocal identification with the state of Israel. I also discussed the variety of Jewish religious denominations on the North American continent.

To my delight, I very soon found out that I was speaking to a well-informed audience, very interested in the topic. The lively discussion that followed my presentation showed that the group members were quite aware of the Jewish identity issues of North America and that they were knowledgeable about the problematic of Israel's definitions of "who is a Jew." The latest developments of a political and religious nature in the Jewish world were discussed and compared with the situation in Poland. At the same time, many questions about American and Israeli Jewish life came to the fore. One participant, I recall, raised the question of Yiddish education in Israel and in America, another participant wanted to know more about the religious proclivities of American Jews. Unfortunately, when the question about the place of Polish Jews in American Jewish consciousness came up, I found it difficult to offer a reassuring answer. At this point, Mr. Krajewski made a comment which I would hear quite often. American Jews, he claimed, see Poland only as a cemetery and have no desire to learn much more about it. To him, he emphasized, Poland is not a cemetery; Poland is a place where he lives and where he wants to build his future.

The next day, it became even more evident to me that this community was not "dead." I was invited by one of the editors of *Midrasz*, Ms. Bella Szwarcman-Czarnota, to continue the conversation with the editorial staff of the magazine. Ulica Twarda 6 [6 Twarda St.], the street where, by the way, my mother and my grandparents lived, and which became part of the Warsaw ghetto, is the center of communal Jewish life in Warsaw. There is the Teatr Żydowski [Yiddish theater], the Spielberg Foundation, the offices of the JDC under Ms. Datner's directorship, the kindergarten, and the offices of two out of the three Jewish magazines that appear in Warsaw. The Jewish press includes *Słowo Żydowskie [The Jewish Word]*, a bi-weekly published in Polish and in Yiddish; the already mentioned *Midrasz*, published in Polish; and *Jidele*, an irregularly published Magazine of Jewish Youth and its Friends. In the editorial offices of *Midrasz* I met Mr. Konstanty Gebert, the editor-in-chief. As Jan Miernowski told me later, Mr. Gebert became famous for his excellent subversive articles in support of Solidarity published under the pseudonym of Dawid Warszawski at the time of Polish struggle against the communist regime. The articles put the secret police on an unsuccessful hunt for the author, even though the pseudonym implied the possibility that the author was Jewish. The identity of Dawid Warszawski was revealed only after the struggle came to its successful conclusion.

*Midrasz* is an attractively edited magazine, printed on glossy paper, decorated with colorful and imaginative illustrations. In response to my compliment for the magazine's graphics, Mr. Gebert explained that this elegant presentation of the magazine intends to transform the gloomy black and white image associated with other Jewish publications. As I learned a few days later at my meeting with the editor of the *Jewish Word*, this message was not lost. Even though sponsored by the Polish Ministry of Culture and Education, which means sparse funding, the cover of the latest edition of the *Jewish Word* boasts a blue and white picture of Jerusalem.

*Midrasz* can afford its luxurious appearance thanks to the sponsorship of the Ronald Lauder Foundation — Polish Mission. But it is not only its external aspect that betrays the magazine's aspiration to keep up with the Western world. The December 1997 issue of *Midrasz* was devoted to the topic of women in the Jewish world; the January 1998 issue explored the problematic of Christians of Jewish origins. These compare favorably with this type of American publications. But the issue was by no means a mere imitation of American socio-cultural media fashion. The problematic of women's position in the synagogue is crucial in the community of "dissimilating" Jews, who grapple with questions of religious observance, mixed marriages, and Jewish education. In a similar way, the issue of converted Jews, whether during the war, as hidden children, or after the war out of conviction, and their place *vis à vis* the Jewish community, shows the extent to which the question of religious identity preoccupies both Jewish and Christian Poland today.

Traditionally, the vitality of any Jewish community has been measured by the education it offers its children. Indeed, Jewish education in Warsaw is gaining momentum. The Lauder-Morasha School is a case in point. This thriving elementary school is convincing evidence that the desire to build a meaningful Jewish future in Poland is both serious and real. Though it may seem unrealistic, I believe that this villa turned into a school in the suburb of Warsaw marks a crucial step in this community's structuring of Polish-Jewish identity. The small but well-taken-care-of house accommodates about 80 Jewish and non-Jewish children, who study secular subjects as well as Jewish history, Hebrew, and stories of the Bible. The entrance and the doors are decorated with signs in Polish, Hebrew, and English; the halls are covered with pictures from Israel and with children's drawings of Torah scrolls and menorahs; the basement houses a kitchen where I saw Polish helpers baking *challahs* for Friday lunch; in the classroom I met children, who, when asked, struggle with Hebrew words. At times, it seemed that such a school could fit very well in American suburban reality. But, incongruous as it may sound, it is in Warsaw. Ms. Helise Lieberman, its dynamic director, who hails from Illinois and New York, explained that the school is part of The Ronald Lauder Foundation project to rebuild Jewish culture in Eastern Europe. Proof that this school is not an artificially implanted fantasy of a rich man lies in the waiting list of about 35 students, in the struggle to obtain a permit to build a real school building from the less than enthusiastic city council, and in planning even further ahead for a future high school.

At the end of my visit, Ms. Lieberman wistfully told me about a typical American Jew who commented to her that all she came to Poland for was to see Auschwitz, and that she could not wait to get out of Poland which to her is nothing but a cemetery. "Isn't this school," Ms. Lieberman asked her, "a small light of hope for the future?" I recalled Mr. Krajewski's comment and realized that his assessment of American Jewish view of Poland might have been correct.

I was told of a similar exchange once again, though in a different context. It was related to me by Mr. Joachim Russek on my visit to Cracow. Mr. Russek is the Director of the Center for Jewish Culture – Judaica Foundation in Kazimierz, a part of Cracow. Now empty of Jews, before the war it was one of the most prominent centers of Jewish life, learning, and culture. "Jewish tourists tell me," said Mr. Russek, "that they pass Cracow only because it is on the way to Auschwitz and there is nothing else they want to see, because Poland means nothing to them except a cemetery. I tell them that if they do not know what was before Auschwitz, and that if they have no awareness of what was lost, they will never understand the full significance of Auschwitz."

At the time of Poland's struggle for freedom, the American Congress agreed to aid Poland with the proviso that two million dollars be allotted to the establishment of the Center for Jewish Culture in Cracow. This money allowed Mr. Russek to reconstruct the facade of the old Kazimierz synagogue and turn the inside into a modern, wonderful cultural center. Now he searches for financial resources to maintain this enterprise, struggling to make the place known without resorting to cheap advertising. His reports on the Center activities show literally dozens of lectures, concerts, exhibitions, and film. A particular achievement is the Festival of Jewish Culture which has become quite well known and which takes place every summer. Mr. Russek also established an intensive study program between Brandeis University in Boston and the Jagiellonian University in Cracow. The program, intended for American students, includes a field study of the landmarks of Jewish culture.

In the beginning of my visit, we told each other something about our personal histories. Thus we established that we were born in the same city, Zabrze or Hindenburg, in Silesia. My twin brother and I were born there because our parents, who had survived in the Soviet Union, had no place to stay in the burned down Warsaw, and turned south. Mr. Russek was born there under more conventional circumstances; his family of coal miners had lived in Zabrze for generations. "You realize," he told me "that I am not Jewish." Anticipating questions which he has heard and answered many times, Mr. Russek explained that he got involved with the Center because he wanted to do really important things. "Jewish culture is part of Polish culture," he said. "If we do not save what is left, if we do not reconstruct what is still remembered, it will be lost forever. I know antisemitism still exists, and I wish the 1946 Kielce pogrom had not happened, but it had and we have to admit it and work together toward something better."

As the evening went on, we kept discussing Polish antisemitism and Jewish prejudices against the Poles. I told him my parents' story and he told me the story of his father, a socialist who never recovered from a years-long incarceration in a concentration camp. We compared our impressions of Israel, and Mr. Russek told me how good he feels in Jerusalem, which he found to be an international city, and how he met old Polish Jews there who told him about Poland. It was an exceptional intellectual and emotional exchange, a true meeting of apparently so different minds.

The next morning I went to Auschwitz. How to tell about this place where one has the unreal sense of touching evil, where one feels surrounded by ghosts; where one cannot help imagining being deported with the others, suffocating in the stench of the cattle wagon, lining up to the tunes of the camp orchestra, being herded on the ramp, entering the "showers"? I wanted a private tour, and Mr. Russek arranged for an excellent guide. Mr. Balys not only knows the history and the geography of the place; he also knows how to present it. I could see the pain in his explanations, the genuine horror at what he was relating, even though he must have gone this route and given the explanation many a time. It was not a tourist season and we were practically alone. I wanted to see everything, and he showed me all he knew, including the underground torture chambers and the execution place, the barracks of the medical experiments, and other places of suffering and horror. Standing there and listening to Mr. Balys' intelligent and sensitive explanations I could grasp fully, maybe for the first time, the dual pattern of physical and psychological mechanism employed by the Nazis. It was a demonic combination, which created a hermetically closed trap. In Auschwitz the question about the passivity of the victims of such a satanically contrived terror looks naive and ill-informed at best.

In Birkenau everything seemed peaceful...until we entered the barracks. Standing there one becomes the victim of one's imagination, the approximation of what it must have been like. Even though indescribably remote from the actual experience, this was the closest I could get to an almost physical sensation of the degradation, the suffering, the impossibility of a dignified death that evolved in this place. Then we walked up to the blown up crematoria and gas chambers, the little ponds into which the ashes were thrown. We stood at the monument whose changed inscription recognizes the majority of the Jewish victims in Auschwitz.

Atop the infamous tower over the entrance to Birkenau, Mr. Balys pointed to the church just across from the prisoners' barracks. He was not pleased with the closeness of the church to the camp, pointing out that the whole area we could see from the tower was in fact camp territory. We had already seen, at my suggestion, the new convent of the Carmelite nuns in Auschwitz, outside of the camp. The convent issue and its politico-theological implications arose again, and I noted that the cross had been removed. However, rapidly unfolding developments shattered the illusory hope that the controversy over the cross had been resolved. As I re-edit these lines, the Polish government and the *Sejm* (the Polish Parliament), supported by the Polish Church, are embroiled in the process of passing a law which would allow them to remove the multiple crosses from the disputed terrain.

Mr. Balys described himself as a retired educator. He had spent a month in Yad Vashem as the guest of the museum and the government of Israel; he loved it and asked me to say "Shalom" to Jerusalem. During our very long and detailed tour, I became convinced that it was by no means material advantage that motivated him to have become a guide of Auschwitz. To my question he answered simply that he believed that showing and explaining the horror of Auschwitz to as many people as possible may prevent another Auschwitz. He said it when we were walking toward the ramp where the selections occurred. At this moment, in this place, where every exchange assumes a special meaning, his answer did not sound at all like a *cliché*.

Of course, the topic of antisemitism, past and present, was unavoidable. While acknowledging that many Poles did not help Jews and that many betrayed Jews, Mr. Balys reminded me that the majority of the Righteous Gentiles honored by Yad Vashem were Poles. The question of the behavior of Poles toward Jews during the war hangs heavily on the conscience of the Poles whom I had the good fortune to meet. They know that Polish antisemitism is still rampant. This certainly does not alleviate the memory of the war. Mr. Balys was emphatic that despite the great theological differences between the two religions, and in spite of great difficulties, the dialogue between the Jews and the Polish Church must go on. We were back to the difficult reality of Polish-Jewish relationships today, a reality that I could observe and even, to an extent, experience during my short stay in Poland.

On my return from Cracow to Warsaw, I met with another well-known intellectual, who is very active in Polish Jewish matters. Mr. Jan Grosfeld, a professor at the University of Warsaw, invited me to his home, where I had an extremely interesting conversation with him and his wife. Mr. Grosfeld represents yet another kind of Jewish existence in Poland. He converted to Catholicism but does not deny his Jewish roots. He reminds us of Jean-Marie Lustiger, the Cardinal of Paris who claims both Catholic and Jewish identity. Lustiger was a hidden child during the war, but he claims that his conversion took place before the war. Mr. Grosfeld, on the other hand, was born after the war to parents who, as I have heard from others, were active Communist party members. He converted as an adult.

Mr. Grosfeld is passionately involved in Jewish affairs. He is a member of the *Rada Episkopatu Polski do Spraw Dialogu Religijnego* [the Council of the Polish Episcopate for Matters of Religious Dialogue]. In fact, Mr. Grosfeld wanted to meet me because we share a common interest. We both wrote on Edith Stein, the Jewish convert and Carmelite nun who perished in the Holocaust and, at the time of my visit to Warsaw, was about to be canonized as a Christian martyr. The affair of the Carmelite convent at Auschwitz was implicitly connected with her martyrdom, and until recently, there was a plaque at Auschwitz commemorating her death. Once again history has been proceeding swiftly, and now as I re-edit this essay, Stein has been officially canonized, becoming St. Teresa Benedicta of the Cross. This act of sanctification makes the connection between the Jewish-born Carmelite Saint and the Carmelite convent affair even more pronounced. The decision to confer the 'highest Church honor upon a converted Jew who died in Auschwitz indicates an intention to infuse the Holocaust with a note of Christian martyrdom. The location of the convent implies an interpretation of the Holocaust in the model of the passion of Christ.

I was invited to talk about Stein at the *Instytut Chrześcijansko-Żydowskiego Dialogu* [Institute of Christian Jewish Dialogue). My presentation was overshadowed by an unpleasant incident which affected the Jewish and the  Catholic community, especially the members of the Institute. A brief summary of the incident gives a good idea of the difficulties confronting those who wish to eradicate the tradition of antisemitism in Poland. First, however, I need to mention that the Polish Catholic Church seems to be working hard at the problem of antisemitism. It is well known that the highest echelons of the Church are encouraged by the Pope to act against bigotry and racism, especially with regard to Jews. It is also well known, however, that though the Pope is venerated in Poland, he is not always obeyed. I believe that it is also of interest to mention that the Church, which has lost authority once the war was won (victory as we know, is sometimes the worst possible disaster), has been trying to regain its power. At the time of my stay in Poland, January 1998, the Sejm was debating the ratification of the concordat with the Church. While some of the speakers declared the ineluctable connection of Poland and the church, others expressed the anxiety of creating a situation less than favorable to minorities. The underlying tone, I believe, was warning against possible exacerbation of antisemitism.

In fact, the episode I am referring to presents us with an example of the extent to which Polish religious antisemitism is played out on the political arena. The crisis began with a sermon given by a priest, Father Jankowski, who is well known for his antisemitic pronouncements. The sermon denounced the presence of minorities in the government while resorting to post-war antisemitic argument of *Żydokomuna*, that is, of Jewish communists conspiring to take over Poland. Even though he did not mention names, Father Jankowski was alluding to Mr. Geremek, who serves as the Minister of Foreign Affairs in the newly formed government. It is important to note that although Mr. Geremek is of Jewish origin, adopted during the war by a Polish family, he is by no means a practicing Jew. In addition, he is former professor and scholar of French literature, a prominent member of the *Solidarność* and now a very highly regarded and respected politician, also active in the European Union. This, however, did not stop Father Jankowski. Since he has been warned before not to speak about politics from the pulpit and not to grant interviews, upon transgressing these two injunctions, the bishop punished Jankowski by forbidding him the pulpit for a year.

I arrived in Warsaw to witness the next chapters of the drama. Jankowski's blatantly antisemitic sermon, which subsequently was published, evoked from the Church a variety of reactions which ranged from dismissing it altogether, to diminishing its importance, to suggesting that the speaker was "a psychiatric case." The course of action changed, however, with a particularly strong article written by another priest, Father Musiał. Father Musiał's extensive article in the respectable *Tygodnik Powszechny*, a paper published by the Church, condemned the tradition of antisemitism in Poland and went so far as saying that statements such as Jankowski's were of fascist nature and led to tragic consequences in history. He also referred to the silence of the Church during the Holocaust and urged a more effective fight against all demonstrations of anti-Jewish hatred.

The next phase of the affair threw the Jewish community into a state of shock. It turned out that Father Chrostowski, who co-chairs, together with Mr. Krajewski, the Institute of Christian Jewish Dialogue, wrote a response to Father Musiał, which in public opinion, amounted to antisemitic propaganda. Chrostowski criticized Musiał's critique of the Church and his reference to the Holocaust, and also had some unpleasant things to say about the disproportionate place of Jews in previous governments. He was clearly referring to a Jewish communist past in Poland.

Needless to say, Father Chrostowski, who was the one to extend the invitation to me to speak about Edith Stein, absented himself from the meeting because of his sudden change of mind concerning the antisemitic pronouncements of Father Jankowski. But others were there, among them Father Czajkowski, who is widely respected for his pro-Jewish attitude. My paper evoked a discussion obviously quite different from the one that followed my presentation on Jewish identity in the home of Ms. Datner. But it was no less animated and probing. The members of the dialogue found it provoking because my approach was phenomenological (Stein was a phenomenologist) rather than theological. Once I established that it is not my intention to present a definitive explanation of Edith Stein, but only explore the philosophical foundations of her ecumenism, my paper was favorably accepted. The most gratifying moments took place after the formal conclusion of the meeting. I got invitations to participate in other meetings, to come again and to give interviews. Some people just came to thank me and an elderly gentleman came up and told me in a very quiet voice: "I was one of those who helped the Jews and I want to give you the poems I wrote about this experience." He gave me two books of his poems and left.

My talk appeared as an article in the February issue of *Midrasz*. All this was, of course, very satisfying. Moreover, it seems very important to mention that the formal part of the meeting ended with making plans for an activity to celebrate the Day of Judaism in the Catholic Church, which has been just approved as an annual event by the Episcopate. Despite the setbacks and the disappointments, there seems to be a very strong determination to continue the dialogue.

The last day in Warsaw was miserable. It was gray, cold and it rained all the time. Most of it was spent in the monumental Jewish cemetery, on an unsuccessful search for the graves of my paternal grandparents, who died in the Warsaw ghetto. The tomb of Esther Kaminska, the founder of the Yiddish Theater and the mother of Ida Kaminska, and that of Y.L. Peretz were reminders of the cultural glory of the Jewish Poland. The memorial that commemorates Janusz Korczak with his children and the memorial in memory of the children of the ghetto were the chilling reminders of how this culture disappeared.

Then it was back to *Umschlagplatz* where my maternal grandparents and other family members must have waited for the transport to Treblinka: the broken trees on top of the front wall of this symbolic train wagon; the crack of hope in the rear wall; the untouched building which was the Gestapo building; the bunker of Mordecai Anielewicz whose location was betrayed; the monument of the Ghetto Heroes made of one enormous slab of marble initially brought to Warsaw by Hans Frank, the Governor General of Poland, and initially intended for a statue of Hitler. It seems that in Poland history does not evolve; rather it shifts rapidly from one extreme to another. Not only are the transformations of hope and despair unpredictable, but often the past seems to overshadow and even to replace the future. What was my part in this turbulence, this maelstrom of an incredible grief of destruction, on the one hand, and, on the other hand, the incredible vitality and energy to go on and rebuild after the destruction?

The last meeting in Warsaw helped me to regain some equilibrium. Just before leaving I met with Mr. Jerzy Halbersztadt, a historian at the University of Warsaw and the Representative of the Washington Holocaust Memorial Museum in Poland. Hastily meeting over a cup of tea in the Bristol Hotel, we were telling each other our family histories. Mr. Halbersztadt, whose parents survived, like mine, by escaping to the Soviet Union, told me about his father who never exhibited any Jewish consciousness, yet always stuck to his name. It was almost uncanny to hear at this moment of departure from Poland a story so similar to my father's. My father, who came to Warsaw after the war to rebuild this city from its destruction, also had his moment of resistance when he refused to accept the suggestion to change his name to appear "less" Jewish. My father was far from any religious orientation and deeply steeped in Polish culture. His name was inseparable from his growing up as a Polish Jew, and this was the part of his identity with which he never parted, even when moving to Israel where, ironically, changes of "Jewishly" sounding names were encouraged and often expected.

So perhaps this was the meaning of my return; perhaps the recognition and acceptance of that aspect of identity which has always been there and which has never been acknowledged will allow me to confront my "unfinished business?" But how has this realization of a vital yet forgotten part emerged? At the moment of saying our goodbyes, Ewa Mierowska was worried that the rainy and bleak weather had spoilt my stay in Poland. "A good stay does not depend on the weather," I heard myself saying gratefully, "it has to do with the people you meet." For the Jews, Poland is in many ways a sad and tragic country, but the people I have met — both Poles and Jews — in their uphill, impossible struggle to reconnect the past and the present do keep the business *unfinished,* thus preventing the metaphor of Poland as Jewish cemetery from materializing. As I was leaving Poland and heading for a brief visit to Israel, my true, though adoptive, home, I felt deeply thankful for having met people who taught me a lesson whose complexity both enriched and made me more complete.

As I mentioned twice before, history seems to be ahead of us, rendering our efforts, experiences, conclusions out of date. Since my visit to Poland, the crosses in Auschwitz have reappeared evoking hopelessness about anti-Jewish sentiments whose voices keep raging even in the deafening silence of Birkenau. Edith Stein has been canonized, and the paradox of a sainthood conferred on a Jewish woman exterminated in

Auschwitz *because* of her Jewishness makes us wonder about the uses and abuses of the memory of the Holocaust dead. It seems that very little progress toward a better world is being made, and solutions are not in sight. And yet, somehow my experience in Poland prohibits despair. My initial decision to open myself up to the old-new experience of Poland allowed me to hear voices other than those of destruction and mourning. The country that is the land of my birth and my childhood was capable, despite the differences and distances that separate me from it, of communicating a teaching. The Krajewskis, the Musials, the Balyses, the Grosfelds, the Russeks, the Miernowskis and the others told me, each in his or her own way, that giving up is a luxury we cannot afford, that the struggle must go on. Living on a land which entombs the most horrific memory in human history, these individuals have not forgotten. On the contrary, they keep the memory alive by drawing upon it to keep up the often losing battle against the forces of hatred that produced it. This is the only way the memory of the Holocaust should be used.

# LIVING IN THE LAND OF ASHES

## KONSTANTY GEBERT

The March of the Living, which takes place each year in Auschwitz-Birkenau, serves forcefully to remind its participants of what Israel was established due to, as well as against. Thousands of young Jews from Israel and the Diaspora come to the site of this former German death camp in southern Poland, on a trip of several days, that brings them also to other sites of martyrdom. Rarely, if at all, do they see monuments of the Jewish life that flourished in that country for centuries before the *Shoah*, and almost never do they meet their peers — young Poles or young Polish Jews — to get a glimpse of what Poland is like more than half a century after the German genocide. The message is clear — Poland is to be seen as place of death only. This, obviously, is quite distressing for those who choose to live here today.

But regardless of the political uses inevitably made of the March, one thing must remain clear in the eyes of Jews and non-Jews alike: it is there to remind us of the fact that Israel was established because Europeans in Europe had murdered the Jewish nation. Consent for setting up the Jewish state was dictated both by a need for expiation and by the necessity of ridding the continent of the survivors. Their presence was an irritant, and the fact they were still being murdered proved all too emphatically that the Germans had merely implemented the desires of the entire continent.

Jews were still killed after the war. The Kielce pogrom in 1946, in which 44 Jews were murdered, might have been the biggest, but it was hardly the only one. Nor do we know the number of Jews butchered in Minsk after the city's liberation by the Red Army, or that of the victims in other towns and villages of Belarus and Ukraine. We do know of small pogroms in Hungary and Slovakia — three Jews murdered here, five there — and of the systematic hunting down of individual survivors. The total toll will never be known. The victims of the post-war killings had barely managed to flee the German statistics of death, but did not manage to make it into the statistics of life. These were counted outside of the Old Continent.

159

Or rather — they could be counted. At the shores of Palestine the Royal Navy intercepted boats laden with Jewish refugees, shot at, and killed them. Those arrested were taken to camps in Cyprus or Europe — sometimes the very same German camps they had managed to flee. In the former Italian colony of Libya, now occupied by the British, a four-day pogrom in late 1945 claimed the lives of at least 167 Jews. The occupying authorities did nothing to stop it. In Palestine itself Jews were killed in Arab terrorist attacks, and responded in kind — including against the British who, now that the common war against Nazism was over, had reverted in Jewish eyes to being but the occupiers: European accomplices of death.

All this needs to be remembered when under Israeli banners thousands of young Jews, oblivious to the Poland they are crossing, march from Auschwitz to Birkenau. It is true that the Germans were the architects and executors of the *Shoah*. But they were aided in that task by numerous Frenchmen and Poles, Lithuanians and Croatians, Hungarians and Italians. Heroic acts of resistance by men and women of all the continent's nations, determined to derail the German machinery of murder, cannot significantly alter this overall picture. Europe had delivered the Jews to the Germans to be exterminated. For a Jew arrested by a French gendarme, who had miraculously managed to flee from a German death camp, and who was then delivered by Polish peasants to Ukrainian auxiliaries, the fact that these nations were also engaged in a war to the death among themselves was inevitably only of secondary importance. And regarding the Jews, the warring nations saw eye to eye.

No one who had not then been a hunted prey can probably understand this experience, a mix of horror, loneliness, alienation, and ice-cold hatred. But the next generations of Jews in Europe can understand it more readily than others. We have inherited sharp eyesight and hearing, and precious few illusions. We take note of each "Jude raus" scribbled on a street in Warsaw, of each neo-Nazi demonstration in Germany, of each Le Pen vote in France. We do know that our citizenship here may be of limited validity. This is also, though not solely, why Israel — all the criticism we might have notwithstanding — is and remains so dear to us. It is only there that our right to life is permanent, inalienable and unassailable.

But young Israelis do not have that training under their belts. Participation in the March of the Living is usually their first trip to the heart of darkness. To the place which, not less than Gothic cathedrals and university reading rooms, is an expression of the deepest essence of

Europe. And when they hear, as they do, occasional cat-calls and insults, when their buses have at times been stoned, they remain convinced that now, as then, genocidal Europe once again is revealing its true face to the Jews.

But such indeed is the message of the March. Its organizers want its participants to believe that Poland, Europe, means death, while Israel is resurrection. They still, as classical Zionists did, want to negate the Diaspora, with the sole possible exception of the North American one, its success story unrivaled since the Golden Age of Spain. This denial of the Diaspora, this hostility toward Jews who have consciously decided they want to live a diasporic life, both hurts and insults us, European Jews.

It hurts not only because of the challenge it poses to our decisions, indeed — to our very identities, but also because of the centrality of the resurrection myth in that particular world-view, and of the trappings of civic religion it has acquired. There already exists a religion based on the myth of death and resurrection. It is not the Jewish religion. Nor is pilgrimage the Jewish way of honoring martyrs. We keep their memory alive by having Jewish children and inculcating them with Jewish values, not necessarily by bringing Jewish children to the sites of their forbears' martyrdom.

But then we do know that the organizers of the March are wrong only in the seeming certainty of their belief that the true face of Europe is genocidal, while we base our relative optimism on the conviction that it does not always have to be that way. But we do know it can. Nor can we discard as a mere coincidence the fact that already thrice this century genocide was attempted in Europe: against the Jews, the Roma, and the Bosnian Muslims. It can hardly be coincidental that all three nations hardly fit the image of the white, Christian European.

But then we also know that the organizers would be less sure of the unrivaled success of the North American Diaspora, if they had attempted to hold the March, say, in Harlem, NY. It is always risky to march rich kids through a poor land.

But especially so if the marchers are taught to despise that land, indeed to hate it. The memorable phrase about hating the Poles "for their part in the atrocities" has been removed from participants' orientation pamphlets two years ago. And yet some of the spirit that had inspired it still lingers. It has also been two years now that young Polish Jews have been allowed to address the March. And yet they still often report being asked, suspiciously, how can they choose to live in this place of destruction and death. As if they were fools at best, traitors at worst.

For the second year in a row the organizers have invited some non-Jewish youth to join the march. I do not know if there is, among them, enough awareness of the magnitude of that gesture. The pain Jews feel when thinking of Auschwitz, when feeling Auschwitz with all the sinews of their souls, when marching from Auschwitz to Birkenau across the land that is mixed with the ashes of our nation, can never be relieved. This March, though a public event, is at the same time the most intimate of Jewish concerns. Non-Jews have now been invited to share that intimacy, for a further refusal would be tantamount to a rejection of their own pain, an insult to their own suffering and will to solidarity.

But it has to be frankly stated that this in no way abolishes the difference between us. The Polish people — thanks to God, but not thanks to its allies — has not been murdered. It still exists. It is a part of that Europe which in its civil war that lasted, with breaks, for half a century, had always found the time to slaughter Jews. There is, of course, no collective responsibility for past actions. But there is collective responsibility for history.

And the history of Europe is a Christian one. Though this statement must be protested against if it is presented in a normative light, it nonetheless remains true as a description. The crosses remain the symbols of that Christian European history. The same crosses which now tower above the walls of the camp. Whose number is growing. And whose presence has led to a terrible and dangerous conflict at Auschwitz.

It is the experience of European Jews that Christianity had prepared the grounds for the *Shoah*. The crosses towering over Auschwitz are to our eyes the symbols of the persecutors, not of the victims. The fact that they have been planted on the grounds of what is the biggest Jewish graveyard in Christian Europe insults us. This word has to be treated in its most literal sense. And I think the Christians have about as much of a chance of convincing Jews that the cross is, in essence, a sign not of oppression, but of love, as — *mutatis mutandis* — the Jews have of convincing Palestinians that the star of David is a sign of powerless victims. And one has to bear in mind that the Middle East conflict has been going on for less than a century, not for millennia, nor has it generated systematic murder and genocide.

This is something the Christians need to understand. And what about the Jews?

We need to understand two things, and neither of them will be easy. The first is that the cross had not been planted solely against us. The second is that there are important Christian reasons for its being there.

Most Jews react to what is happening at Auschwitz and Birkenau as if it concerns them, and them alone. They are barely cognizant of the Polish, non-Jewish martyrdom which also occurred there. Polish senator Władyslaw Bartoszewski has repeatedly experienced this himself, when foreigners say: "I did not know you are Jewish" upon learning he had been an inmate in Auschwitz.

For the Jews, Auschwitz as the site of their martyrdom is such an overpowering presence that there is simply no space left for other people's signs, symbols or values. But we do need to understand that for the Poles, Auschwitz is the symbol of their martyrdom. The fact that, as a nation, it had suffered incomparably less than the Jews, is irrelevant here. There is no discussing, given the depth of emotions on either side. The crosses insult us – but this is not the main reason for their being there.

And yet the organizers of the cross-building campaign are in no way oblivious to the fact that their crosses insult and cause us pain. They indeed see in that one more reason for planting them there, on that spot, symbolically reclaiming martyred Polish soil from the domination of the foreigner. Antisemitic pamphlets are being distributed; hate is being spread. The Jews, say some of the organizers, are simply engaged in their age-long pursuit — the hatred of all that is Polish.

And yet, even if the antisemites, as it is ardently to be desired, would no longer sully that place of martyrdom by their presence, the issue would not disappear. These crosses have been planted there to commemorate the martyrdom of Polish Christian Europeans at the hands of German Christian Europeans. For the Christians, the Christian cross belongs in such a place. It does not, however, belong in a Jewish cemetery.

Some solutions have already been advanced. During a radio talk show I participated in, a woman listener called to suggest that the best thing would be for Jewish ashes to be excavated and transported to Israel. She added that Christians would be happy to cover the cost of the operation. I listened to her very carefully, hoping to detect hatred in her voice. But no — the lady was imbued with Christian love and willingness to attain a compromise. The same spirit as seen in the declarations of another Polish gentleman, who suggested that, since the sight of the cross is offensive to Jews, the issue would be best solved by heightening the inner perimeter wall of the camp, which runs between the field of crosses and the camp itself. He, too, was willing to volunteer resources to that end.

But this cannot work. The walls between Christian and Jew, between the Star of David and the Cross, need to be lowered, not raised. Nor is it possible to extract Jewish ashes from the soil, water and air of Europe, to return them to their pristine purity. We shall remain here, though at times one side, or the other, believes it would be better to separate. We shall remain here, just as — *mutatis mutandis* — the empty grave of Jesus of Nazareth will remain in the heart of Jerusalem, though Jews would certainly prefer not to see crosses on their soil. And yet nobody throws those crosses out of Jerusalem.

But in Auschwitz, where not one Jew died, but over one million, there should be no crosses. Not one.

There is no good solution to the question, but there is a precedent. Father Maximilan Kolbe, a Christian priest (and a pre-war antisemite), died a martyr's death in Auschwitz, volunteering to substitute for another prisoner, who had been sentenced to death by starvation. Kolbe had been made a saint by the Catholic Church, and today there is a chapel in his death cell, replete with Christian icons and crosses. They insult no one, for those who would be insulted by their presence simply do not go to that site. And my prayers in Auschwitz are not disturbed by the awareness of their invisible presence. They are disturbed by my awareness of where I stand. A smaller cross, one that would not be visible above the inner perimeter of the camp, would be an insult to those alone who want to feel insulted, who seek it out to confirm their hostility and pain.

I understand their feelings; I also understand the feelings of those who are jarred by the sight of the crosses on top of the church at Birkenau, very visible from the campgrounds. But that church, as opposed to the crosses at Auschwitz, does not stand on the grounds of the camp proper. There is a limit to what we can realistically demand in the name of our pain.

And so we must talk. We must negotiate deadlines and dimensions, compare the costs of political confrontations and those of making concessions. There is no hope that the unseemly presence of the crosses in that particular place will, in itself, be understood. The ideas of deporting human ashes or heightening the wall as a way of solving the conflict shows just how deeply — half a century after the ovens were extinguished — Auschwitz still poisons human souls.

Nor can we, as the Chief Rabbi of Poland has suggested, simply state "we do not care" what the other side wants. We have to care even — indeed, especially — is we find it unacceptable. So let us calmly negotiate, testing the limits of possible compromise. But we should harbor no illusions that both sides negotiate on the grounds of common values. Our experiences differ, and so does the way we see the world.

And this, precisely, is our defeat. A defeat both for Jews and for Europe. For it turns out that Auschwitz — a place everyone should approach with terror in the heart, whose gates one should cross only at extreme risk to one's soul, and where no one should dare plant his or her symbol or mark — has become domesticated. The horror flowing from it has been contained through the conjoint efforts of political contests and mass tourism to that ghastly Disneyland.

And yet we should feel that horror all the time. Indeed, it is the lack of horror that should elicit our horror, for we now know that it was possible. Only this horror can be a barrier, even if fragile and flimsy, against the return of the nightmare. Not necessarily against the Jews this time: there still are the Roma, the Bosnians, the immigrants. When Europeans no longer fear themselves, all others have grounds for fear.

The March of the Living will, as every year, exit through the main gate at Auschwitz, and turn right, turning its back to the crosses located at the other end of the road. It will march toward the dumping fields of human ashes at Birkenau. There they will weep and light their memorial candles. And then they will drive off and fly away. And Breathe. And be reborn.

None of that will be possible for us, Jews and non-Jews, inhabitants of the land of the ashes.

# THE CHALLENGE OF SOLIDARITY

## SUSAN E. NOWAK

---

The controversy surrounding the establishment of a Carmelite convent at Auschwitz, and the subsequent erection of crosses, indisputably exposed the tensions confronting contemporary Jewish-Catholic relations.[1] Jews and Roman Catholics committed to interreligious dialogue recognize that these tensions fundamentally challenge the integrity of Jewish-Catholic relations. Of great concern is the fact that throughout the negotiation process the Roman Catholic Church adopted contradictory attitudes, behaviors, and positions. It became painfully apparent that the root of the contradictions was the church's odious legacy of anti-Judaism and antisemitism. As the negotiations continued it became equally clear that, if left unaddressed, this legacy would undermine the credibility of contemporary Roman Catholicism and the viability of Jewish-Christian relations.

## THE LEGACY OF THEOLOGICAL ANTI-JUDAISM

> Let us remember. This crime was perpetrated in a Europe nourished on the Christian faith... To earn the right to pray at Auschwitz we must confess how weak and how brutish was the response of our conscience in the face of the perversions of the Nazis and the mortal danger suffered by the Jews at that time... We cannot deny responsibility shared by Christians in the history which led to the *Shoah*.[2]

In 1998 the Vatican presented, *We Remember: Reflections on the Shoah*, a document ten years in the writing. The anxieties and concerns raised by the protracted drafting process were eased by reports that the document would directly address the ways in which theological teachings directly influence not only the beliefs, but especially the attitudes, practice, and behaviors of church members. To be sure, the credibility of the proposed document was strengthened when Vatican spokesperson Joaquin Navarro-Valls announced that it would deal both with historical judgments and theological issues concerning the Church, the Holocaust, and antisemitism.[3] The Vatican announcement was deeply welcomed by those concerned about the future relationship of Judaism and Christianity. It buoyed hopes that Roman Catholicism was readying itself to acknowledge its responsibility for teachings that fostered theological anti-Judaism and antisemitism over the centuries.

In particular, Navarro-Valls' announcement seemed to indicate a willingness to confront historical documentation which might well expose the lack of Roman Catholicism's resistance to, if not its active collaboration with, the Nazis during the Holocaust, as well as the direct link between its teachings and its failure to combat effectively the genocide of the Jewish people.[4] Expectations were raised that the document would not be encumbered by a flawed hermeneutic which attempts to exonerate the Church as a whole by holding up those precious few Roman Catholics who did risk all in order to resist Nazism and save Jews from annihilation.[5] Most especially, it was hoped that the Church was ready to teach *by example* that all who participated in the *Shoah* must confront their past choices and actions and commit themselves to a process of ethical, theological, and philosophical self-critique for the sake of a new and different future.[6]

To the disappointment of many Christians and Jews, *We Remember* fell well short of these hopes. While it is important to recognize its achievements, strongly evident in the initial sections, it is equally important to identify the deep flaws that pervade the latter sections. *We Remember* bears sad witness to the fact that the time has not yet arrived when the Vatican can dare the demands of theological self-critique.

The controversy precipitated by the establishment of a Carmelite convent at Auschwitz reveals in yet another setting the consequences of the Church's failure to accept responsibility for its anti-Judaic teachings and the destructive behaviors they spawned.[7] As the controversy progressed, it became evident that the appropriateness of an "Auschwitz convent" was not the only issue at stake. At the heart of the controversy lay questions regarding the Church's commitment to its most recent teachings on theological anti-Judaism and antisemitism and the integrity of its participation in institutional Jewish-Catholic interreligious dialogue.[8] There was great concern that the attitudes, statements, and actions on the part of ecclesiastical officials involved in the convent negotiations corroborated charges that Roman Catholicism has only superficially altered its teachings on Judaism and the Jewish people.[9]

Throughout the controversy it was argued vehemently by some that prayers and acts of repentance undertaken by the Carmelite nuns as reparation for the failure of Christianity during the Holocaust could not be construed as insensitive or harmful.[10] Others, however, believed equally as strongly that the nuns' mission exposed the insidious theological supersessionism (i.e., appropriation of another's history and memory, equalization of suffering, and collapse of religious and national identities) underlying and distorting the seemingly well-intentioned actions of the Carmelites and the Catholic Church.[11]

For the latter group, the painful and protracted nature of the controversy (i.e., the Church's failure to initiate dialogue regarding the convent's establishment; non-compliance with the timeline of the two Geneva Agreements; erection of an eight meter cross on the convent building; disputation over authority and jurisdiction among members of the Church hierarchy; publication of accusatory and prejudiced statements; equation of national Polish identity and Roman Catholic identity) clearly reveals the extent to which theological supersessionism continues to shape the Catholic theological worldview.[12] They argue, correctly, that theological supersessionism distorts the Church's perception of the critical issues at stake. As a result, equivocation[13] and contradiction[14] obstruct the Church's understanding of the symbolic centrality of Auschwitz within the Jewish community worldwide,[15] thwart its efforts to address the Holocaust as a Christian catastrophe,[16] and impair its recognition of the uniqueness of the Jewish experience during the *Shoah*.[17]

In particular, the direct correlation between distorted understandings of key theological concepts (i.e., election, covenant, messianism, fulfillment, eschatology, and mission) and the Church's negative perception of Judaism and the Jewish people is obscured.[18] In the most extreme expressions, this correlation has allowed the Church to perceive itself as the newly elect messianic people, the successor of Israel, and the locus of salvation for all peoples. Denying the theological legitimacy of an ongoing covenantal relationship between God and Judaism was the next logical step. Covenantal relationship and election no longer resided with the "faithless" Jews, but with the Church, the "True Israel." Constructed as the "purely carnal Israel," Judaism was identified with everything unredeemed, evil, and demonic. Its continued existence was reduced to one purpose: testimony to God's continuing covenantal relationship with Christianity. Jewish suffering, whether caused by socio-cultural marginalization and/or politico-religious persecution, is understood as a consequence of a willful forfeiture of election and the covenantal relationship.

It must be emphasized that until the analyses of Christian theologians such as Rosemary Radford Ruether and Franklin Littell were given prominence, Christianity did not acknowledge the ways in which theological supersessionism influenced its interpretations of ecclesial identity and mission or justified centuries of Christian antisemitic behavior. It was blind to the reality that presenting Judaism as the theological symbol of unredeemed humanity justified reinterpreting the particularity of Christian historical revelation as a "universal particularity," which thereby legitimated the suppression of religious pluralism. The writings of Ruether and Littell, among others,[19] challenge Christians to address this flawed hermeneutic and rectify its influence on the Church's commitment to Jewish-Christian interreligious dialogue.[20]

The convent controversy and the debate over the cross/es has made this reality painfully evident both to the Jewish community and to Roman Catholics committed to Jewish-Christian interreligious dialogue, and they clearly and publicly acknowledge such a hermeneutic as antithetical to the principles of mutuality, equality, diversity, and respect for difference so essential to dialogue. As the controversy began to reach its long overdue resolution, statements and actions by ecclesiastical officials signaled a willingness to reassess the influence of the Church's theological anti-Judaism upon its perception and treatment of Judaism and the Jewish people.[21] After almost a decade of accusation, blatant prejudice, and defensive posturing, they buoy hopes that the Church will repudiate this influence and initiate the development of a credible Catholic theological worldview.[22] For those Roman Catholics committed to a stance of solidarity with the *Shoah's* victims, this task is an imperative.

## *TESHUVAH* AND THE DEMANDS OF SOLIDARITY

That antisemitism has found a place in Christian thought and practice calls for an act of *teshuvah* (repentance) and of reconciliation on our part as we gather here in this city, which is a testimony to our failure to be authentic witnesses to our faith at times in the past.[23]

Solidarity denounces the dichotomy of theology, or theory, and transformative action, or practice. Hence, it requires a community to understand that praxis defends the right to difference, dissimilarity, and distinctiveness so essential to the achievement of justice. Solidarity fosters critical self-reflection upon the power and privileges which sustain relationships marked by exclusion, victimization, and indifference. It also challenges the community to reconstruct its values, self-understanding, and structures in light of the experiences of those who are devalued and despised. Never is it enough for individuals or communities merely to acknowledge the systemic connections between ideological definitions of normativity, location within societal structures, and vulnerability to marginalization and violence. Rather, they are charged with the responsibility for mandating the reconstruction of these connections according to the principles of justice, inclusivity, co-responsibility, and plurality.

Roman Catholic theology and practices need to address this understanding of solidarity. This demands that Roman Catholicism assume two arduous, but quintessential, tasks. First, it must undertake public acts of *teshuvah* (repentance) for its perpetuation of theological anti-Judaism and its consequent antisemitic behaviors. Second, it must assume responsibility for reconstructing its theological worldview. Both tasks require a radical revision of its self-understanding and identity in light of the legacy of Christian triumphalism and the tragic history of Jewish-Christian relations.

## THE RECONSTRUCTION OF CHRISTIAN THEOLOGY AS AN ACT OF *TESHUVAH*

We are especially disheartened by those among Catholics who in some way were the cause of the death of Jews. They will forever gnaw at our conscience on the social plane. If only one Christian could have helped and did not stretch out a helping hand to a Jew during the time of danger or caused his (*sic*) death, we must ask forgiveness of our Jewish brothers and sisters.[24]

Reconstructing the Church's worldview in this way requires recognition of the ways in which Catholic notions of ecclesial identity, witness, and mission have been distorted. Only then can Roman Catholic thinkers reinterpret, with any confidence, the concept of covenant, a notion of obvious theological significance to both Christians and Jews.[25] Next, recognition must lead to reformulation. Reinterpreting notions of covenant necessitates reformulating central christological tenets accordingly. This may well be the most crucial task facing the Church today. Third, reformulation must precipitate similar developments of praxis. Reconstructed notions of covenant and christology will impact enormously and positively the Church's construction of Judaism and the Jewish people.

The task of theological reconstruction must begin with the reinterpretation of the concept of covenant because, historically, the Church's notion of covenant became exclusive in scope, dualistic in structure, and divisive in effect.[26] The dictates of external authority supported an ethic based upon the prerogative of rights and encouraged a sacramental understanding that emphasized ritualistic sacrality. Within this theological worldview, not only did Judaism became the *Other* which forfeited its covenantal election, but also Christianity claimed for itself greater responsibility for God's ongoing covenantal purposes. Even though the Church never went so far as to claim that Judaism was totally excluded from the covenantal relationship, its self-understanding was rooted in the theological assertion that it had eclipsed Judaism as God's elect. This self-understanding, in turn, reinforced the Church's negative construction of Judaism and the Jewish people.

The theological concept of solidarity can open the way for a fundamental transformation of these distorted understandings. First and foremost, this concept champions the intrinsic interrelation between theological formulation and right living. It focuses our attention and efforts on the fact that the truth of theological formulations is inexorably bound to action on behalf of justice and peace. This premise directs both the "deconstructive" and "reconstructive" dynamic of solidarity. The "deconstructive" task, addressed above, recognizes the ways in which religious triumphalism, patriarchal projection, and theological exclusivism distort understandings of covenant. This reverses the intrinsic interconnection between linear, hierarchical, and exclusionary understandings of covenant and the marginalization, degradation, persecution, and annihilation of Jews as the *Other*. Moreover, it reveals the link between an androcentric-patriarchal ethic of dominance-subjugation (with its predilections for external authority, the prerogative of rights, and ritualistic sacrality) and Roman Catholicism's failure to eliminate theologies which represent Christianity as the "completion" of Judaism.

The critical principles of justice, inclusivity, co-responsibility, and plurality, central to the "reconstructive" task of solidarity, provide the theoretical underpinnings for a theological worldview that validates the covenantal status of both Judaism and Christianity. Liberated from a constricted vision of theological exclusivism, the Church could then affirm the authenticity of Judaism's distinctive witness to God's covenantal relationship with humankind. Released from the destructive influence of hierarchical dualism, Roman Catholicism could publicly celebrate Judaism's long history of intimate relationship with God and its commitment to covenantal obligations and responsibilities. Disengaged from the defensive posture of patriarchal projection, the Church would be freed to confront the ways in which anti-Judaic teachings and antisemitic behaviors have profaned its witness to God's covenantal promises. Dissociated from an ethic of domination-subjugation, Catholicism could acclaim the fecundity of Judaism's ongoing witness to covenantal responsibilities, obligations, and rights. Consequently, for the first time in its history, the Church could accept *in praxis* the legitimacy of Judaism's covenantal status.

Within Roman Catholic systematics, a theology of covenant is inextricably linked to christology and ecclesiology. Thus, I argue that the theological concept of solidarity as a primary hermeneutic will foster the reconstruction of formative identity notions, such as redemption, repentance, and mission. Furthermore, this hermeneutic will make it very clear that *critical praxis,* rather than doctrinal definitions, provides the primary foundation for christological beliefs, ecclesiological commitments, and covenantal faith. At a minimum, it highlights those aspects of traditional christology and ecclesiology which have sustained, as well as those which have challenged, religious oppression. At its best, it illumines those aspects which have acted as a critical force of transformation.[27]

The construction of the figure of Jesus provides an important case in point. Christologies rooted in solidarity emphasize the full humanity of Jesus. They do not present Jesus as a demiurge or give disproportionate attention to his divinity; they acknowledge him as fully human and divine in a way that allowed him to live in solidarity with humanity precisely as a full human being. Jesus' life-activity reveals the nature of God and opens up a way of life for all humankind. His words and actions reveal God as the source of good and the foe of evil. Jesus' life choices make it clear that God does not will suffering, but stands with humanity in solidarity against the forces of oppression. The course of Jesus' life illuminates his belief that

God's cause is whatever promotes justice, peace, and wholeness. Through Jesus God is revealed, once again, to be self-communicating, effective love expressed in solidarity with humanity.[28]

Within this theological worldview, the words and actions of Jesus express the gracious, free initiative of God on behalf of humankind. To follow Jesus in community is to stand in solidarity with Jesus, who is in solidarity with God, who is in solidarity with all people, particularly the poor and marginalized. In fact, the full redemptive significance of Jesus' death can only be grasped if it is understood as a consequence of his life-activity.[29] Likewise, the intrinsic relationship of Jesus' life-activity and death has direct implications for interpretations of the cross.

Paradoxically, the cross is both sheer negativity and the locus of the divine presence, an understanding that transforms traditional presentations of the resurrection. Resurrection is endowed with a critical force, testifying to God's radical identification in mercy and compassion with all those who suffer exclusion, violence, and death. The resurrection reveals God's vindication of Jesus' solidarity with the oppressed and verifies Jesus' claim that the very being of God is liberating love.[30]

This understanding of resurrection provides a new interpretative paradigm for traditional christological beliefs. The resurrection is interpreted in light of the cross, but the cross must be interpreted in light of Jesus' life-activity. The meaning of resurrection and cross are diminished if they are divorced from Jesus' stance of radical solidarity with God and the oppressed. Their critical force lies precisely in their claim that ultimate victory will be achieved over the forces which threaten human dignity and freedom. The intrinsic interconnection of Jesus' life, death, and resurrection stands as the guarantor that something definitive did happen in Jesus.

Herein lies the foundation for Roman Catholicism's eschatological hope: what happened to Jesus is promised to those who stand in solidarity with the God of solidarity. This eschatological promise challenges the ecclesial community to actualize redemption through a commitment to *critical praxis*. Consequently, christologies rooted in solidarity give great attention to the social, cultural, religious, and political exigencies of Jesus' context, his response to these exigencies, and his relationship to God. To do otherwise, is to render interpretations of Jesus' redemptive significance inadequate, if not meaningless.

Reconstructing the figure of Jesus in this manner presents a formidable challenge to Catholic ecclesiologies. It charges them with the responsibility of critical reflection, particularly upon the Church's self-understanding and *praxis*. Within this theological worldview, acts of solidarity are a contemporary source of ecclesial identity. Life-activity becomes a definitive witness to God's vindication of Jesus' solidarity, at the same time that it informs Roman Catholicism's notions of identity, community, and unity and decisively shapes its understanding of mission, sacraments, authority, discipleship, and interreligious dialogue.

Ecclesiologies after the *Shoah* must confront the history of human suffering, listening closely to the experiences of the victims, reflecting critically on the behavior of the perpetrators, and considering solemnly the morality of the bystanders. After the Holocaust the Church cannot assume a stance of neutrality in the face of the mass murders, brutality, and enslavement that continue to devastate human relationships, mock justice, and destroy hope. It must proclaim the memory of God's solidarity with Jesus, who was in solidarity with all of humankind, as a *subversive memory of hope* for those who still suffer marginalization, endure persecution, and fear extermination.[31] It must lift up the memory of the victims who have been robbed of their voice, stand with them in their suffering, and testify on their behalf. Empowered by the subversive memory of God's solidarity with those named and treated as the *Other*, the Church must challenge every system which threatens human dignity, seek to transform every structure which denies freedom, and strive to correct every ethic which thwarts the achievement of peace. If it does not do so, it stands guilty of collusion with oppressive centers of power that threaten to reduce history to a history of human suffering, victimization, and genocide.

Ecclesiologies after the *Shoah* must compel the Church to undertake a critical two-fold task. First and foremost, it must commit itself to the rigors of critical self-reflection. Catholicism bears a special responsibility to examine, repudiate, and transform the aspects of its self-understanding which have justified its long history of religious triumphalism and oppression. The direct connection between the Church's failure to stand in solidarity with the victims of the *Shoah* and, until very recently, with the Jewish community in its memorialization of that tragic event makes it imperative that Catholicism confront its history of denigration of Judaism and its betrayal of the Jewish people. It is particularly crucial that Roman Catholicism, as a community rooted in the sacraments of Eucharist and Reconciliation, reflect upon these historical failings during sacramental celebrations.[32]

Second, the Church must challenge the world's nations to listen and respond to those who have suffered persecution, faced annihilation, and been denied the right to speak on their own behalf. Ecclesiologies rooted in solidarity demand that the Church do more than merely expose corrupt centers of power or rhetorically denounce their illicit use of privilege and prestige. These ecclesiologies require that it engage, *in word and action*, the struggle to transform the victimizer, the persecutor, and the murderer. Consequently, the critical force of the Church's mission is directly dependent upon its willingness to address the social dimensions of sin and to confront the objective forces which hold people in bondage.

Roman Catholicism need look no further than its own history of theological anti-Judaism and antisemitism to understand the urgency of this task. The *Shoah*, the Auschwitz convent controversy, and the Cross/es dispute provide the proper data for critical reflection upon the Church's role among the world's nations. Each event indisputably reveals the tragic results that occur when the Church fails to confront the perpetrators of bigotry, prejudice, violence, and death.

## CONCLUSION

> The most important way to overcome the difficulties that still exist today is the establishment of a dialogue which would lead to the elimination of distrust, prejudices, and stereotypes, and to mutual acquaintance and understanding based on respect for our separate religious traditions as well as opening the way to cooperation in many fields. It is important, moreover, that while doing this we learn to experience and appreciate the proper religious contexts of Jews and Christians as they are lived by Jews and Christians themselves.[33]

The future credibility of Roman Catholicism rests with a crucial choice: will the Church continue to ground its message and mission in religious triumphalism or will it submit itself to the transformative power of solidarity? The dynamics surrounding the *Shoah*, the Auschwitz convent controversy, and the Cross/es dispute raise questions about the Church's ability to meet the demands of solidarity. These events reveal Roman Catholicism's inability to acknowledge the validity of Judaism's covenantal status, the vitality of its growth as a tradition, and the legitimacy of its right to memorialize the *Shoah* without the intrusion of Christian symbols.[34] It is given further expression when Catholicism resists confronting those forces within itself which breed unmitigated nationalism, domination, and persecution.

However, there are voices within the Church who signal the possibility of a different future because they do not turn away from the skewed dynamics which continue to surface in Jewish/Christian relations. In fact, they take responsibility for their transformation. These voices offer reason to hope that Roman Catholicism possesses the will to undergo the rigors of *teshuvah* for the sake of a credible future.

If these voices are able to lead the Church to submit itself to the transformative power of *teshuvah*, its words and actions will become a source of *teshuvah* as *tikkun olam* (the repair of the world). Freed from a vision of an exclusivistic covenant, Roman Catholicism will be able to stand in solidarity with Judaism and the Jewish people. Together, these two religious traditions, distinct from one another and yet historically interrelated, will be able to unite in solidarity on behalf of all who suffer oppression, exploitation, and death. There could be, in our time, no stronger witness to the liberating, transformative love of the God of solidarity.

## ENDNOTES

1. This chapter will not summarize either the chronology of events or the analyses of the issues involved. Numerous articles, editorials, and books offer a multitude of insights into the events, issues, and personalities involved. For a well-documented account with a detailed bibliography see: Carol Rittner and John K. Roth, eds. *Memory Offended: The Auschwitz Convent Controversy.* (Praeger Publishers: New York, 1991). Hereafter this work will be cited as *Memory Offended*.
2. Bernard Dupuy, OP in the name of the French bishops, September 1986 as quoted by Sergio I. Minerbi, "Pope John Paul II and the *Shoah*," Yehuda Bauer, ed., *Remembering for the Future: The Impact of the Holocaust and Genocide on Jews and Christians.* (Oxford: Pergamon Press: 1989), 2980.
3. Ron Kampeas "Vatican Prepares Document Acknowledging Guilt for Antisemitism," *The Jewish Ledger* June 2, 1994. It should be noted that the Vatican distinguished this document, which was announced by Pope John Paul II in 1987, from the document being prepared by the Polish and German bishops. Navarro-Valls emphasized that the Church's repudiation of all forms of antisemitism is clearly stated in the new Catechism and statements by Pope John Paul II. See: "On File," *Origins: CNS Documentary Service* 24 (June 9. 1994): 50.

4. For an overview of papal positions regarding the Nazi Regime, the Jewish victims of the *Shoah*, and the Church's role during the Holocaust see: Monty Noam Penkower, "Auschwitz, the Papacy, and Poland's `Jewish Problem,'" *Midstream* XXXVI (August/September 1990): 14-19. (Hereafter, this work will be cited as "Poland's 'Jewish Problem'"). For a recent reference to the repudiation of the documentation's charges by Vatican historians see: "On File," *Origins: CNS Documentary Service* 24 (June 9, 1994): 50.

5. This dynamic was clearly evident in the remarks made by Pope John Paul II during the meeting of the Pope, Jewish leaders and others on April 7, the day of the Vatican concert to commemorate the *Shoah:* "We must be deeply grateful to all who work to secure ever wider and fuller recognition of the 'bond' and 'common spiritual patrimony' which exist between Jews and Christians (*Dignitatis Humanae,* 4). In the past these links have inspired deeds of courageous solidarity. In this regard, as a matter of historical fact, one cannot forget that in my own homeland, as in other countries and also here in Rome, in the terrible days of the *Shoah,* many Christians together with their pastors strove to help their brothers and sisters of the Jewish community, even at the cost of their own lives." See: "Concert at the Vatican: Commemorating the Holocaust," *Origins: CNS Documentary Service* 23 (April 28, 1994): 783-784.

6. The Holocaust is of great significance for all peoples, non-Jews as well as Jews. Sufficient attention has not yet been given by non-Jews to the impact of the Holocaust upon the course of human history. It is essential that every dimension of this catastrophic event be scrutinized, whether concerning aggressive perpetrators, silent accomplices, active resisters, or ravaged victims. Only in this way can humankind regain the moral will to sustain the transformation of ideologies dependent upon domination, exploitation, and victimization. For analyses which directly address this problematic see: Rittner and Roth, "Introduction," *Memory Offended,* 3-4. and Elie Wiesel and Carol Rittner, R.S.M., "An Interview, August 29, 1989," *Memory Offended,* 113-116.

7. Some who supported the location of the convent in the *Theatregebäude,* or Old Theater, the building that stored the *Zyklon-B* gas used for genocidal purposes during the war, argued that the building was located outside the camp boundaries. However, documentation attests to the fact that the official boundaries of the Auschwitz concentration camp, as established by UNESCO, included the Old Theater as part of Auschwitz I. For arguments representing both sides of the boundary dispute, see: Waldemar Chrostowski, "Controversy Around The Auschwitz Convent," *Christian Jewish Relations* 22 (1989): 21-36; Rittner and Roth, eds. "Introduction," *Memory Offended,* 1-15; Solomon, "The Carmelite Convent at Auschwitz," 42-44.

8. Some of the documents most frequently cited as premier examples of the Church's changed teachings are as follows. The Vatican II document, *Nostra Aetate,*

promulgated on October 20, 1965, is hailed as the document which marks the radical shift in the Church's teaching regarding Judaism and the Jewish people. With it came the first official acknowledgment of Roman Catholicism's legacy of theological anti-Judaism and antisemitism. Although the language and scope of *Nostra Aetate* is qualified, i.e., the Council chose not to use the term "deicide" within the final version of the document, the document explicitly condemns antisemitism and states that the Jewish people bear no collective responsibility for the crucifixion of Jesus Christ. The 1975 *Guidelines* statement of the American Catholic bishops charged theologians with the responsibility of re-examining the nature of Judaism's covenantal relationship and Christianity's interpretation of that relationship. It was unprecedented in its call for theologians to achieve an understanding of Judaism and the Jewish people which reflected Jewish understandings. "Confessions on the Holocaust," the1975 document promulgated by the German Bishops, is considered by some one of the most moving documents to-date. The 1983 statement issued by the Joint National Commission for Catholic-Jewish Religious Dialogue in Brazil lays down six objectives intended to promote a practical and workable framework of understanding between the two traditions. For articles which raise questions regarding the integrity of the church's participation in interreligious dialogue see: Michael Berenbaum, "The Struggle for Civility: The Auschwitz Controversy and The Forces Behind It," *Memory Offended*, 83-90; Brumberg, "The Problem That Won't Go Away," 31-34, 93-94; Deborah McCauley, "*Nostra Aetate* and The New Jewish-Christian Feminist Dialogue," R. Brooks ed., *Unanswered Questions: Theological Views of Jewish-Catholic Relations* (Notre Dame, Indiana: University of Notre Dame Press, 1988), 189-210.; Deborah McCauley and Annette Daum, "Jewish-Christian Feminist Dialogue: A Wholistic Vision," *Seminary Quarterly Review* XXXVIII (1983): 147-190 (Hereafter, this work will be cited as "Jewish-Christian Feminist Dialogue"); Steven F. Windmueller, "The *Shoah* – Antisemitism and Christian-Jewish Relations," *Journal of Jewish Communal Service* 65 (Fall 1988): 3-8.

9. Although *Nostra Aetate* signaled the Church's readiness on the level of official teachings to affirm the validity of the other major religions, the final version of the document did not include a condemnation of all Christian persecutions or seek forgiveness from the Jewish people for the suffering they endured throughout those persecutions. Instead, the document focused upon fostering future relations characterized by "that mutual understanding and respect which is the fruit above all of biblical and theological studies, and of brotherly (*sic*) dialogues." See "Declaration on the Relationship of The Church to Non-Christian Religions," In Walter M. Abbott (ed.) *The Documents of Vatican II.* (N.Y.: Guild Press, 1966), 657. It is cogently argued that this focus reveals the problematic which has plagued the reconstruction of Roman Catholic teachings since the promulgation of *Nostra Aetate*. The failure to address concretely and assume responsibility for the

behavioral consequences of Roman Catholic theological teachings has allowed the Church to evade the task of a thoroughgoing reconstruction of every aspect of Roman Catholic theology. Christine Gudorf provides an interesting development of this argument from the vantage point of psychology in her article "Catholics and Auschwitz: Guilt and Beyond," *Christianity and Crisis* 49 (October 23, 1989): 327-328. Claire Huchet-Bishop sets forth a similar analysis in "The New Road," *Memory Offended*, 147-150. The International Catholic-Jewish Committee offers some hope that the Church may address this failure, by calling for a deepening of the Church's assimilation of *Nostra Aetate*. The Committee acknowledged that this presupposes not only a systematic uprooting of antisemitism, but also an explicit act of repentance on The Church's part. See: "Uprooting Antisemitism", *Origins: CNS Documentary Service* 20 (September 20, 1990): 235.

10. These arguments fail to engage a rigorous examination of the issues at play. They primarily give voice to three reactions: concern that the "goodwill" motivating the Roman Catholic participants is not recognized, surprise at the negative reactions of Jewish organizations, and indignation that the Roman Catholic participation in the negotiations was not received with gratitude. That a theology of supersession, albeit unconscious, shapes these reactions is revealed by their dualistic, hierarchical framework. Judaism and Catholicism are placed in a relationship of oppositionality from which there can emerge only one "winner." Each tradition is also endowed with characteristics that connote their relative power and location within the convent controversy. The Jewish "side" is characterized as "other," "weak," "helpless," and "foreign," while the Catholic-Polish "side" is characterized as "us," "strong" "householder," and "host". Ultimately, this framework cannot facilitate a just resolution to the controversy because it is grounded in an unacknowledged, but operative interplay of power, dominance, privilege, normativity, and sovereignty. For striking examples of this mode of argumentation see: Chrostowski, "Controversy Around The Auschwitz Convent," 21-36 and Paul Lewis, "Furore over Convent Near Auschwitz," *Christian Jewish Relations* 19 (March 1986): 45-48.

11. The following authors provide insightful analyses into the various dimensions of this problematic. Stanisław Krajewski, "The Controversy over Carmel at Auschwitz: A Personal Polish-Jewish Chronology," *Christian Jewish Relations* 22 (1989): 38-39. Hereafter, this work will be cited as "Chronology;" Burton Levinson "Winter Chill on a Springtime Visit to Rome" *ADL Bulletin* 46 (June 1989): 2; Daniel Polish "Catholic-Jewish Relations and The Auschwitz Controversy" *Ecumenical Trends* 16 (October 1987): 169-171; Rittner and Roth, eds. "Introduction," *Memory Offended*, 1-15; Ady Steg "The Jewish-Christian `Summit,'" *Christian Jewish Relations* 19 (1986): 47-51; David Warszawski, "The Convent and Solidarity," *Tikkun* 4 (November/December 1989): 29-31, 93; Elie Wiesel, "A Year

of Blood and Ashes," *Baltimore Jewish Times* September 29, 1989 Hereafter, this work will be cited as "Blood and Ashes."

12. The degree to which theological supersessionism shapes the Roman Catholic theological worldview is given further testimony by the lack of direct participation by the Carmelite nuns themselves in the negotiations. The limitations imposed by their cloistered lifestyle notwithstanding, it is most significant that questions were not raised about the appropriateness of a male superior representing the nuns or that the actual positions held by the nuns regarding the controversy have remained primarily a matter of speculation. For the texts of two interviews with Sister Teresa, the Mother Superior of the Carmelite convent around which the controversy swirled see: Leon Klenicki, *ADL on The Frontline* 2 (October 1992): 16 and Francis A. Winiarz, "We're Not Moving a Single Inch," November 1, 1989," *Memory Offended*, 259-262.

13. The equivocal nature of the Church's stance toward Judaism and the Jewish people was evident during the 1994 Vatican concert commemorating the Holocaust. There is no doubt that the concert was a momentous event. The Pope spoke movingly of the suffering endured by the Jewish people, honored the courage and tenacity of the survivors, and appealed to members from both traditions to join together on behalf of justice and peace. However, in neither of his public speeches did the Pope admit to the Church's complicity during the *Shoah*. He did not allude to the fact that this commemoratory event was being initiated by the very Church which not only disseminated derogatory and false teachings about Judaism and the Jewish people, but also chose a cautious and passive posture during the *Shoah* itself. Thus, the concert continued the thrust of *Nostra Aetate* by focusing upon the *future* of Jewish-Catholic relations in a manner which did not address the tragic course of that historical relationship. Other examples of the Church's equivocation are readily found in statements made during the controversy by Cardinal Franciszek Macharski of Cracow and the June 7, 1979 and June 24, 1988 papal sermons of Pope John Paul II. For analyses of the statements and sermons see: Adler, "Controversy": 9-10; Montague, "The Carmelite Convent": 1-3, 5, 7-8, 12-13; Wiesel. "Blood and Ashes": 73 For texts of the statements and sermons see: "Documentation," *Christian Jewish Relations* 22 (1989): 112-140; Montague "The Carmelite Convent": 2-3, 7-8, 19; and Rittner and Roth eds., *Memory Offended*, 243; 247-248.

14. A comparison of papal meetings with various dignitaries discloses the Church's contradictory position toward Judaism and the Jewish people. On September 15, 1985 Pope John Paul II met with Jewish leaders; a year later he made an historic visit to the Great Synagogue of Rome. However, he also chose to schedule a meeting with Kurt Waldheim, the former Austrian president and World War II German officer who was accused of Nazi sympathies and collaboration, and to award Waldheim knighthood in The 147-year-old Order of Pius IX in July of 1994.

Another example can be found in the Pope's willingness to meet with the PLO Chairman, Yassir Arafat, while steadfastly refusing to establish diplomatic ties with Israel until 1994. For discussions of this contradictory stance see: Adler, "Controversy": 4-5, 9-16; Penkower, "Poland's `Jewish Problem'": 14-15, 17-18; A. M. Rosenthal, "On My Mind," *The New York Times* August 12, 1994; Wiesel, "Blood and Ashes": 73.

15. Several authors thoughtfully address the symbolic significance of Auschwitz for the Jewish community, as well as the complexities of the Jewish-Catholic relationship in Poland. See: Gerhard M. Riegner and Stanisław Musial, "Documentation: Auschwitz Convent – The Second Geneva Meeting," *Christian Jewish Relations* 20 (1987): 53-59 and John Pawlikowski, "The Auschwitz Convent Controversy: Mutual Misperceptions," *Memory Offended*, 63-72.

16. For a discussion regarding the Church's reticence to acknowledge this fact see: Penkower, "Poland's `Jewish Problem'": 14-19.

17. Monty Noam Penkower offers persuasive documentation regarding the failure of Popes Pius XII and John Paul II to recognize and honor this uniqueness. The actions and words of Pope John Paul II provide contemporary examples. For a concise overview of Pope John Paul II's attempts to defend and rehabilitate Pius XII's role in the Holocaust years see: Penkower, "Poland's `Jewish Problem'": 15-16 and Minerbi, "Pope John Paul II and the *Shoah*": 2975. For papal statements which defend Pius XII's actions concerning Judaism and the Jewish people during World War II see: "Lessons of World War II," *The Tablet* September 2, 1989: 1011-1012 and "Overcoming Difficulties of The Past," *Origins: CNS Documentary Service* 8. (April, 12, 1979): 691. Monty Noam Penkower critically analyses the Pope's failure to acknowledge the singularity of the Jewish experience during the *Shoah* the following example illustrates this failure. "When stopping in 1979 before a Hebrew memorial tablet at Auschwitz, he paid homage to the `sons and daughters of a nation destined for a complete extermination,' only to speak a few moments later, in front of a tablet with the inscription in Polish, of `six million Poles [who] perished during The last war, one-fifth of a nation.' Three million Jews were denied their identity in the statistical service of six million Poles. In 1987, visiting the death camp of Majdanek, John Paul II again made no reference to the Jews – who had perished as Jews" (Penkower, "Poland's `Jewish Problem'": 16-17).

18. The inflammatory sermon delivered by Cardinal Józef Glemp, Primate of Poland, at the shrine of the Madonna of Częstochowa, followed by his interview with *La Repubblica*, an Italian journal, provide tragic, but unmistakable examples of this correlation in public statements made by ecclesiastical officials. For a complete text of the sermon in English see: "Documentation," *Christian Jewish Relations* 22 (1989): 121-128. Daniel Polish offers a compelling analysis of the consequences of the cardinal's sermon for Jewish-Christian Relations, see: Daniel F. Polish, "Catholic-Jewish Relations and the Auschwitz Controversy," *Ecumenical Trends* 18

(December 1989): 169-. Two sermons of Pope John Paul II, given on the 2nd and 9th of August 1989, provide further examples of an unreflective perpetuation of this correlation. For English translations of these texts see: Adler, "Controversy": 14 and Rittner and Roth eds. *Memory Offended*, 245-246 and 249. Stanisław Krajewski offers a compelling testimony regarding the tragic impact of this correlation upon Jews who claim their identity as Poles in Poland. See: Krajewski, "Chronology": 37-54.

19. The writings of Gregory Baum, Alice L. Eckardt, A. Roy Eckardt, Eugene Fisher, Deborah McCauley, and John Pawlikowski figure prominently in this regard. Each thinker has contributed important insights regarding the development of Christian anti-Judaism and antisemitism, as well as to the justification of their devastating consequent behavioral responses.

20. Deborah McCauley and Annette Daum offer an incisive critique of the distorted theological presuppositions which skew the participation of both Roman Catholicism and Judaism in institutional interreligious dialogue. See: McCauley and Daum, "Jewish-Christian Feminist Dialogue": 147-190.

21. I point to two examples. First, Cardinal Johannes Willebrands, President of the Vatican's Commission for Religious Relations with the Jews, stated definitively that the relocation of the convent and the establishment of a Center for Information, Education, Meeting, and Prayer had papal approbation. For a text of the announcement see: "Vatican Commission's statement 19 September 1989," as quoted in "Documentation: The Carmelite convent at Auschwitz: Statements February 1987 to December 1989," *Christian Jewish Relations* 22 (1989): 137. Second, the Pastoral Letter issued by the Polish Bishops in 1990, significant in and of itself due to Catholic Poland's history of anti-Judaism and antisemitism, calls for such an examination. For a complete text in English translation see: Rittner and Roth, eds. *Memory Offended*, 263-266.

22. Stanisław Krajewski and Stanisław Musiał, S.J. urge us not to overlook the significance of the convent's eventual relocation. They argue that the Church's decision to move the established institution, in response to the request by the Jewish community, is without precedent throughout the entire history of Jewish-Catholic relations. See: Stanisław Krajewski, "Chronology": 48. It may be argued that the Vatican's agreement to establish formal diplomatic ties with Israel offers another hopeful sign. It is significant that in both cases the Church has followed its proclamations with action. See: Msgr. Claudio Celli and Yossi Beilin, "The Vatican-Israel Fundamental Agreement," *Origins: CNS Documentary Service* 23 (January 13, 1994): 526-528.

23. Archbishop Edward Idris Cassidy, President of The Holy See's Commission for Religious Relations With the Jews, September 1990 as quoted in "Uprooting Antisemitism," *Origins: CNS Documentary Service* 20 (September 20, 1990): 235.

24. Polish Pastoral Letter, November 30, 1990, "Pastoral on Jewish-Catholic Relations," as quoted in Rittner and Roth eds. *Memory Offended*, 265.

25. The problematic surrounding the current Roman Catholic interpretation of "covenant" has begun to be addressed by Roman Catholic thinkers. For succinct discussions of this problematic see: Gabriel Moran, "Backward and Forward," *Memory Offended*, 75-82 and Rittner and Roth eds. "Introduction," *Memory Offended*, 1-15.

26. For an insightful analysis of the effect of patriarchal projection and religious triumphalism on institutional Jewish-Christian interreligious dialogue see: McCauley and Daum, "Jewish-Christian Feminist Dialogue": 147-190.

27. Analyses by Roman Catholic theologians regarding the collusion of traditional antisemitism with oppressive centers of power are indebted to the insights of the Frankfurt School, particularly those of Jürgen Habermas and his notion of a hermeneutic of suspicion. Analyses by the following Roman Catholic theologians illustrate the multifarious use of Habermas' notion within contemporary Roman Catholic theology: Johann Baptist Metz, *Faith in History and Society: Toward a Practical Fundamental Theology* (N.Y.: The Seabury Press, 1980); Rosemary Radford Ruether, *Faith and Fratricide*; Edward Schillebeeckx, *Christ: The Experience of Jesus as Lord* (N.Y.: The Crossroad Publishing Company, 1977) Hereafter this work will be cited as *Christ*., *Jesus: An Experiment in Christology* (N.Y.: The Crossroad Publishing Company, 1981) Hereafter this work will be cited as *Jesus*., *Church: The Human Story of God* (N.Y.: The Crossroad Publishing Company, 1990) Hereafter this work will be cited as *Church*.; and Schussler Fiorenza, "Critical Theory and Christology": 63-110.

28. Edward Schillebeeckx was one of the first Roman Catholic theologians to undertake a thorough reconstruction of the figure of Jesus and its implications for Roman Catholic ecclesiology. The Schillebeeckxian trilogy sets out in detail the shift in Roman Catholic understandings of God, Christology, and ecclesiology which result from his reconstructive efforts. For a detailed development of Schillebeeckx's theological programmatic see: *Christ, Jesus, and Church*.

29. For a concise analysis of the inadequacies inherent in theologies which interpret the redemptive significance of Jesus' death in isolation from his life-activity, see: Schüssler Fiorenza, "Critical Theory and Christology": 63-110 and Schillebeeckx, *Christ*, 793-801.

30. Edward Schillebeeckx's explication of the significance of the resurrection is a stellar example of the positive contributions which the concept of solidarity can make to Roman Catholic systematics. See: *Christ* and *Jesus*.

31. Johann Baptist Metz has demonstrated the contributions which narrative theology can make to the development of a credible Roman Catholic ecclesiology. For a more detailed discussion of his theological vision see: *Faith in History and Society*.

32. Johann Baptist Metz and Edward Schillebeeckx articulate compellingly the intrinsic interconnection between praxis undertaken on behalf of the poor and ostracized, liturgical celebration, and authentic faith in God. See: Baptist Metz, *Faith in History and Society* and Schillebeeckx, *Christ* and *Church*.

33. Polish Pastoral Letter, November 30, 1990, "Pastoral on Jewish-Catholic Relations" as quoted in Rittner and Roth eds. *Memory Offended*, 266.

34. Pope John Paul II's sermon in Warsaw during June of 1987 exemplifies this inability. The Pope spoke of suffering as a purgative experience which engenders hope during his address to representatives of the Polish Jewish community in Warsaw. He evidenced no awareness that he was imposing a Christian understanding of suffering upon his interpretation of the Holocaust. For a complete version of the text in English translation see: "Remarks by the Pope to the Jews in Warsaw," *Origins: CNS Documentary Service* 17 (September 10, 1987): 200.

# PRAYERS OF VICTIMS,
# VICTIMS OF PRAYERS

## DAVID PATTERSON

Controversy and outcry followed in the wake of the establishment of a Carmelite convent at Auschwitz in 1984, and the discussion has continued unabated, despite the establishment of a new interfaith center in the area to take the place of the convent.[1] Given Christianity's violent history of antisemitism and its silent complicity in the creation of Auschwitz, many believed that this site covered with Jewish ashes was not the place for Christian prayers.[2] How could those who were deaf to the pleas of the Jews now seek the ear of God — unless it was to seek atonement for the Church itself? But that did not appear to be the aim of the Carmelites' prayers. On the contrary, "the nuns were praying for the murdered and the murderers alike" on a site that "through the martyrdom of thousands of Catholics, has become a sacred place."[3] On the other hand, it has been argued that there is room for prayer everywhere, that, indeed, the Carmelites' devotion to prayer could help to mend the world precisely in a place where the world was severely wounded. Therefore, it is maintained, the charges leveled against the Church, the objections to the convent, and Polish assessments of the situation were generally characterized by misunderstanding and overreaction.

This latter position is represented by a book first published in 1990 in response to the turmoil created by the convent; it is *The Convent at Auschwitz* by Władysław Bartoszewski, who attempts to defuse the whole affair by pointing out the unnecessarily extreme reactions on both sides and by clarifying the issues. Bartoszewski does, however, lay most of the blame for the conflict on the Poles, arguing that the main reason for the controversy surrounding the convent "was an almost total lack of understanding of Jewish matters on the part of the Poles."[4] Another important book on the controversy is *Memory Offended: The Auschwitz Convent Controversy*, edited by Carol Rittner and John K. Roth (1991), who take the position that Christianity's supersessionism contributed to the Holocaust and that, just as Christianity cannot supersede Abraham's Covenant, a

Carmelite convent cannot supersede the murder of Abraham's children. If such a thing should come about, then the victims whose prayers the Christians ignored would once again become the victims of Christian prayer. Nevertheless, Roth and Rittner maintain, there is a serious need for mutual understanding between Christians and Jews, and contributing to such an understanding is the primary aim of their book.[5]

While both of these volumes play important roles in the debate over the convent at Auschwitz, both could create the mistaken impression that since the convent has been removed, the issue has been resolved. Such is not the case. For the issues raised by the convent at Auschwitz run deeper than the nuns' cloister and are older than the murder camp. As we shall see, it is an issue concerning the difference between Jewish notions of prayer and Christian notions of prayer. Moreover, it is a difference that reveals something about why Jews, without exception, were targeted for murder and why Christians, with notable exceptions, either did nothing or participated in the murder.

## THE *MITZVAH* PRAYER IN THE FORM OF A DEED

As the words *deomai* in Greek and *precari* in Latin suggest, prayer, on the Christian view, is generally associated with supplication, entreaty, and pleading; Christian prayer is prayer *for*, an asking for something, either for oneself or for another. In keeping with the Gospel's injunction to take their prayers to their closet (Matthew 6:6), Christians have developed cloistered orders devoted to prayer; thus some Christians take their prayers to the interior of the convent and to the interior of the soul, isolating themselves from the human community. As the Christian stands alone before God in judgment, where he is either damned alone or redeemed alone, so does he pray alone before the Father, the Son, and the Holy Spirit.

Jewish thinking and teachings about prayer are quite different, as the Hebrew word for "prayer," *tefilah*, and its cognates suggest. While the root *pilel*, may imply supplication, it also has meanings associated with decision, thought, analysis, and judgment; its cognate *naftulim* means "struggles" or "wrestlings," so that here prayer is not a request submitted for oneself but an encounter — at times adversarial — between God and the soul, as when Jacob wrestled with the angel at Peniel. If prayer is for the sake of redemption, it is for the redemption of the community and not merely for the self. Therefore Jews do not retreat to the cloister to pray; rather, they pray in a *minyan*, standing as a community before the Holy One.

There are other features of Jewish thinking on prayer that one does not find in the Christian tradition. The Baal Shem Tov, founder of Hasidism, maintained that prayer and the *Shekhinah*, God's Indwelling Presence, are of a piece; in the words of a *tsaddik*, "Men believe they pray before God, but this is not so, for the prayer itself is divinity."[6] The prayer takes hold of the one who prays and sets a task before him; to pray is to be commanded to act. Through prayer, therefore, we do not speak to God – God speaks to us, declaring "Hear, O Israel" through our own lips, just as He speaks to us and commands us, through our study of Torah. That is why in the Jewish tradition, unlike the Christian tradition, we are taught that Torah study is a form of prayer; and yet, the Talmud teaches, the *deed* born of Torah study is greater than the study itself (see *Berakhot* 7b). Hence, says Rabbi Schneur Zalman, "Whoever says that he has nothing but Torah — thus no deeds of kindness — he has not even Torah."[7] And if he has not even Torah, he has not even prayer. If, as Abraham Joshua Heschel argues, the true content of prayer is the response to it,[8] then there is no prayer without the deed – without the *mitzvah*. For according to Jewish thought, the response to prayer is not God's reply to a request but our engagement in action.

What is a *mitzvah*? In the words of Heschel, it is "a prayer in the form of a deed."[9] It is part of our dialogue with the Holy One: what we *do*, we *say* to God. Such thinking is as central to Jewish thought as it is alien to Christian thought. For a *mitzvah* is not just a good deed; it is a *commanded* deed. The Christian encounters God as love; the Jew responds to God as the *commandment* to love and therefore to *act* in a certain manner.[10] With the accent on the inner intensity of love, a Christian, says the apostle Paul, is "justified by faith and not by doing something the Law tells him to do" (Romans 3:38); the Jew, on the other hand, understands the commandment of Torah to be a blessing and the deed of kindness to be his being.[11] Indeed, the talmudic sage Rabbi Chanina teaches us that one who acts because he is commanded is greater than one who acts without being commanded (Avodah Zarah 3a). The *Chasidei Umot Ha-Olam* — the Righteous among the Nations — are not those who are filled with faith or who pay lip service to God; they are those who perform *deeds* of loving kindness for human beings, as commanded by God. There is no other way to answer "Here I am!" to the One who asks each of us, as He asked Adam,

"Where are you?" From a Jewish standpoint, those who curl up in the cloister of prayer are absent from God because they are absent from their neighbors. And when we are absent from our neighbors, with hands clasped in "prayer" instead of reaching out to help, our neighbors die.

As Christians, the Carmelites of Auschwitz signify the ones who drew their shades and turned their backs while the Jews were led to the gas chambers, not just in the Vatican but in cities and towns throughout Europe. Having begun with Paul's rejection of the Jewish teaching on the preeminence of the *mitzvah* — of the prayer in the form of a deed commanded by God — the Christians ended as the accomplices of those who targeted both the Jews and Jewish teaching for annihilation.

The issue surrounding the convent at Auschwitz, then, does not go away when the convent goes away. For it is not just a matter of insensitivity or even of ignoring Christian complicity in the Event. Rather, it concerns the relationship between prayer and deed that is antithetical to Jewish teaching, which in turn is antithetical to Nazi teaching. Among the things slated for destruction by the Nazis was the Jewish accent on the *mitzvah*, not the Christian accent on faith. This is not to say that Nazi teaching and Christian teaching come to the same thing. But the Nazis did set out to destroy prayers and a view of prayer — the prayer in the form of a deed — that the Christians in their cloisters have themselves rejected. Hence the Nazis generally did not view the cloistered Christian as a threat to their extermination project. But those who offered water to Jews awaiting deportation in the heat — those who performed a *mitzvah* — were threatened with death.

## THE NAZIS' ASSAULT ON THE *MITZVAH*

In the Holocaust the assault on God's Chosen people is quintessentially an assault on God Himself. The assault on God, in turn, often takes the form of an assault on the Torah through which He commands and sanctifies His Chosen people with *mitzvot*. Indeed, just as he declared God and prayer to be one, the Koretzer Rebbe taught, "God and Torah are one. God, Israel, and Torah are one."[12] One means employed by the Nazis for destroying the Jews and their teachings concerning the *mitzvah* was the destruction of Torah scrolls wherever they could find them. Rabbi Shimon Huberband points out, for instance, that whenever Jews were found with Torah scrolls, they were tortured and the scrolls were burned or desecrated.[13] And in his diary from the Vilna Ghetto Zelig Kalmanovitch writes, "A war is being waged against the Jew. But this war is not merely directed against one link in the triad (of Israel, God, and Torah) but against the entire triad: against the Torah and God, against the moral law and Creator of the universe."[14] Waged against Israel, God, and Torah, the war against the Jews is a war against the *mitzvah*, against the prayer in the form of the deed — against places of prayers that might be made into deeds.

Synagogues were made into latrines, stables, scrap depots, and other such facilities; in many cases, however, the Nazis were not content merely to desecrate the houses of prayer but put them to the torch, often with Jews inside the building, and thereby consigned God Himself to the flames. In her memoir of the Holocaust, Judith Dribben makes this point by recalling the utterance of a Nazi as he triumphantly gazed upon a synagogue ablaze with Jews crowded inside: "The Jewish God is burnt to ashes!"[15] One realizes, then, why Adam Czerniakow, labored to save the Great Synagogue in Warsaw. From November 1941 to March 1942 he records his fear that "the Synagogue cannot be saved,"[16] his effort to "save the Synagogue, so far without success,"[17] and his sorrow that "the Synagogue could not be saved."[18] Of course, what is to be saved in the attempt to save a synagogue is not just a wooden structure but also a realm of sanctity and prayer, a place — the *makom* of *Ha-Makom* — through which the deed that begins as a prayer may enter the world even as the world is being undone. The assault on the synagogue is not an assault on a building or a space but on the commandment and the encounter between God and the soul that characterizes prayer: in order to assail God, the Nazis launched an attack on the prayer that is itself divinity.

The diarists of the Warsaw Ghetto bear witness to the Nazis' assault on Jewish prayer. On the eve of Tisha B'Av 5700 (1940) Chaim Kaplan writes, "Public prayer in these dangerous times is a forbidden act. Anyone caught in this crime is doomed to severe punishment. If you will, it is even sabotage, and anyone engaging in sabotage is subject to execution."[19] Of course, the prayers subject to the Nazis' assault are not only those said in a *minyan* but those that take the form of deed or ritual. Rabbi Huberband notes that in Warsaw the use of the *mikveh* "was punishable by death as an act of sabotage."[20]   To forbid the use of the *mikveh* is to forbid other prayers that take the form of deeds: it prohibits wives from joining with their husbands and both from joining with the Creator in the process of bringing life into the world. To be sure, the first commandment to appear in the Torah is the commandment to bear life into the world (Genesis 1:28); it is this commandment, this *mitzvah*, that makes holy matrimony holy. Thus the relation of Israel to God is often understood in terms of the conjugal relation that belongs to the sanctity of marriage. The *Midrash Tanchuma*, for example, tells us that the two tablets given at Sinai signify Israel as a bride come to meet her groom, the Holy One.[21]     Therefore, when we wrap the *tefillin* around our fingers each weekday morning, we declare ourselves to be "betrothed" to God. Since the sexual union of husband and wife, for which the *mikveh* prepares them, is a sacred expression of this sacred relation, the Nazis' desecration of the *mikveh*, is a violation of the marriage of Israel to God, a marriage whose "knot" is tied by the *mitzvot*.

The marriage that declares life to be sacred is the foundation for the home as a center of sanctity, that is, as a *dwelling* place through which the Indwelling, the *Shekhinah*, may enter into the world in the mode of commandment. Thus, just as the places of prayer came under assault, so did the place of dwelling, a place whose *dwelling* is constituted by deeds of kindness and hospitality. One of the most significant symbols of the home's sanctity is the *mezuzah*, which is attached to the door posts of the home and contains portions of the Torah that command us to act in a certain manner. The *mezuzah* is embossed with the letter *shin*, which stands for *Shaddai* or "Almighty" and is one of the names of God. And so we realize the importance of the *mezuzah*: it is the sign of God's presence at the threshold of the home, a sign of the sanctity of home and family. The destruction of the *mezuzah*, then, signifies an attempt to destroy the name of God and with it the Guardian of Israel Himself. Here Warsaw archivist Emmanuel Ringelblum notes, "At the beginning of the Ghetto period, *men of valor* (Nazis) tore down the *mezuzot* from the door posts of Jewish apartments."[22] This destruction of the *mezuzah* is an assault not only on the particular homes violated but on the very notion of home as the site from which life derives its value: home is the place where our name is first uttered, where we are first called upon to act for the sake of another, where we first engage the *mitzvah*.

There is a connection, then, between the assault on the home and the assault on those Jews who engaged in the observance of the *mitzvot*; where one comes under attack so does the other. That is why the Nazis took Hebrew artifacts and *tefillin*, as Rabbi Huberband points out, and "ripped them and burned them. They confiscated *talis kotons* in order that they be used by Jews to clean toilets."[23] And: "The Germans collected *taleysim*, *talis kotons*, and *kitls*. These holy garments were given to Jews to wash floors, automobiles, and windows."[24] When a Jew puts on these holy garments or lays *tefillin* with the appropriate prayers on his lips, his very body is transformed into a cry of "Here I am!" before the One who commands him to observe these *mitzvot*. It is a saying of *Hineni!* That means "Here I am, ready to act!" The destruction and desecration of such ritual objects, then, are tied to the assault on the *mitzvah*, which is precisely an assault on Torah, Israel, and God.

Because doing a *mitzvah* is definitively linked to the Jew's being — that is, to the Jew's *body*, and not just the clothing — the features of the body exemplifying the observance of the *mitzvot* came under severe attack. Among Jewish men, for example, the feature that distinguishes the face as a face turned toward God is the beard. Thus Rabbi Huberband notes, "If a bearded Jew was caught, his life was put in danger. They tore out his beard along with pieces of flesh, or cut it off with a knife and a bayonet."[25] Similarly, describing an *Aktion* staged in the Lvov Ghetto, David Kahane writes, "First they seized old men with beards and sidelocks. Not even a work card could save a bearded Jew."[26] The Talmud tells us that the beard is the glory of the face (Shabbat 152a). If it is the *glory* of the face, then it makes the face into a sign of the Holy One, who sanctifies the life of the human being through His commandments; and if the face is such a sign, then, in the words of Emmanuel Levinas, "the face is what forbids us to kill."[27] The commandment prohibiting murder is the most fundamental of the *mitzvot* and is just the one that the Nazis must eliminate, if they are to get rid of God, Torah, and Israel. For this project they must eliminate the greatest of all the *mitzvot*, namely the commandment asserting that all the *mitzvot* may be violated in order to save a human life.

Thus Auschwitz comes to symbolize the murder not only of the Jews but also of the *mitzvot* that they embrace and by which they are sanctified, the *mitzvot* that prohibit murder and command us to save lives. And this is just the point where the Carmelite convent enters into an ongoing complicity with the Nazis.

## THE CONVENT'S COMPLICITY IN THE ASSAULT

The Nazis' assault on the *mitzvah* is an assault on the Jews' being *in the world*, which suggests that the Jews' crime was the ontological crime of *Dasein*, of being there. But it was also a metaphysical crime, for it lay neither in simply being there nor in having committed a transgression but in signifying that we are commanded from on high — commanded by One who transcends the justifications of race — to *do* something *in the world*. Where prayer takes the form of a deed, human life is a participation in life and in the creation of life. As indicated in the preceding section, many of the *mitzvot* resolve around getting married, having children, and establishing homes - that is how we live *in the world* and join our voice to the voice of the Creator to declare that life is good. The assault on the *mitzvah* that came with the murder of the Jews entailed the murder not only of mothers, fathers, and children but also of the very notion of mother, father, and child. "Children were old, and old men were as helpless as children," Elie Wiesel once stated it.[28] To become a mother was a capital crime.

How could Carmelite nuns possibly become accomplices to such an assault? After all, "their lives," explain Rittner and Roth, "are dedicated deeply and profoundly to confronting the world and God at an intense spiritual level. In the best and most loving dimension of their tradition, they live an enclosed life of voluntary poverty, sacrifice, and prayer."[29] If the Nazis seek to rule *over* the world, the Carmelites seek to rise *above* it; as for the Jews, they seek to dwell *in* it. Yet both the *over* and the *above* are opposed to this *in*. Although their reasons are quite different from those of the Nazis — reasons of faith and devotion to God, and not reasons of race and devotion to the Führer — the Carmelites' position is also antithetical to a Jewish mode of being *in the world*. Indeed, the world is just where the cloistered order strives *not* to be: among them there are no mothers, no marriages, no homes, no families. Opposed to Jewish being-in-the-world, such a view is in keeping with Paul's teaching that "the man who sees that his daughter is married has done a good thing, but the man who keeps his daughter unmarried has done something even better" (1 Corinthians 7:38). Hence the Carmelites take the vows of chastity and do not marry. The Talmud, by contrast, teaches that a man who is not married is a man without Torah (*Yevamot* 62b) and that a husband and wife have not fulfilled the commandment to have children until they have had two boys and two girls (*Yevamot* 62a). To be sure, from a Jewish standpoint, it is unintelligible to align oneself with the "most loving dimension" of a tradition and at the same time "live an enclosed life;" to love is to love people, and you cannot love people by shunning their company or by refusing to have children.

None of this is to equate Carmelites with Nazis. But it is to suggest that their view of the world and of the ideal life could play into the hands of the Nazis. For it could play into the hands of an indifference toward the condition of this world — and toward the plight of Jews in this world — as one turns away from this world to prepare to enter the next. This attempt to turn one's face toward God ends by turning one's back on humanity. The result can be a proliferation of the illness of indifference that contributed to the murder of the six million.

The convent's complicity in the assault on the *mitzvah* is characterized by the silence of its prayers — by the silence of its walls — in the face of the silenced prayers of the Nazis' victims. From the standpoint of the victims, the silence of the cloister's walls is the silence of indifference, the silence that profanes the Name and robs the world of its face. "Silence," says the sixteenth-century sage Ovadiah Sforno, "on the part of one who has the power to protest is tantamount to admission (consent), for regarding he who is silent (it is as though) he agrees with the action."[30] Time after time, the outcry over the silence that Sforno declares to be a consent to evil finds its way into the memory and the testimony of the victims of that silence. Filip Muller, for example, writes, "The whole world knew (of Hitler's intention to exterminate the Jews), and knowing it remained silent."[31] And in Vladka Meed's memoir we read, "The world has turned a deaf ear to what's going on here. We must do everything ourselves."[32] The deaf ear is the mute mouth that refuses a reply to the supplications of the human face. The one who thus grows deaf and mute loses his own face to become the faceless spectator, like those who from behind their blinds looked on as children crying out for water were herded into trains. The Jewish confrontation with the convent has little to do with a longing for revenge or a desire to make the Catholics "feel guilty"; nor is it merely a matter of tolerance or sensitivity. Beyond that, it is an insistence that this Christian *Other* assume a face through some kind of response *in deed* to the face of the Jewish victim.

To be sure, the encounter with the faceless indifference of the world, as it appears in Holocaust memoirs, is not so often between Jew and Nazi as it is between Jew and Christian neighbor, those decent people with whom the survivor had perhaps enjoyed the semblance of a human relationship. "Acquaintances, friends, neighbors," says Frida Michelson, for instance, "quit talking to us. When we met on the street, heads turned away. It was as if we already did not exist."[33] Isabella Leitner, to cite another example, writes, "You, my former neighbors, I cannot live with you again. You could have thrown a morsel of sadness our way while we were dragging ourselves down Main Street."[34] And Nathan Shapell remembers how people he and his family had known all their lives were transformed into strangers who treated the Jews as if they had some disease. "They withdrew from us, and some made a special point of insulting and betraying us," he relates. "Yet each Sunday found them at their places of worship, and I wondered what they said to their God when they lifted their voices in prayer."[35]  Similarly, one wonders what the Carmelites could be saying to God. And one fears what their silence is saying to the world. For in this silence lies the convent's complicity.

The silence of the cloister stands in stark contrast to the silence of the ashes that cover Auschwitz. The ashes cry out while the cloister and its inhabitants turn away, like the "good Christians" of Auschwitz. Commenting on the people of the town of Auschwitz, Charlotte Delbo recalls, "None of the inhabitants of this city/had a face."[36] Representing a retreat from the world and therefore a rejection of the *mitzvah*, the convent aligns itself with that silent facelessness. The world is made of people. The world void of face is made of people rendered faceless, beginning with "good Christians."  Delbo issues this indictment when she cries out, "You who wept for two thousand years/for one who suffered three days and three nights/ what tears will you have /for those who suffered/many more than three hundred nights and many more than three hundred days?"[37] It was in Poland, in the heart of Catholic Christendom, that the death factories were most relentlessly fueled by the death of indifference — not only at such infamous sites as Chełmno, Treblinka, and Majdanek but throughout the nation, in city and town. Vladka Meed, for example, relates that after the *szmalcownicy*, the blackmailers of Warsaw, would leave a Jewish victim in the street, Christian passersby would look on for a moment and then resume "their Sunday stroll. Why did the Poles remain silent?"[38] Recalling those Polish faces void of humanity, those eyes that met his during an evacuation march, Shapell writes, "I... searched their faces for — for what? Horror? Sympathy? Would I never learn? I saw instead smiles and even laughter. On the few serious faces no sign of emotion was displayed."[39] These and other examples demonstrate that the facelessness that arose within the Third Reich infects and feeds on the soul of Christendom, so that one need not be a Nazi to abet the Nazis, even – or perhaps especially – after the event, when the cries of the victim are no more than a fading memory. Void of any sign of caring that would impart to it a face, the convent remains in an elsewhere that, from the standpoint of the victim, is nowhere. It is as though the convent were a sign of the absence of God. And if the Nazis wanted to convince the Jews of anything, it is that God had abandoned them.

Where, then, does all this leave the Christians and the Jews in relation to one another?

## TOWARDS A DIALOGUE BASED ON DEED

In the context of the Auschwitz convent controversy, we discover that the deepest differences between Christians and Jews lie not in concepts of God and the Messiah but in the understanding of prayer and *mitzvah*, which in turn leads to an important difference in the emphasis placed on realms of life. Briefly stated, it seems that Christians practice piety in order to find their way, individually, into God's kingdom, while Jews labor as a community in order to draw God into this kingdom. And where does He enter? Through the portal of the *mitzvah*. The convent signifies the idea that the best way to find one's way into God's kingdom is through faith, prayer, and purification. The Jews, on the other hand, realize that such practices are of no use to the victims of the Holocaust or to the humanity that has survived the Holocaust. Striving to bring God into this world — if not for the victims, then for the humanity that remains — Jewish thought revolves around the *mitzvah*: the prayer in the form of a deed, the act of loving kindness, the attempt to save a life. From a Jewish point of view, the prayer taken to the closet in the fervor of faith and the longing for purification is a luxury that, in the shadow of Auschwitz, humanity cannot afford.

*Where, then, does this leave the Jewish-Christian dialogue?*

If dialogue is dialogue, then it is about seeking the truth; if it is about seeking the truth, then it is about embracing the Good; and if it is about embracing the Good, it is about *doing* good — and not about power, condemnation, or self-justification. Now the evidence that their practice of the *mitzvot* did not save the Jews from being murdered is irrefutable; equally irrefutable is the evidence that their faith, prayers, and piety did not prevent Christians from becoming either the active or the passive accomplices to that murder. The question for those who seek the Good, however, is not "Am I going to survive?" but "Am I going to kill? Am I going to tolerate murder by folding my arms, remaining silent, or retreating to the fortress I call a home?" Even when they were murdered, Jews could retain their Judaism; but when they stood by and did nothing, Christians lost their Christianity. Unless prayer is understood as a deed, as a *mitzvah* — that is, as something we practice and not something we recite — it will never bring us a step closer to God. For it will continue to distance us from one another.

It was indicated above that, as a form of prayer, a *mitzvah* is part of a dialogue with God. If that is the case and if the path to God leads through our fellow human beings, then the *mitzvah* should be part of our dialogue with human beings. And it should be central to the dialogue between Christians and Jews. But in order for the *mitzvah* to take on such a significance, the teaching that "man is not justified by works of the law but through faith in Jesus Christ" (Galatians 2:16) — a teaching exemplified by the Auschwitz convent — must be replaced by the teaching that human beings are indeed justified by works of the law, by *mitzvot*, since chief among those works is saving lives. If, in other words, the *mitzvah* is to be central to Jewish-Christian dialogue, then we all must understand our salvation not in terms of our faith in a redeemer but in terms of our treatment of one another. Such a move poses serious problems for Christians. For it implies that Christians must abandon all projects of converting the Jews; that faith in the Christ does not by itself lead to God; and that there are paths to redemption *other than* those leading through the Christ. Once again we are reminded that the righteousness of the Righteous among the Nations did not lie in their concern for saving Jewish souls or in their faith in Christ; it lay in their *mitzvot*, in their deeds of lovingkindness. That example, and not Christian doctrine, will best serve the interests of Jewish-Christian dialogue.

Jews too, however, face certain difficulties in opening up a dialogue with Christians based on *mitzvot*. And the example of the *Chasidei Umot Ha-Olam* is helpful here as well. The righteousness of these Righteous did not lie in their concern with the guilt of those whom they helped or with what those in need might have done in the past. The question that makes their actions righteous is not "What have you done?" but "What must I do?" Similarly, if the *mitzvah* is to be central to Christian-Jewish dialogue, then

Jews must turn their attention away from Christian guilt, Christian crimes, and antisemitic Christian teachings. That does not mean we should be silent in the face of the Auschwitz convent or that we must forget the millions of our people who were murdered. But it does mean that we must not become obsessed with the convent and that we must not get lost in the concentrationary universe. It means that we must go from crying out to the Christians, "Look at what you've done to us!" to asking, "What can we do for each other?" It also means that Jews must get past the general notion that the Christians can do more for us than we can do for them. Jews have been victims of Christians, yes. But we are their victims no more. We are not needy —we are needed.

Of course, there are those who will ask why Jews or Christians should be interested in any dialogue whatsoever. There are those who will say that the differences and the history between the two are so irreconcilable as to make any true dialogue impossible. Better, it will be said, just to leave each other alone, to simply "tolerate" one another and leave it at that. As long as the *mitzvah* remains in the margin, such a position is easily maintained. But once they place the *mitzvah* at the center of their relationship, then Christians and Jews will realize not only that they need each other but also that the world needs both. They need each other not to serve each other's interests but to serve a suffering humanity that both are *commanded* to serve. I have heard good Jews declare that they will not support Christian children's funds, and I have heard good Christians assert that they have no reason to support Jewish schools. Once the *mitzvah* becomes central to the relationship, however, the accent is no longer on *Christian* or *Jewish* but on *children* and *schools*. And then, of course, there is a world in need of every witness to the Holy One, blessed be He, a world ruled by various forms of nihilism, materialism, relativism, and post-modernism. The real danger of the Auschwitz convent, then, lies in its offense not only to the memory of the murdered but also to the memory of what is most dear. For the Auschwitz convent epitomizes a position that precludes an accent on children and schools and a testimony steeped in the needs of loving kindness.

With the *mitzvah* at the center, therefore, the question guiding Jewish-Christian dialogue is not "How can we serve one another?" but rather "How can we help each other serve those whom God's Law commands us to serve?" — to serve by feeding, clothing, sheltering, comforting, and healing bodies, and not by saving souls. "The material needs of my neighbor," Rabbi Israel Salanter reminds us, "are my spiritual needs"[40] As a Jew once said to his followers, "I was hungry and you gave me food, I was thirsty and you gave me drink, I was a stranger and you welcomed me, I was naked and you clothed me, I was sick and you visited me, I was in prison and you came to me" (Matthew 25:35-36). He did not say, "I was a sinner and you saved my soul."

In the *Sifre* we hear God cry out, "When you are My witnesses, I am God; but when you are not My witnesses, I am not God."[41] Mother Theresa exemplified the response to this outcry. When she left her convent to serve a suffering humanity, she declared that God had spoken to her. When asked what He said, she did not reply that He ordered her to go forth and help those poor people. As she explained it, God said, "I am thirsty." From the ashes of Auschwitz God cries out: "I am thirsty! I am cold and hungry! I am tortured, murdered, and betrayed!" The convent at Auschwitz represents a deafness to that outcry, a deafness that now makes those victims of murder into victims of prayer by making their prayers unheard. And their prayers to God are God's prayers to us. The convent, therefore, threatens to make us deaf to God, to the One who cries out, "I am thirsty!"

There lies the abiding danger of the Auschwitz convent. And of Auschwitz itself.

## ENDNOTES

1. An agreement to establish such a center was reached on 22 February 1987; ground breaking for the center took place on 19 February 1990.
2. "When our brothers and sisters met their death at Auschwitz," said Montague, "they were surrounded by a total silence on the part of the world and a very significant silence on the part of the Church. We cannot tolerate that prayers should take place, even in the best of intentions, in this place, from those who could have, at the right time, raised their voice for our brothers and sisters and did not do so." See A. Montague. "The Carmelite Convent at Auschwitz: A Documentary Survey," *IJA Research Report* (London), No. 8 (October 1987), pp. 5-6.
3. Władysław T. Bartoszewski, *The Convent at Auschwitz*. (New York: George Braziller, 1991), p. 155.
4. *Ibid.*, p. 159.
5. See Carol Rittner and John K. Roth, "Introduction: Memory Offended" in *Memory Offended: The Auschwitz Convent Controversy*. ed. Carol Rittner and John K. Roth (New York: Praeger, 1991), p. 10.

6. See Martin Buber, *The Legend of the Baal Shem*, tr. Maurice Friedman (New York: Schocken, 1969), p. 27. Said the Koretzer Rebbe a disciple of the Baal Shem, "God and Prayer are One." See Louis I. Newman, *The Hasidic Anthology*. New York: Schocken, 1963), p. 147.

7. Schneur Zalman, *Likutei Amarim Tanya*, tr. Nissan Mindel, et al. (Brooklyn: Kehot, 1981), p. 415.

8. Abraham Joshua Heshchel, *Man's Quest for God: Studies in Prayer and Symbolism* (New York: Charles Scribner's Sons, 1954), p. 16.

9. *Ibid.*, p. 69.

10. "God is love," the Christians are taught in 1 John 4:16; on the idea that God is the commandment to love, see Emmanuel Levinas, "The Paradox of Morality" in *The Provocation of Levinas: Rethinking the Other*, ed. Robert Bernasconi and David Wood (London: Routledge, 1988), pp. 176-77.

11. In the blessings that are part of Jewish prayers God is the One who "sanctifies us with His commandments and commands us" to do something. As for the relation between being and doing, A. J. Heschel explains that, according to Jewish understanding, man is what he does, not what he believes; see A. J. Heschel, *Between God and Man*, ed. Fritz A. Rothschild (New York: Free Press, 1959), P. 164.

12. Newman, p. 147.

13. Shimon Huberband, *Kiddush Hashem: Jewish Religious and Cultural Life in Poland during the Holocaust*, tr. David E. Fishman, ed. Jeffrey S. Gurock and Robert S. Hirt (Hoboken, NJ: Ktav, 1987), p. 44.

14. Zelig Kalmanovitch, "A Diary of the Nazi Ghetto in Vilna," tr. and ed. Koppel S. Pinson, *YIVO Annual of Jewish Social Studies* 8 (1953): 52.

15. Judith Dribben, *And Some Shall Live* (Jerusalem@ Keter. 1969), p. 24.

16. Adam Czerniakow, *The Warsaw Diary of Adam Czerniakow*, ed. Raul Hilberg, Stanisław Staroń, and Josef Kermisz, tr. Stanisław Staroń et al. (New York: Stein and Day, 1979), p. 301.

17. *Ibid.*, p. 335.

18. *Ibid.*, p. 337.

19. Chaim Kaplan, *The Warsaw Diary of Chaim A. Kaplan*. Tr. and ed. Abraham I. Katsh (New York: Collier, 1973), p. 179.

20. Huberband, p. 61.

21. *Midrash Tanchuma*, Vol. 1 (Jerusalem: Eshkol, 1938), p. 411.

22. Emmanuel Ringelblum, *Notes from the Warsaw Ghetto*. tr. and ed. Jacob Sloan (New York: Schocken, 1974), p. 152.

23. Huberband, p. 44.

24. *Ibid*, p. 35.

25. *Ibid.*

26. David Kahane, *Lvov Ghetto Diary*. tr. Jerzy Michałowicz (Amherst: University of Massachusetts Press, 1990), p. 45.

27. Emmanuel Levinas, *Ethics and Infinity*. tr. Richard A. Cohen (Pittsburgh: Duquesne University Press, 1985), p. 86.

28. See David Patterson, *In Dialogue and Dilemma with Elie Wiesel.* (Wakefield, NH: Longwood Academic, 1991), p. 21.

29. Rittner and Roth, p. 6

30. Sforno, *Commentary on the Torah*, Vol. 2, tr. Raphael Pelcovitz (Brooklyn: Mesorah, 1989), p. 709.

31. Filip Muller, *Auschwitz Inferno: The Testimony of a Sonderkommando*. tr. Susanne Flatauer (London: Routledge, 1979), p. 36.

32. Vladka Meed, *On Both Sides of the Wall*. tr. Benjamin Meed (Tel-Aviv: Hakibbutz Hameuchad, 1973), p. 136.

33. Frida Michelson, *I Survived Rumbuli*. tr. Wolf Goodman (New York: Holocaust Library, 1979), p. 38.

34. Isabella Leitner, *Fragments of Isabella*. ed. Irving Leitner (New York: Thomas Crowell, 1978), p. 16. Notice that Leitner seeks neither prayers nor heroic action but just a *facial* expression: a look of sadness.

35. Nathan Shapell, *Witness to the Truth*. (New York: David McKay, 1974), pp. 50-51.

36. Charlotte Delbo, *None of Us Will Return*. tr. John Githens (Boston: Beacon, 1968), p. 98.

37. *Ibid.*, p. 13.

38. Meed, p. 113.

39. Shapell, p. 111.

40. Quoted in Levinas, *Nine Talmudic Readings*. tr. Annette Aronowicz (Bloomington: Indiana University Press, 1990), p. 99.

41. *Sifre on Deuteronomy* (New York: Jewish Theological Seminary, 1993), pp. 405-06. My translation.

# HISTORY REMEMBERED: AN ANTI-JEWISH EXPOSITION OF THE GOOD FRIDAY LITURGY IN DURAND'S *RATIONALE*

## TIMOTHY M. THIBODEAU[1]

## DEFINING THE PROBLEM

In his *Who Killed Jesus?*,[2] New Testament scholar and cofounder of the Jesus Seminar, John Dominic Crossan, offers an impassioned critique of Raymond E. Brown's highly acclaimed magnum opus, *The Death of the Messiah*.[3] Crossan contends that Brown has sidestepped the contentious issue of the historical accuracy of the Passion narratives presented in the four canonical Gospels. In his own scholarly works, Crossan argues that these well-known accounts of the arrest, trial, and execution of Jesus were "prophecy historicized," or anti-Jewish "Christian propaganda" cast in the rhetoric of historical narrative.

The religious community—"relatively powerless Jews," to quote Crossan—which liturgically recited or reenacted these finished narratives came to remember them as "history." However, when Christianity and rabbinic Judaism became separate religions, and the Christian Church became co-terminus with the later Roman Empire, these same stories had lethal consequences.[4]

Anti-Jewish Passiontide sermons evolved into the burning of synagogues with the approbation of bishops.[5] Sadly, by the Middle Ages, the labeling of the Jews as "Christ Killers"[6] was a norm, which took a deadly turn for the worse in the increasingly frequent and more widespread violence, perpetrated by Christians against European Jews.[7]

As a medievalist who specializes in the liturgical rites of the Latin Church and their formal exposition in medieval commentaries on the liturgy,[8] I was instantly drawn, as I read the introduction to Crossan's book, to a rather curious story he recounts from medieval France, which he discovered in a footnote in Brown's study. In the eleventh-century

Passiontide ceremonies of the Cathedral of Toulouse, the mockery and abuse of Jesus by the Roman soldiers and Jews was symbolically reenacted on Easter Sunday.[9] Intrigued by this strange tale, I did the requisite research to identify the medieval source and uncover the precise details of the story.[10]

An obscure French monastic chronicler named Adhémar of Chabannes (988-1034) provides a short narrative of this macabre ritual in his brief history of the Franks.[11] According to an entirely erroneous local legend, which he tacks onto his account, Adhémar says that Jewish traitors handed over Toulouse to a Muslim army from Spain in the previous century (when the city, never, in fact, fell to the Moors!). This act of treachery was supposedly the impetus for the ritual "striking of a Jew" on the steps of the Cathedral of St. Stephen on Easter Sunday. Both Crossan and Brown neglected to note that Adhémar's description of the Toulouse ritual is preceded by a much more disturbing Good Friday incident in Rome:

> At that time [1020], on Good Friday, after the veneration of the cross, Rome was imperiled by an earthquake and terrible windstorm. Immediately, some Jews secretly told the lord pope that at that hour, Jews in the synagogue were mocking an image of the crucifix. After making a careful inquiry and discovering exactly what had happened, Pope Benedict [VIII] immediately condemned to death the authors of this desecration. When they were beheaded, the violent winds stopped.

> At the same time Hugues, chaplain of Aimeri the viscount of Rochechouart, was with his lord in Toulouse for Easter. [Hugues] administered a blow to the head of a Jew, which had been the custom there every Easter; when his skull was struck, his eyes immediately were knocked out from his wicked head and fell to the ground, whereupon he immediately died. He was carried away from the basilica of St. Stephen to the Jewish synagogue where he was buried.[12]

The following essay was born of my prolonged reflection on this disturbing, palpable manifestation of the "historical remembrance" of Christ's Passion, narrated and solemnly commemorated in the medieval liturgy of Good Friday.[13] My aim is to discuss the formal commentary on this liturgy by William Durand of Mende (born in southern France c. 1230, he died in Rome on 1 Nov. 1296).[14] Near the close of the thirteenth century, this Provencal bishop composed what was destined to become the best known commentary on the liturgy produced in the Middle Ages, the *Rationale divinorum officiorum* or "Reasons for the Divine Offices."[15]

Divided into eight books,[16] Durand's mammoth treatise unquestionably remains the epitome of the medieval allegorical tradition of liturgical commentary.[17] The nineteenth-century liturgist and founder of the monastery of Solesmes, Prosper Guéranger, declared that we "can consider the *Rationale* to be the final word on the medieval understanding of the divine cult [or liturgy]."[18] Indeed, the manuscript evidence for the dissemination of the text—about 200 complete Latin copies from all over Europe; over 95 fragments; several medieval vernacular translations (including Old French and Old High German)—clearly reveals that the *Rationale* was one of the most popular liturgical treatises of the entire medieval period. A "best seller" by medieval standards, the *Rationale* also enjoyed the honor of being only the second "non-inspired" (i.e. non-Biblical) book to come off the press of Faust and Schoeffer in Mainz in 1459 (it was only preceded by the Psalter, the complete Bible, and Donatus' Latin grammar).

Taking his cue from previous centuries of liturgical exposition, Durand provided a running commentary on the prayer-texts, ceremonies, and liturgical vessels of the Good Friday Liturgy. While he never advocated violence against the Jews or their persecution, Durand's exposition of this liturgy refined and codified a medieval exegetical tradition of reading the Passion stories as "history remembered," to use Crossan's phrase. In expounding on the liturgical use of these stories, Durand articulated a systematic and vehement anti-Jewish theology.[19] "Blind" Jews, "perverse" Jews, "hard-hearted" Jews, and "pestilential" Jews are stock phrases that easily flow from his pen when he explains the rationale for the form and content of the Good Friday liturgy.[20]

This codification of an anti-Judaic theology in the *Rationale* is particularly troublesome for a modern audience when we consider that the genre of Mass exposition was, by design, a didactic or catechetical literature written for the formal instruction of the clergy. As a liturgical manual, the *Rationale,* as Durand's title indicates, provided a carefully argued and fully developed "how and why" of current liturgical practices. Thus, in commenting on one of *the* holiest days of the Church year, Durand enshrined a vociferously anti-Jewish reading of the Passion narratives as history, with potentially dreadful consequences.

## MEDIEVAL EXPOSITIONS OF THE LITURGY

Formal expositions of the liturgy were among the earliest Christian writings. The Patristic era witnessed the proliferation of Greek and Latin treatises, letters, and homilies on what we would today call liturgical or sacramental theology.[21] Because of its paradigmatic sacramental nature and its integral connection with Christian catechesis and initiation, Baptism received the lion's share of attention in these Patristic liturgical commentaries.

Beginning with the Carolingian era (c. 750) in medieval Europe, a large corpus of new Latin liturgical exposition appeared as a direct consequence of the systematic liturgical reforms directed by the Carolingian monarchs. These treatises continued the patristic tradition of explicating the rite of Baptism but increasingly began to include extended treatment of the Mass, the Divine Office, and the temporal cycle or church year. This comes as no surprise since the Frankish monarchs Pepin, Charlemagne, and Louis the Pious mandated full-scale reform of the monastic, cathedral and parochial liturgy, demanding conformity with the *usus Romanus*, or the liturgical texts, ceremonial, and chants of the diocese of Rome.[22]

It was within this milieu that the prolific Carolingian author, Bishop Amalarius of Metz (c.775/80-852/53), produced a gargantuan corpus of liturgical exposition that came to dominate the hermeneutics of nearly every Latin liturgical expositor of the Middle Ages, including William Durand. Amalarius' work is noteworthy because he was the first medieval liturgist systematically to interpret the entire liturgy — the temporal cycle; the Mass; the canonical hours; the ordination rites — allegorically.[23] In his magisterial history of the Roman Mass, Josef Jungmann notes that Amalarius' enduring contribution to medieval liturgics was his elucidation of various forms of allegorical interpretation of the liturgy. Jungmann notes that he most often employed "typological allegory" (fulfillments of Old Testament prophecies in Christ's ministry, life and death) and "rememorative allegory" (linkage, remembrance, and reenactment of key events in Salvation history).[24]

Amalarius depicts the liturgy, then, as a dramatic "iconographic" representation of the unfolding of "Salvation history." The Mass, in particular, functioned as an iconographic set of "portraits" of key events in this sacred history. In his *Expositio Missae* (c. 813-814), Amalarius outlines the Mass liturgy in bold typological strokes. For example, the *Introit* or opening prayer symbolizes the Old Testament Prophets who predicted Christ's coming; the *Kyrie* or "Lord have mercy," represents John the Baptist proclaiming Christ's advent; the *Gloria in excelsis* or "Glory to God in the highest," refers to the company of angels who brought tidings of great joy to the shepherds watching their sheep (and the allegories continue down to the final blessing of the priest).[25] Of course, the eucharistic liturgy is paradigmatic for Amalarius, with its Canon of the Mass figuratively representing the Last Supper and Christ's sacrificial death on Calvary. Jungmann found that the Amalarian exegesis of the eucharistic liturgy even dominated late medieval liturgics and the pictorial arts:

> Despite [vacillations], the fundamental theme of all Mass allegory was the *suffering* [my emphasis] or the life and suffering of Jesus. Our Lord's command, 'Do this in commemoration of me,' was never lost sight of even in the plain and simple devotion of the centuries; rather it had been fulfilled in a sort of figurative fashion. Significant in this respect is the picture of St. Gregory's Mass, a theme repeatedly utilized by artists of the late Middle Ages. While Gregory is at Mass our Lord appears to him above the altar as a man of suffering, with the instruments of His Passion.[26]

A recent study of late medieval piety in England further underscores Jungmann's thesis. In a brilliant analysis that makes admirable use of documentary, architectural, and artistic sources, Eamon Duffy convincingly argues that medieval spirituality is anchored in the liturgy and particularly the Mass:

> The liturgy lay at the heart of medieval religion, and the Mass lay at the heart of the liturgy. In the Mass the redemption of the world, wrought on Good Friday once and for all, was renewed and made fruitful for all who believed. Christ himself, immolated on the altar of the cross, became present on the altar of the parish church, body, soul, divinity, and his blood flowed

once again to nourish and renew the Church and the world. As
kneeling congregations raised their eyes to see the Host held
high above the priest's head at the sacring, they were transported
to Calvary itself, and gathered not only into the passion and
resurrection of Christ, but into the full sweep of salvation history
as a whole.[27]

In the Prologue of the *Rationale*, Durand provides an excellent
example of the continued influence of the "Amalarian," allegorical reading
of the liturgy:

> Allegory is present when what is said literally has another
> meaning spiritually; for example, when one word or deed brings
> to mind another. If what is said is visible, then it is simply an
> allegory; if it is invisible and celestial, then it is called anagogy.
> Allegory also exists when an unrelated state of affairs is shown
> to exist through the use of strange or alien expressions; for
> example when the presence of Christ or the sacraments of the
> Church are signified in mystical words or signs: [when Isaiah
> says] 'A branch shall come forth from the root of Jesse' [Isa
> 11:1], by which he clearly means: 'The Virgin Mary shall be born
> of the stock of David, who was the son of Jesse.' Mystical deeds
> can signify in the same fashion the freedom of the people of
> Israel from Egyptian slavery by the blood of the [paschal] lamb,
> which signifies the Church snatched away from the clutches of
> the devil through the passion of Christ.[28]

This passage is noteworthy not only for its definition of allegory, in
both its broad and technical sense, but also for a demonstration of the
Christian "supersessionist" mentality that was such an essential component
of medieval Biblical exegesis and liturgical exposition.[29]    While Durand
knew that the Old Testament had a "literal" or "historical sense," when
commenting on the liturgy, he invariably read the Hebrew scriptures
through a typological or allegorical lens (as did virtually every medieval
Biblical exegete). Note, for example, Durand's allegorical exegesis of Isaiah
11:1, with his emphatic statement of what the Hebrew Prophet *clearly means!*

For medieval liturgical expositors, the rites of the Church were
prefigured in the Old Testament and then nullified or superseded with the
new Christian rites. In his commentary on the Good Friday liturgies, which

I will treat at length below, Durand provides a succinct example of what I mean by a "supersessionist mentality" which was rooted in a purely allegorical or typological reading of Hebrew Scriptures:

> Two lessons are read, because Christ died for two peoples, namely the Gentiles and the Jews; or, for the salvation of both the flesh and the soul. One lesson is taken from the law, another from the Prophets, because Christ's passion was foretold by the Prophets and prefigured by the Law and the Patriarchs. Abraham figuratively sacrificed the body of Christ when he sacrificed a ram.[30]

St. Paul's declaration in his First Epistle to the Corinthians would also be taken quite literally by a medieval liturgist as a validation of this supersessionist theology of the Christian paschal mystery: "Christ our Paschal [lamb] has been sacrificed; let us therefore celebrate the feast not with the old leaven, nor the leaven of malice and evil, but in the unleavened bread of sincerity and truth [I Cor. 5:7-8]."[31]

## THE GOOD FRIDAY LITURGY

The "three days" of sacred mysteries—hence the term *Triduum*—were, for Durand and his contemporaries, the summit and quintessence of the Christian liturgical calendar.[32]   He refers to these solemnities as a time of the "strictest fasting and silence," as if the Church celebrates a funeral.[33] Pierre Jounel notes that these three days—Holy Thursday, Good Friday and the Easter Vigil—were treated with utmost solemnity as early as the fourth century. The *Triduum sacrum* was considered the most sacred liturgical celebration of the year by both St. Ambrose and St. Augustine.[34] While providing a succinct chronology for the development of this medieval service,[35] Jounel notes that the Good Friday Liturgy originated in Jerusalem at the end of the fourth century; the earliest evidence for the liturgy in Rome comes from the seventh-century Gregorian Sacramentary and a contemporaneous evangeliary. This early Roman liturgy consisted only of Biblical lessons and a prayer of the faithful. From the eighth century, the adoration of the cross was added to the papal service. By the tenth century, communion of the people was added in Germanic lands, but in the thirteenth century this practice disappeared; communion was only received from a pre-consecrated host by the presiding bishop or priest.

In Durand's commentary the basic outline of the liturgy is as follows: biblical readings; reading of the Passion narrative (from the Gospel of John);[36] prayer of the faithful; adoration of the cross; communion only by the presiding priest.[37]    In discussing why the priest alone receives communion on this day, Durand notes that the postcommunion prayer is omitted as well. He justifies this silence with a rather strange allegorical reading of the Cain and Abel story, which is typologically linked to the cry of the Jews for Christ's blood in the Gospel of Matthew:

> The priest receives communion in silence, hence the postcommunion [prayer] is not recited because while we are consuming that blood which we consume, that blood cries out from our mouth on our behalf to the Lord. We are that earth which opened its mouth and drank the blood of Abel — that is, Christ — which  was shed by Cain — that  is, the Jewish people — and  thus they were made a wandering and exiled people, as is written: *Destroy them in your truth* [Ps. 58:12]; and they [the Jews] are accursed by their own curse: *His blood be on our heads and our sons' heads* [Matt. 27:25]. [38]

The Good Friday liturgy contains nine "prayers of the faithful," ranked in a hierarchic order, which precede the ritual of the adoration of the cross. There are nine such petitions, which remained invariable in the Roman Mass from the ninth century to the *Missale Romanum* (1570) of Pius V.[39]  Prayers are offered for the Church; the pope; all ranks of the clergy; the Holy Roman Emperor; all catechumens; the infirmities of all people; heretics and schismatics; the Jews; and the pagans. Since some of these petitions are prayed on behalf of groups for whom we would not normally expect the Church to pray, Durand feels obliged to offer some sort of justification for this practice:

> We must not pray for those whom we know are not saved, or for those who remain in hell, nor for Judas who gave up hope [of salvation]; but we pray for ourselves and all ranks of the Church, and for neophytes, for the Gentiles, for the Jews, for heretics and schismatics, that Christ will impart his grace to them, and convert them to the faith. Christ prayed for both his

friends and enemies, therefore the Church likewise regularly
prays for all.[40]

Not only are the prayers invariable, their recitation follows a very precise,
and for Durand, equally unalterable set of rubrics. First, the priest sings
each petition, which begins with *Oremus* or "Let us pray;" the prayer itself is
recited, and then the deacon says, *Flectamus genua* or "Let us kneel;" while
the congregation is kneeling, another short prayer is recited by the
celebrant; after a short space of time he once again says, "Let us pray," at
which point the congregation stands for the next prayer.

Oddly, Durand provides *no* commentary on the majority of these
petitions; in fact, he does not even bother to list all of them. He does,
however, have a good deal to say about the prayer for the Jews (whom he
associates, in one instance, with the pagans!). His commentary on the
petition for the conversion of the Jews contains some of his most overtly
anti-Jewish statements. The text of the prayer itself can be found in the
Missal of Pius V (1570), or the so-called "Tridentine Mass," and was recited
until the liturgical reforms of the Second Vatican Council:

> Oremus et pro perfidis Judaeis: ut Deus et Dominus noster
> auferat velamen de cordibus eorum; ut ipsi agnoscant Jesum
> Christum Dominum nostrum[41]

> Let us pray for the faithless Jews, that our Lord and God
> will remove the veil from their hearts, that they might recognize
> Jesus Christ our Lord.

In this context, the term *perfidis Judaeis* quite literally means "faithless Jews,"
or Jews who lack the (true) Christian faith. But the boundaries of
translation, particularly for a medieval Christian author, are far more
capacious than narrow etymological definitions would have us believe. For
Durand this term easily conjures other meanings: Jewish dishonesty,
deceitfulness, obstinacy, or treachery. A careful reading of Durand's
discussion of the petition for the Jews provides ample proof that he
collapses all of these multiple meanings of the term *perfidis* into one concept
of "Jewish faithlessness" which implies a persistently stubborn or
contemptuous disbelief in Christ on the part of the Jews.

Durand tells us that in the first seven petitions, the congregation kneels and responds "Amen" at the conclusion of each prayer. When, however, the Church prays for the Jews, and then the pagans, he argues emphatically that it would be unbefitting for the congregation to kneel or even to respond "Amen." His rationale speaks for itself and should therefore be quoted in full:

> It is fitting that when praying for these [i.e. the first seven petitions], the Church genuflects during the prayers, so that through a bodily disposition, it shows devotion and humility of mind, indicating that at the name of Jesus, every knee shall bend [cf. Phil. 2:10], because all nations bend their knees—unless [the Church] is praying for the Jews. This is because they mocked Christ by genuflecting, saying: 'Prophesy for us, O Christ: who struck you?' [Mt. 26:68]. Therefore, in averting this mockery, the Church does not genuflect when praying for them, that it might avoid imitating these actions. Besides, because no prayer can dispel their blindness until the full number of nations has entered [the Church], the Church should not pray for them eagerly, nor should [it] genuflect....

> Also, in the prayers for pagans and Jews, the response should not be 'Amen,' as some said, and this is because these [two] are outside of the corporation [collegium], or the body of the Church, and the faithful people should not display affection for those, who, as the Apostle, to the Corinthians says: 'What have I to do with judging those outside?' [1 Cor. 5:12]. While it is permitted to pray that their hardness [of heart] will be converted, nevertheless, because this [conversion] cannot be completed until the end of the world, as the Apostle testifies when he says: 'Until the full number of Gentiles shall enter and thus all Israel shall be saved' [Rom. 11:25-26], therefore, the response for their prayers should not be 'Amen'.[42]

This same exegetical frame of mind is displayed in Durand's brief remarks on the ceremony of the Veneration of the Cross. In one of the most dramatic and captivating rituals bequeathed to us by the medieval Franco-Germanic Church,[43] Durand notes that the priest carries a veiled cross in procession, standing in persona Christi, or in the place of Christ.[44] While he solemnly processes, the Improperia and the Hagios ho Theos are sung.

The former are the "Reproaches" which begin, *Populo meus, quid feci tibi* ("My people what have I done to you?"); the latter is a Greek and Latin hymn, sung antiphonally, praising "God's holiness." Durand explains that even though the cross bore an inscription proclaiming "Jesus of Nazareth, King of the Jews," written in Latin, Greek and, Hebrew [cf. Joh. 19:19], the Church prays *only* in Greek or Latin. The Greek and Latin language are used today to "adore Christ,"[45] but "the Hebrew ceases to praise God."[46] Besides, "the Hebrew language contradicts and even blasphemes against the others."[47]

The veil is then removed from the cross before it is adored, "as a sign that the perverse Jews stripped the Savior naked."[48] The congregation, which is barefoot out of respect for the cross,[49] "reverently pays respect and devoutly kisses the very symbol which the "wicked Jews ridiculed."[50] Durand also observes that in some churches, the cross—which he calls the *vexilla Ecclesie*, or "battle standard of the Church"—is "held up high to symbolize Christ's victory. Until now they have been carrying the cross singing antiphons, bearing it so that they may respond in Greek and Latin and devoutly adore the Cross, because the crucified Lord passed from the faithlessness of the Jews to the confession and devotion of the nations."[51]

When Durand comments on the Passion narratives and the prayer-texts or rites that refer to "the Jews," he *never* takes this to mean the "Jewish leaders" or the "Sanhedrin," or "some of the Jews, who were wicked," but *the* Jews, which should be taken as *all* Jews. Sadly, it was a short step for medieval Christians to move from speaking about the Jews of old as killers of Christ, to characterizing *all* Jews, who willingly persist in their "faithlessness," as being somehow collectively guilty, through their continued unbelief, for Christ's death. Professor Crossan undoubtedly recognizes the fluidity of the boundaries of theological debate between rival religions and broader cultural or ethnic stereotypes. These differences can be lethal when one group overtakes the other. "Antisemitism," he declares in the opening line of his book, "means six million Jews on Hitler's list but only twelve hundred on Schindler's list."[52]

Modern Roman Catholicism, or at least official Catholic theology since the Holocaust, has openly disavowed the vitriol of patristic and medieval Christian antisemitism. To this author, one of the most dramatic and sincere manifestations of this new spirit of ecumenism—or maybe even contrition—is the petition for the Jews in the Good Friday liturgy of the *Novus Ordo* or New Missal of Paul VI (1969):

> Let us pray for the Jewish people, the first to hear the word of God, that they may continue to grow in the love of his name and in faithfulness to his covenant... Almighty and eternal God, long ago you gave your promise to Abraham and his posterity. Listen to your Church as we pray that the people you first made your own may arrive at the fullness of redemption. We ask this through Christ our Lord.

## ENDNOTES

1. I wish to express my gratitude to Susan E. Nowak, who shared her own expertise in Jewish-Christian studies with me, helping me to understand the problem of Christian antisemitism within a broad conceptual framework. Thanks also to my wife Susan Corazza Thibodeau for reading and critiquing early drafts of this essay.

2. *Who Killed Jesus? Exposing the Roots of Antisemitism in the Gospel Story of the Death of Jesus.* (Harper, San Francisco, 1995).

3. *The Death of the Messiah: From Gethsemane to the Grave. A Commentary on the Passion Narratives in the Four Gospels.* 2 vols. (Doubleday, New York, 1994).

4. "[B]y the fourth century, Christianity was the official religion of the Roman Empire, and with the dawn of Christian Europe, anti-Judaism moved from theological debate to lethal possibility. Think, now, of the passion-resurrection stories as heard in a predominantly Christian world. Did those stories of ours send certain people out to kill?" *Who Killed Jesus?*, xii.

5. I have in mind the burning of a synagogue in Callinicum (Syria) in 388 by a local bishop and monks. Ambrose of Milan vigorously defended this act in a correspondence with the Emperor Theodosius. For the political and social context of these events, see Peter Brown, *Power and Persuasion in Late Antiquity: Towards a Christian Empire* (Madison, WI, 1992), esp. 103-117; see also Robert L. Wilken, *John Chrysostom and the Jews: Rhetoric and Reality in the Late Fourth Century* (Berkeley, 1983); Lee Martin McDonald, "Anti-Judaism in the Early Church Fathers," in *Antisemitism and Early Christianity. Issues of Faith and Polemic*, ed. Craig A. Evans and Donald A. Hagner (Minneapolis, 1993), 215-252.

6. Jeremy Cohen, "The Jews as the Killers of Christ in the Latin Tradition, from Augustine to the Friars," *Tradition* 39 (1983), 1-27.

7. A succinct and brilliant account is provided by R.I. Moore, *The Formation of a Persecuting Society.* (New York, 1987), esp. 27-45; 80-90. Other important works include: Bernhard Blumenkranz, *Les Auteurs chrétiens latin au moyen âge sur les juifs et le*

*judaisme.* (Paris, 1963); B.S. Bachrach, *Early Medieval Jewish Policy in Western Europe* (Minneapolis, 1977).

8. There is an enormous amount of literature on medieval liturgical exposition. Among the most important works are: Adolf Franz, *Die Messe im deutschen Mittelalter. Beiträge zur Geschichte der Liturgie und des religiösen Volkslebens.* (Freiburg, 1902/Darmstadt, 1963; Joseph Jungmann, *The Mass of the Roman Rite. Its Origins and Development* trans. Francis A. Brunner (1951-1955; reprint ed. Westminster, MD, 1986) 2 vols.; Roger E. Reynolds, "Liturgy, Treatises on," *Dictionary of the Middle Ages* 7 (1986), 624-633; Cyrille Vogel, *Medieval Liturgy. An Introduction to the Sources.* trans. and rev. by William G. Storey and Niels K. Rasmussen (Washington, D.C., 1986).

9. See J.H. Mundy, *Liberty and Political Power in Toulouse, 1050-1230* (New York, 1954), 8-9. Mundy is Brown's original source for this story; Mundy also provides important information about the Jews of Toulouse in the eleventh and twelfth centuries. In the early fourteenth century, the Jewish community of Toulouse suffered grievously at the hands of the Dominican Inquisitor, Bernard Gui (c. 1261-1331). See Yosef Hayim Yerushalmi, "The Inquisition and the Jews of France in the time of Bernard Gui," *Harvard Theological Review* 63 (1970), 317-376.

10. *Who Killed Jesus?*, ix; *The Death of the Messiah* vol. 1, 575 n. 7. Both authors provide only the sketchiest of accounts; both versions are faulty on the circumstances and details of the story, since neither author notes that this ritual actually led to the violent death of a Jew in 1020.

11. *Ademari Historiarum Libri III*, ed. G. Waitz, in *Monumenta Germaniae Historica, Scriptores* IV, (Hannover, 1841), 106-148. This terrible tradition came to an end in the early 1100's, through an official commutation to an annual sum paid to the cathedral clergy. Béziers, Arles, and Chalon-sur-Saône had similar traditions which were also changed to money payments to the clergy at about the same time. See Mundy, *Liberty and Political Power*, 225 n. 21.

12."His diebus in parasceve post crucem adoratam Roma terrae motu et nimio turbine periclitata est. Et confestim quidam Iudeorum intimavit domno papae, quia ea hora deludebant sinagogae Iudeorum Crucifixi figuram. Quod Benedictus papa sollicite inquirens et comperiens, mox auctores sceleris capitali sententia dampnavit. Quibus decollatis, furor ventorum cessavit. Quo tempore Hugo, capellanus Aimerici vicecomitis Rocacardensis, cum eodem seniore suo Tholosae in pascha adfuit, et colaphum Iudeo, sicut illic omni pascha semper moris est, inposuit, et cerebrum ilico et oculos ex capite perfido ad terram effudit; et statim mortuus, a sinagoga Iudeorum de basilica sancti Stephani elatus, sepulturae datus est." *Ademari Hist.* 3.52, 139.

13. This reflection was greatly aided by a correspondence and phone conversation with Professor Crossan himself, who discussed the basic outline of this article. While I have used his book as a springboard, so to speak, for my own work, this

does not mean that I am in agreement with his thesis that the Passion narratives are, on the whole, "a-historical."

14. For Durand's life and works see: Victor Le Clerc, "*Guillaume Duranti, Évêque de Mende, surnommé le Spéculateur,*" *Histoire Littéraire de la France* (Paris, 1895) vol. 20, 411-480; Michel Andrieu, *Le Pontifical Romain au moyen-âge III: Le Pontifical de Guillaume Durand,* Studi e Testi 88 (Vatican City, 1940); Louis Faletti, "Guillaume Durand," *Dictionnaire de droit canonique* 5 (1953), 1014-1075. The most up-to-date bibliography of Durand scholarship can be found in *Guillaume Durand Évêque de Mende (v. 1230-1296): Canoniste, liturgiste et homme politique,* ed. Pierre-Marie Gy (Paris, 1992).

15. Guillelmi Duranti, *Rationale divinorum officiorium I-IV; V-VI Corpus Christianorum, Continuatio Mediaevalis* vols. 140, 140A ed. T.M. Thibodeau and A. Davril (Turnhout, 1995; 1998). Anselme Davril and I are publishing a critical edition of the entire commentary in three volumes.

16. 1). The Church building and its various parts, and other sacred places (e.g. cemeteries);    2). The ministers of the Church, their ordination rites and their pastoral and liturgical functions; 3). The liturgical vestments of bishops, priests and other ministers; 4). The Mass; 5). The Divine Office; 6). The Sunday liturgy, the Dominical feasts and the Lenten fasts (a treatment, essentially, of the Temporal cycle); 7). The Saints' feasts (or Sanctoral cycle); 8). The calendar and *computus.*

17. I have discussed the importance of the *Rationale* in the medieval genre of liturgical exposition in my: "William Durand: 'Compilator Rationalis'," Ecclesia Orans 9 (1992), 97-113.

18. *Insitutions liturgiques* (Paris, 1840), vol. 1, 355: "*On peut considérer ce livre comme le dernier mot du moyen-âge sur la mystique du culte divin.*"

19. For the difference between Anti-Judaism and Antisemitism, see J. Gager, *The Origins of Antisemitism: Attitudes Towards Judaism in Pagan and Christian Antiquity* (Oxford/New York, 1983), and G. I. Langmuir, *Towards a Definition of Antisemitism* (Berkeley, 1990). In distinguishing between the two terms, Gager employs antisemitism (p. 8) "to designate hostile statements about Jews and Judaism on the part of Gentiles" that "betray very little knowledge about Jews or Judaism, and tend to be sweeping generalizations." According to Langmuir, Anti-Judaism is "primarily a matter of religious and theological disagreement." While such nuanced distinctions are appropriate, they are nonetheless highly problematic. For medieval and early modern European authors, the step from anti-Judaic polemic (theological debate or attack) to antisemitism (broad and denigrating statements about the "character" of Jewish people) is quite easy and follows its own pernicious logic. See, for example, Heiko Oberman, *The Roots of Antisemitism in the Age of Renaissance and Reformation,* trans. James I. Porter (Philadelphia, 1984).

20. Durand's comments on the liturgical recitation of the Lamentations of Jeremiah are typical of his approach: "These [lamentations] are recited to note the blindness and hardness [of heart] of the Jews who refuse to understand or believe the thing

most clearly noted literally, namely the passion of the Son of God." *("[Dicuntur] ut per hoc notetur cecitas et duritia Iudeorum qui res tanquam alphabetum notissimas, uidelicet passionem Filii Dei, intelligere et credere nolunt...")* Rat. VI, 72, 14, CCCM 140A, 340

21. See Vogel, *Medieval Liturgy*, 10-11, for a detailed list of Patristic texts on the liturgy.

22. Vogel, *Medieval Liturgy*, 62-134, for a discussion of the history and development of the Romano-Frankish and Romano-Germanic Sacramentaries.

23. I have treated the complex nature of medieval liturgical allegory and its relationship to patristic modes of the Scriptural exegesis in my: *"Enigmata figurarum*: Biblical Exegesis and Liturgical Exposition in Durand's *Rationale,"* Harvard Theological Review 86 (1993), 65-79. One should also note that the Christian religion itself rests on an allegorical or typological reading of the Hebrew Scriptures which, in the literal or historical sense, may have an entirely different meaning.

24. Jungmann, *The Mass of the Roman Rite* I, 87-92. For a more recent discussion of liturgical theology and "salvation history," see I. H. Dalmais, "The Liturgy as Celebration of the Mystery of Salvation", in A.G. Martimort, *et al.*, eds., *The Church at Prayer: An Introduction to the Liturgy*, trs. Matthew J. O'Connell (Collegeville, Minn., 1987) vol. 1, 253-272.

25. J.M. Hannsens, ed., *Amalarii episcopi opera liturgica omnia* vol. 1, *Studi e Testi* 138 (Vatican City, 1948), 255-281; summarized by Jungmann, *The Mass of the Roman Rite* I, 89-90.

26. Jungmann, *The Mass of the Roman Rite* I, 116-117. For a more critical appraisal of the dangers of unchecked allegorism in later medieval culture see Johan Huizinga, *The Autumn of the Middle Ages*. trs. Rodney J. Payton and Ulrich Mammitzsch (Chicago, 1996), esp. 173-202.

27. *The Stripping of the Altars. Traditional Religion in England 1400-1580* (New Haven and London, 1992), 91. Duffy's book is rich with examples of various late-medieval devotions to the suffering of Christ or his wounds. Duffy also discusses the circulation of Eucharistic miracle stories; he notes that "the classic medieval representative of culpable unbelief, the ultimate outsider, is of course, the Jew, and unbelieving Jews regularly feature in Eucharistic miracle stories." Duffy, 105.

28. "Allegoria est quando aliud sonat in littera et aliud in spiritu, ut quando per unun factum aliud intelligitur. Quod si sit uisibile est simpliciter allegoria, si inuisibile et celeste tunc dicitur anagoge. Est etiam allegoria quando per alienum sermonem alienus status designatur, ut cum Christi presentia et Ecclesie sacramenta uerbis uel misticis rebus designantur. Verbis ut ibi: Egredietur uirga de radice Yesse, quod aperte sonat: Nascetur uirgo Maria de stirpe Dauid qui fuit filius Yesse. Misticis rebus ut populus ab egyptiaca seruitute per agni sanguinem liberatus, significat Ecclesiam passione Christi a demoniaca seruitute ereptam. Et dicitur allegoria ab aleon grece, quod est alienum et gore, quod est sensus quasi alienus sensus." *Rationale*, Prohemium, 10, CCCM 140, 7.

29. The definitive study of history of Biblical exegesis remains Henri De Lubac's *Exégèse Médiévale: Les quatre sens de l'Écriture* (Paris, 1959-1964) 2 vols. in 4 parts.

30. "Leguntur autem due lectiones, quia pro duobus populis Christus passus est, gentili uidelicet et hebreo; uel pro salute carne et anime. Vna sumpta est ex lege, altera ex prophetis, quia Christi passio a prophetis fuit prenuntiata et a lege et patriarchis prefigurata. Abraham enim carnem Christi figuatiue immolauit quando arietem immolauit." Rat. VI, 72, 2, CCCM 140B, 369

31. "Pascha nostra immolatus est Christus, itaque epulemur non in fermento veteri neque in fermento malitiae et nequitiae sed in azymis sinceritatis et veritatis." Biblia Sacra iuxta Vulgatam Versionem, ed. R. Weber and B. Fischer (Stuttgart: Duetsche Bibelgesellschaft, 1983).

32 For an excellent overview of the historical development of the Easter liturgies, see P. Jounel, "The Easter Cycle," in Martimort, *The Church at Prayer* (Collegeville, Minn., 1986), vol. IV, 33-76. See also Josef A. Jungmann, *The Early Liturgy to the Time of Gregory the Great*, trs. Francis A. Brunner (Notre Dame, 1959), esp. 253-265.

33. "Sane hac die Ecclesia artissimum ieiunium et silentium agit; nullum tamen officium sollempniter celebrat, sed hora nona conuenit ad adorandum crucem; non ad misse officium quo hec dies caret, sed quasi ad funeris obsequium dicendum." Rat. VI, 77, 1, CCCM 140A, 369

34. Jounel, "The Easter Cycle," 46-47; Augustine's phrase is *sacratissimum triduum crucifixi, sepulti et ressuscitati.*

35. *Ibid.* 49-50. For a more exhaustive and technical treatment of the development of the various liturgical books used for these rites, see Vogel, *Medieval Liturgy*, 31-224.

36. Durand explains that John's Gospel is recited because the author was present for the crucifixion and stood by the cross. *Rat.* VI, 77, 8, CCCM 140A, 372.

37. VI, 77, 26, CCCM 140A, 383.

38. "[C]um silentio sacerdos communicat: unde postcommunio non cantatur, quia nobis sumentibus sanguis ille quem sumimus de ore nostro pro nobis ad Dominum clamat. Nos enim sumus terra illa que aperuit os suum et bibit sanguinem Abel, id est Christi, quem effudit Cayn, id est iudaicus populus, unde factus est uagus et profugus super terram, iuxta illud: 'Disperde illos in ueritate tua; et factus est maledictus illa maledictione: Sanguis eius super nos et super filios nostros.'" Rat. VI, 77, 26, CCCM 140A, 383. Note that Durand changes the Vulgate rendering of Ps. 58:12—Disperge, "Disperse"—to Disperde, "Ruin" or "Destroy."

39. The form and content of the Good Friday Liturgy, codified in the Missal of Pius V, remained in place for almost four centuries. In 1955, Pius XII issued a General Decree, through the Sacred Congregation of Rites, *Maxima redemptionis nostrae,* which restored a patristic scheme of the liturgical services of the Triduum, while also altering the rubrics for portions of the nine intercessory prayers. The

text of the prayer for the Jews remained the same but the custom of neither kneeling nor responding "Amen" was abolished. In the *Novus Ordo* or reformed Mass of Vatican II, promulgated by Paul VI (1969), the prayer itself was radically altered; I cite this prayer in my conclusion.

40. "Et ex hoc uidetur quod non debemus rogare pro eis quos scimus non esse saluandos, aut pro illis qui in inferno remanserunt, nec pro Iuda qui desperauit; sed oramus pro nobis et pro omni gradu Ecclesie, et pro neophytis, pro gentilibus, pro Iudeis, pro hereticis et schismaticis, ut Christus gratiam suam infundat, et ad fidem conuertat: Christus enim orauit pro amicis et inimicis, ideo Ecclesia statim similiter orat pro omnibus." VI, 77, 12, CCCM 140A, 374.

41. Missale Romanum, ex decreto sacrosancti concilii Tridentini restitutum (New York, 1945), 175.

42. "Sane, Ecclesia pro hiis orans flectit genua in orationibus, ut, per habitum corporis, deuotio/nem et mentis humilitatem ostendat; insinuans etiam quod in nomine Iesu omne genu flectendum est, quoniam omnes nationes sibi genua curuant, nisi quando pro Iudeis oratur. Quia enim ipsi illuserunt Domino flexis genibus, dicente: 'Prophetiza nobis, Christe, quis te percussit?' ideo in detestationem huius illusionis, Ecclesia pro eis orans genua non flectit, ut uitet opera simulata. Preterea, quia eorum cecitas nulla poterit oratione depelli donec plenitudo gentium subintrauit, ideo non est pro ipsis uehementer orandum nec genua flectenda..Sed et in orationibus pro Iudeis et paganis non respondetur 'Amen,' ut quidam dixerunt, et hoc ideo quia cum illi sint extra collegium, siue corpus Ecclesie, et fidelium populus non ostendit affectum suum ad eos, iuxta illud Apostoli ad Corinthios: 'Quid michi de hiis qui foris sunt iudicare?' Per 'Amen' enim affectus exprimitur. Preterea, licet pro illis oretur ut eorum duritia conuertatur. Quia tamen hoc impleri non poterit usque circa finem seculi, Apostolo testante qui dicit: 'Donce plenitudo gentium introeat, ut omnis Israel saluus fiat;' ideo ad orationes pro illis non respondetur 'Amen'." Rat. VI, 77, 13, CCCM 140A, 374-375.

43. Theodor Klauser, *A Short History of the Western Liturgy. An Account and Some Reflections*, 2nd ed., trs. John Halliburton (Oxford/New York, 1979), 81. Klauser notes that some of the most dramatic and imaginative elements of medieval worship were introduced to the roman liturgy by Franco-Germanic liturgical reformers in the Carolingian era.

44. "Consequenter post orationes, sacerdos crucem uelatam baiulat ad dextrum cornu altaris, ibique crucem super humeros tenens, in persona Christi, Iudeis improperat beneficia Domini, dicens: 'Popule meus, quid feci tibi?'" VI, 77, 13, CCCM 140A, 375.

45. "*greca et latina que Christum adorant...*"VI, 77, 14, CCCM 140A, 376.

46. "*hebraica nunc silet a laude Dei...*" VI, 77, 14, CCCM 140A, 375.

47. "*Hebraica uero contradicit et adhuc blasphemat predictas.*" VI, 77, 15, CCCM 140A, 376. Here Durand might not only be speaking figuratively. He may well have in mind the accusation made against the Jews in the thirteenth and fourteenth century that their "Benedictions" contained "Maledictions" against the Christian faith. Durand's younger contemporary, the Dominican Inquisitor Bernard Gui (d. 1331), conducted many inquisitorial proceedings against Christian heretics and Jews in Toulouse. In his *Practica inquisitionis*, a well known inquisitor's manual, he claims that the Jews blaspheme against the Christian faith and the Church in their daily (Hebrew) prayers: "The prayer which they recite three times a day contains many maledictions and imprecations against Christians and against the Roman faith, which they call a damned and depraved kingdom. They pray that God destroy it and all Christians, although they do not expressly use the word 'Christians'; but by all the words they make it understood that this is what they mean, as is clear form this word '*minim,*' which means 'heretics'." Cited in Yosef Hayim Yerushalmi, "The Inquisition and the Jews of France in the time of Bernard Gui," *Harvard Theological Review* 63 (1970), 358-359.

48. "*Deinde crux denudatur in signum quod peruersi Iudei Saluatoris denudauerunt.*" VI, 77, 16, CCCM 140A, 376.

49. "*Nudis etiam pedibus adoratur... ut cum afflicto pro nobis nos affligi ostendamus.*" VI, 77, 22, CCCM 140A, 378. Interestingly, Durand neither mentions nor comments on the threefold *Ecce lignum crucis*, "Behold the Wood of the Cross," sung as an antiphon by the priest, to which the congregation responds, *Venite adoremus*, "Come, let us adore." This antiphonal singing, as the priest processes with the cross, precedes the act of veneration in the Franco-Germanic liturgy; it also is the order followed by the Roman Missal of Pius V (1570).

50. "*Subsequenter ipsa crux denudata salutatur et adoratur, quia eum cui perfidi Iudei illuserunt, chrsitiani reuerenter salutando et deuote osculando uenerantur.*" VI, 77, 20, CCCM 140A, 378.

51. "*Crux quoque revelata, et etiam uexilla Ecclesie, in quibusdam locis diriguntur in altum ad Christi uictoriam designandam. Adhuc crucem baiulantes, antiphonas canentes, crucem illo deferunt ut grece et latine respondeatur, et deuote adoretur, quia et Dominus crucifixus transiuit a perfidia Iudeorum ad confessionem et deuotionem gentium...*" VI, 77, 19, CCCM 140A, 377-378.

52. Who Killed Jesus?, ix.

# INTERVIEW WITH ELIE WIESEL

## 28 October 1998

### Alan L. Berger

---

**A.B.:**  You have said that no religious symbols should be at Auschwitz. Why?

**E.W.:**  Because Auschwitz should be a place where people come together. Not where they go apart. The moment you bring religion into Auschwitz, people go apart from one another. Secondly, because it creates problems. They are questioning God. One should continue questioning God. Those who were there and question, it is one thing. Those who have not been there and come to question, it is another. So it is best for it to be a place of meditation. But for a Jew to see crosses there is painful. After all, the cross has a past. And the past is not the same for the Christian as it is for the Jew. The cross was a symbol of compassion and love and mercy for the Christian. It was a symbol of persecution for the Jew. So why does one have to repeat and emphasize it? The best thing is not to have crosses there – or any other religious symbol.

It was I who discovered the crosses in Birkenau. At first, I did not know how to feel about them. I was there five or six years ago and all of a sudden from a distance I saw the crosses. I realized there were twelve or fifteen huge crosses. Some of them glued together with Stars of David. The curator said that young Catholics, boy scouts, with good intentions, with very good intentions, came years ago and planted them to show Jews and Christians that they had a common past.

So I said what I had to say, that this is not the place for crosses. I came back, and began writing, and agitating. At first the Jewish organizations refused to listen. They did not want to be involved. I went to see several cardinals. Finally a breakthrough came when I received messages from the then Polish Prime Minister Włodzimierz Cimoszewicz inviting me to come and take part in a ceremony commemorating the Kielce pogrom. I answered I would come provided he promises me that the crosses will be removed. Letters followed through mutual friends. Finally, he sent me, black on white, a promise that the problem will be solved to my

221

satisfaction. I came for three hours to Poland, and in my address in Kielce I said some harsh things about the crosses. And I also thanked the Prime Minister for his promise. That unleashed a campaign of antisemitism, you cannot imagine. Against him. Against me. Against Jews in general.

I had to write in *Gazeta Wyborcza*, a "Letter to a Catholic Friend," to explain my position. Eventually, the Minister of Culture removed the crosses. There remained one big cross at Auschwitz, called the "papal cross." The World Jewish Congress asked me what to do since there was a plan, a project to rebuild certain places in Auschwitz and to formalize relations. My feeling was that Jews should not negotiate in the shadow of a cross. As a result, all of a sudden, because of this, the extreme right wing, the extreme fanatic wing of Catholicism in Poland, decided to punish us Jews; they planted seventy crosses. And, again, more crosses. At one point there were nearly three hundred crosses around Auschwitz. This was meant to keep us frustrated. If we said anything, they would plant crosses. The basic problem has not been resolved, although now only one cross remains.*

I must confess that good people in Poland, at the highest level, are terribly embarrassed by this latest incident. But before that, there were the crosses in Birkenau which, to me, were more important because they were located in the Field of Ashes which is where the Hungarian Jews were exterminated. The President of Poland, Kwaśniewski, told me at a conference in Davos that only the Church can help. Both he and the Prime Minister, they do not know what to do. They were embarrassed. Everybody who has a conscience was embarrassed by it. That's where we are.

**A.B.:** The claim has been made, by a certain official in Auschwitz, that the reason Elie Wiesel does not want crosses in Auschwitz is because he does not believe in God. Could you comment on this astounding claim?

**E.W.:** Whoever made that claim lacks something. Elie Wiesel does not want the crosses because he does believe in God.

**A.B.:** You have frequently observed in your writings and lectures that a repressed past returns to haunt the repressor. How is the Pope – and the Vatican – repressing the bitter and unhappy history of the Church's response during the *Shoah*? Do you think it has to do with the Pope's commitment to the doctrine of papal infallibility?

**E.W.:** I cannot speak for the Pope. I cannot even interpret him. It is incredible. Perhaps he is too convinced of his own infallibility. But then, the

---

* Editors' note: This is the situation as of January, 2002.

Pope, I think, came a long way. Soon after he became Pope, he came to New York, to address the United Nations: he never mentioned the word Israel in his speech.

He went to Auschwitz and never mentioned the word Jew. He did mention Edith Stein and Maximilian Kolbe as representing Auschwitz. He never mentioned the word Jew. So I published a critical appreciation of his behavior, it appeared in the *London Jewish Chronicle*. As he grew older, he improved. He did host a *Shoah*-concert at the Vatican. I was invited. I did not go. But this is the point, he did something. His speeches now reflect a deeper understanding of Jewish suffering. He went to Jerusalem, visited the Wall and Yad Vashem. He does speak about the singularity of Jewish victimhood.

Edith Stein? I confess to you, I was much less shocked than some Jewish leaders who protested against her becoming a Catholic saint. What right do I have to interfere with Christianity? If they want to take a Jewish woman who converted and make her a saint, it is their business and not mine. It is their affair.

I heard that the Pope also wants to canonize Pius XII. That I am against. What was the difference of opinion between the Third Reich and the Vatican during the Holocaust? When you study the documents, you will see that all of the conflicts and the tensions were about who decides who is a Jew. A converted Jew remains still a Jew to the Germans, yes. For the Vatican, no. That was the difference. The Vatican did not go out of its way to help Jews, as such. To the extent that it interceded in Berlin, it did so for converted Jews. That's their business. For me, Edith Stein is not a saint. But for them...

**A.B.:** Could you comment on what some have seen as mixed papal signals? His March document, *We Remember: A Reflection on the Shoah*, acknowledges that there was a Holocaust and calls for *teshuvah* (repentance). Yet the document is troubling in its failure to take history and historical responsibility seriously. One gets the sense of *pilpul.*\*

**E.W.:** He always defends Pius XII. Why? He could simply not speak about him. But John Paul II defends Pius XII on every occasion. That makes it difficult to give credence to his other statements, to his positive statements. If he really feels that there is enough proof to counterbalance our suspicion of Pius XII, then let him open the archives. Why does it take so long?#

---

\* *Pilpul* is a method of interpretation, associated with Talmud study, that involves casuistry and mental acrobatics.

# Editors' note: See footnote 25, pp. 18-19 above.

**A.B.:**    There are certain voices within the Church calling for more openness. Cardinal O'Connor recently called for opening the Vatican Archives. In Poland itself, Reverend Stanisław Musiał is a strong supporter of Jewish-Catholic dialogue and strenuously opposed to antisemitism.

**E.W.:**    Cardinal O'Connor was my friend. As is Cardinal Lustiger. More liberal voices are being heard.

**A.B.:**    You have spoken of an ominous trend in de-Judaizing the Holocaust. At first, people spoke of the six million Jews. Then it was the six million, plus five million others. It next became eleven million, including six million Jews. Do you see the issue of the crosses as another attempt to de-Judaize the *Shoah*?

**E.W.:**    Yes. There is no doubt about that. I can tell you that highly influential Polish personalities who came to see me said that there is a strong tendency to Christianize the Holocaust. They themselves are Christians, good Christians. They say, look, this is the only way for Christians to cope with the Holocaust, with Christianity's role in it; after all, those who committed the crimes were Christians. Or at least born Christians. Whether they practiced Christianity is one thing; some of them did practice. It is not for me to decide who is a Christian and who is not. But the fact is they were born in Christian families. Most of them were baptized. And *that* is something wrong, even from the Christian viewpoint. Therefore, I think the only way they say they can cope with this is to say that the Holocaust was not only a Jewish tragedy. It is a universal, thus also a Christian tragedy. People often refer to it as "man's inhumanity to man." I do not like that. It is man's inhumanity to Jews, not to Man.

**A.B.:**    What do you think has been learned about Jewish-Catholic and Jewish-Polish relations — if anything — either from the Carmelite controversy or from the current crisis?

**E.W.:**    I believe in cooperation. We should maintain dialogues and create bridges, links with Poles who are worthy of it. There are good people there, too. After all, during the war, the Żegota organization helped Jews. We should never forget that. It is true that many Poles denounced Jews. There are not many, but there are some who did risk their lives to save Jews. And there are people today who would like nothing better than to create these dialogues and these forums. I think we should encourage such efforts. The history of Polish-Jewish relations is not only a history of sadness. Some Polish kings were quite liberal in their dealings with the Jews. It is said that one of the kings even had a Jewish mistress.

## The Future

**A.B.:** What can the second generation in Poland do, especially in light of the phenomenon in that country of "new Jews" (people who are discovering that they were born to Jewish parents who gave them to Christians during the Holocaust in order to spare their lives)?

**E.W.:** They must first learn to develop a passion for learning which characterizes the Jewish People, learning of our past. They should do it together. They should create an organization, an institution, a link, to meet – once a day, once a week, to learn from each other, and to discuss common concerns. Not to feel alone. They are traumatized, so they should vanquish solitude. And then, of course, join the Jewish community. This is a decision they must make, since they are Jews. They must fulfill the obligations of the Jew, and link themselves to Jewish destiny.

**A.B.:** How can young Jews and Catholics in America, and elsewhere, respond? Can they do anything? Should they do anything?

**E.W.:** They should somehow tell them that we are here. And we are ready to receive them, to embrace them, and to be with them. When Jews go to Poland, they should meet with Polish Jews. I think that they should be considered by us as brothers and sisters.

**A.B.:** In view of the remarkable symposium, "The Claims of Memory," held in honor of your seventieth birthday, is memory a bond or a barrier in light of such vastly different –Jewish and Polish Catholic – memories of Auschwitz?

**E.W.:** Whose memories? We all have memories. The killers have their own. All of us should tell the truth. I do not want the Polish memory to be my memory. I do not want my memory to be their memory. The truth is they should confront their own conscience. And say this is what our compatriots have done, good or bad. Some good. Some not so good. Somehow, they all fuse into one past. All the memories merge into one, and that is God's memory.

# APPENDICES

# A CONVENT AND CROSS
# IN AUSCHWITZ

## A Declaration by the Jews and Christians Discussion Group in the Central Committee of German Catholics

## SIDIC

---

## THE FACTS

For the past five years the "Carmel of Auschwitz" has been a source of painful controversy between Catholics and Jews. During Pope John Paul II's visit to the Benelux countries in May 1985, an association known as *"Kirche in Not/Ostpriesterhilfe,"* which helps support the Church in Eastern Europe, solicited donations with a pamphlet bearing the title "Your gift to the Pope: a convent in Auschwitz". The pamphlet referred to the existence of a convent of barefoot Carmelite nuns in the building of the old "theater" of the Auschwitz concentration camp. This building, adjacent to the fence around the Auschwitz I concentration camp, was the place where the *Zyklon B* poison gas was stored during the years of extermination and was part of the overall Auschwitz complex comprising Auschwitz-Birkenau (Auschwitz II), the extermination center three kilometers away, and many other camps.

The disclosure that the building houses a Carmelite convent evoked an immediate protest from the Jewish community, first in Western Europe, then in Israel and other parts of the world. Prominent Catholics, too, raised objection. In order to defuse the situation, senior Catholic and Jewish representatives met to discuss the matter. In a joint statement issued in Geneva on 22 February 1987, the two sides agreed to establish a Centre for information, education, contact and prayer outside the boundaries of the Auschwitz and Birkenau camps. The Centre was also to be the home of the convent of Carmelite nuns. But although it was agreed that the project would be completed within two years, there were no signs of any action being taken.

After the two years had expired, the time limit was extended by six months. In this period, too, there were no signs of any steps being taken to

229

build the center and relocate the convent. In the autumn of 1988, however, a cross about 7 meters high was raised in the convent's compound, opposite the place where Polish martyrs were murdered.

The controversy escalated in the summer of 1989 through the activities of local Jewish groups. The situation did not improve until the Vatican Commission for Religious Relations with Jewry endorsed the Geneva agreement on 18 October 1989. And the tension was further eased when the Polish Government called for an early solution to the problem. The fact that a plot of land has meanwhile been purchased is a hopeful sign.

Apart from relocating the convent and building the Centre, it is necessary to clarify the differing Jewish and Christian interpretations of symbolism and spirituality, which are the real source of the conflict. This is the purpose of the following comment, especially in the light of the debate on this problem in the Federal Republic of Germany.

## COMMENT

No other name recalls Hitler's extermination camps more vividly than Auschwitz. Originally built to eliminate the Polish intelligentsia, it became the site where millions of people were murdered: Poles, Russians, Hungarians, Germans, Dutchmen, Belgians, French, Sinti and Romany, or "Gypsies," but above all, Jews, merely because they were Jews. Unlike the other camps, Auschwitz, being the largest Jewish cemetery in Europe, symbolizes the Holocaust, the *Shoah*, that is to say, the attempt to exterminate the Jewish people.

Especially in German-speaking countries, Auschwitz also stands for the catastrophe in Christian-Jewish history and exhorts a change in the Christian attitude. What the theologian Johann Baptist Metz said at the 1978 Catholic Convention in Freiburg is an obligation we Christians still have to honor: "We Christians can never go back beyond Auschwitz; but on closer examination, we are no longer able to go forward beyond Auschwitz by ourselves, only together with its victims".

This is why we in particular, Catholics and Jews, who have been discussing our problems for the past twenty years, are saddened by the conflict that has arisen over the founding of a Carmelite convent in the Auschwitz extermination camp. It has damaged — because those promises have not been kept — the credibility of the Catholic Church. The conflict has at the same time strained the bond of unity within the Catholic Church. It has shown how heavy the burden of history weighs on us all, though, of course, in quite different ways upon Christians and Jews. But we have also learned that our perceptions of each other's faith and way of life are quite different. It is difficult, therefore, to respect them and to take them seriously.

To the Jews among us, Auschwitz is the very place and name which stands for the *Shoah*, the manifestation of evil, of the incomprehensible silence of both God and man. It is no place for subsequent symbols or quick interpretations, for in the Auschwitz of today the reality of the past is present. Auschwitz is a tangible symbol. "One need only stoop to find the ash that fell from the sky at that time and scattered the wretched remains of thousands and thousands of Jewish children, silently and wisely, into the four winds. On the soil of Auschwitz we can hear the voice of memory which "burns but never dies' away" (Elie Wiesel). If something is added as a symbol, it may diminish the force of Auschwitz's message. The symbolism of Auschwitz has the most telling effect if it is kept free from additional symbols. This absence and avoidance of symbols also manifest a solidarity with all the victims, as explained by Theo Klein, head of the Jewish delegation to the official talks on the "Carmel" conflict. "We (Jews)," he said "have never denied that Poles, Russians, 'Gypsies' and others died there. We do not insist that Auschwitz be made a synagogue... (The dead) were Catholics and Protestants, Jews, Muslims and free thinkers. None of these groups can claim an exclusive right to commemorate them." Auschwitz must be protected from any group or institution laying claim to the truth and seeking to use Auschwitz for its own purposes.

Our respect for those who suffered and died at Auschwitz, but also for the Jews as the people of God's covenant, forbids us Christians at this site to resort solely to our Christian forms of liturgy and spirituality. In exercising this restraint, the renunciation of symbols can be a positive sign. There are dimensions and depths of suffering — and of suffering in relation to God — which make silent abhorrence and reflection the appropriate response.

We Christians must appreciate the seriousness of the question which non-Christians ask about our theology of the Cross, which has changed for us from a pillory to a token of redemption. Throughout history many non-Christians, especially Jews, have experienced the Cross as a symbol of persecution, through the Crusades, the Inquisition and the compulsory baptisms, the "s. Thus we must learn to realize that for many people the Cross means something quite different from the message we intend it to give. Our symbols, intentions and criteria cannot serve as the standard for all others.

We Christians, too, can perceive Auschwitz devoid of symbols as a symbol in itself. Its emptiness can serve as an eloquent remembrance of the forsakenness, the lack of solace and the terror of the many who had to live and die there. A convent might cover up a Christian presence to a degree that was not there before. Those who ask what it is about Christian nuns praying and making atonement there that is so disturbing to the Jews must learn to understand that it is improper for us to subsequently adopt Auschwitz for Christianity or even give the impression of doing so. Prayer for the victims of Auschwitz is independent of the place Auschwitz; expiation for past atrocities is not tied to the place where they were perpetrated.

True, it is a tradition of Christian piety going back to the early history of the Church to erect the Cross or a church at places of martyrdom or over the graves of martyrs. But that tradition cannot be continued at Auschwitz. It would seem presumptuous because the dead at Auschwitz are not "our" martyrs, even though there were men and women among them who died as Christians. Furthermore, it would distort the fact that it was baptized people who became perpetrators. However understandable the longing of Christians to place the abysmal suffering of Auschwitz under the Cross of Christ so that the light of hope from the Resurrection may radiate over this place of incomprehensible God-forsakenness and contempt for mankind; however great the seriousness with which the Polish people wish to make that site a symbol of their own martyrdom and renewal, Auschwitz must and for all time be preserved as the place where millions of Jews died, abandoned by an indifferent world and by the Churches, who, after all, live with the Jewish people in one and the same Covenant of God.

We Christians must genuinely accept the burden of history. "For history is not something external; it is part of the Church's own identity and can remind us that the Church, which we profess to be holy and mystery, is also Church guilty of sin, which needs to stop and reconsider" (German language Bishops Conferences marking the 50th anniversary of the pogrom of November 1938). In memory of Auschwitz we Christians must understand:

- that the murder of millions of Jews is so closely associated with the name of Auschwitz that the voices of the members of precisely that people must not be ignored when "deciding" on Auschwitz;

- that we have forfeited much of our credibility because, as religious communities, we at that time – in spite of the exemplary conduct of individuals – ignored the suffering of the Jewish people;

- that we must strive to change our attitude and renew our relationship with the Jewish people;

- that Auschwitz also stands between the Polish and the Jewish people and needs to be remembered as a place of Polish suffering;

- that — and this may be the most difficult of all — ours are not the only criteria, nor the only appropriate ones, no matter how sincerely we consider them to be the true ones.

As Jews and Christians we are convinced that Auschwitz must not be allowed to become a place of superficial inspection or ideological instruction. It will not be easy to preserve it in such a way that it keeps alive the memory of the victims and enables visitors to show respect in their own different ways. The proposed Centre outside the camp should help achieve this aim. This undertaking and the transfer of the convent and the cross are necessary steps which can demonstrate the seriousness of the Catholic renewal in terms of the Church's continuing affinity with the Jewish people. The decisive change in the relationship of the Catholic Church with the Jewish people (and with individual Jews), which, as Pope John Paul II said on visiting the great synagogue in Rome, began with the Second Vatican Council faces the test: whether we Christians as the "Church after Auschwitz" are prepared for and capable of reversal, of *Umkehr*. This must be proved precisely at Auschwitz.

# THE CROSS IN
# JEWISH CHRISTIAN RELATIONS

## Edward H. Flannery

The year 1096 was a fateful year for the Jewish People. It was the date of the first Crusade, that religio-military campaign, called by Pope Urban II, to rescue the holy places from the hands of the Muslim "infidels". The Crusade acquired its name from the word *crux*, the Latin root of the word cross. As the recognized symbol of the Christian faith, it was the banner behind which the crusaders undertook their march to the Near East. Seized with religious fanaticism, these "men of the cross," their banner aloft and *"Deus vult"* [1] on their lips, massacred many Jewish communities along their way: the "infidel at home" as Jews were described at the time. In some cases an option was allowed, baptism or death. The cross no longer aloft was now used, we might say, as a hammer to force Jews to the front. Ten thousand Jews are estimated to have been killed. It was the first massive flow of Jewish blood, a flow that did not cease until merged with that of the six million of the *Shoah* in our own time.

The harrowing experience left the Jewish Community stunned, angered and depressed. Christians were now seen as assassins, inhuman and capricious. The breach between Christians and Jews was widened beyond repair and, as oppressions and massacres continued, so remained until the second half of the present century. And the Cross remained for Jews a symbol of anger and fear.

Interestingly, these and other such historical data might never have come to my attention but for a personal experience that took place a few years earlier in New York City. I was in the company of a young Jewish couple. Spying a huge cross shaped with lighted windows on the Pan Am building during the Christmas season, the young lady remarked, "That cross makes me shudder." When asked what she meant, she simply said: "it's like an evil presence" This young lady, I knew, was not anti-Christian. I quickly saw that she was actually doing me a confidence, in her hope that she could for the first time unburden herself to a Christian of a deep source of fear and anger *vis à vis* this Christian symbol without fear of a rebuff. The episode was my introduction to Jewish-Christian relations, and also the first of a number of such instances in which Jews confided to me their discomfort with crosses and crucifixes in public places or in buildings hosting Jewish-Christian conferences and workshops. In recent days the ecumenical problem that the Cross poses has come to the surface. In the controversy over the Carmelite convent at Auschwitz, a dispute arose about the towering cross erected near the convent, but on that occasion nothing was said on either side except that the cross should or should not be there.

## THE CROSS: AN ECUMENICAL PROBLEM

The foregoing stories give some indication of the chasm that Christians have carved between Jesus and His people and of the depth of alienation that has affected Jewish-Christian relations throughout the centuries. They also present an ecumenical problem that still confronts us today. When an especially sacred symbol of one faith-tradition is seen by one as a sign of love and redemption but by the other as a source of hatred and fear, both are faced with an ecumenical problem of the first order.

The stories, however, provide no hint of the theological origin of the unfortunate episodes they relate, which will be our main concern in this essay, for it is only in an understanding of the theology of the Cross that these scandalous happenings can be adequately appraised, and only therein will the ecumenical problem be resolved. It is an oddity of the Jewish-Christian dialogue, now a quarter of a century old, that the problem of the different reactions of Christians and Jews to the Cross has been given a wide berth. It has rarely been touched but indirectly, as, for example, part of the scriptural problem of Jewish involvement in the crucifixion, passion plays, and antisemitic practices. This issue of SIDIC is one of the first to take up the issue *ex professo*.

It is understood that throughout this essay the Cross is to be identified with the Cross of Christ Crucified as conceived in Christian teaching. One is aware of C.G. Jung's investigations of the cross as a pre-Christian archetypal symbol of religious mythology in which it appears as a multifaceted symbol that includes such images and representations as the Tree of Death, the Tree of Life, the Mother, Life itself, et cetera. Among other examples, Jung notes those medieval legends which transform the Tree of Death into the Tree of Life and medieval artists' portrayals of Christ hanging on a tree rooted in the grave of Adam[2]. Such hybrids of

Christian doctrine and ancient mythical symbolism are not to be understood reductively, having, as they do, no historical connection with the crucifixion of Jesus on a Roman cross at the end of the first third of the first century of the Common Era. There is, however, nothing to prevent one from discerning here a psychological support for Christian faith and piety emanating from the depths of the human psyche. *Gratia perficet naturam.*[3]

## ANTI-JUDAISM IN CHRISTIAN THEOLOGY

### SOME DISTINCTIONS

The alienation of Christians and Jews began in theology, specifically in theological anti-Judaism. This harsh term has, by wide consensus, been accepted to denote no more than theological disagreement with tenets of Judaism. A distinction is necessary, however. A first kind of anti-Judaism comprises those inevitable disagreements that Christianity had with Judaism by virtue of its own beliefs. No negative effect is necessarily involved in such disagreements. Another stage is that composed of differences which, owing to the level of their negativity and intensity of effect, exceed the bounds of acceptable theological disagreement and move, as it happened in the earlier centuries, into the realm of defamation. Anti-Judaism in such cases becomes Christian antisemitism. Defamatory references appear, for example, in passages of the New Testament where Judaism and some of the Jewish leadership are branded as reprobate, rejected of God, and satanic. They pose a serious scriptural and pastoral problem for Christianity that has not been solved.

### CHARGE OF DEICIDE

Such passages pale in significance when compared to the charge of deicide that evolved in the course of the anti-Judaic/antisemitic polemic that followed in their wake. This deplorable accusation defined the crucifixion of Jesus as the handiwork of the Jewish people. Jews were soon publicly portrayed as Christ killers, hence slayers of God (deicides), accursed, and scattered throughout the world in punishment for their blasphemous crime. This theological myth proved to be the most virulent motivator of the millennial oppression and murder of Jews throughout Christian history. For Jews, understandably, the tragic fate visited upon them became largely symbolized by the Cross, the gibbet of Jesus' death - a symbol of hate and fear.

The Second Vatican Council's rejection of the deicide accusation in its statement on the Jewish People in *Nostra Aetate*, 4, in 1965 is, to be sure, an initiative in which to rejoice. Nonetheless, it is possible to savor it with mixed reactions. Despite its obvious merits, it is difficult not to view it as too little too late. After all, the accusation had already done its frightful damage, and well before the statement was issued, reasonable and informed persons had consigned it to the dustbin of history. Moreover, one may question whether the statement and others that followed are sufficiently imbued with, or have been followed up by, that spirit of repentance and reparation which the part played by the Church and by Christians in the age-long oppression calls for. This observation is not intended to make light of this and other statements and initiatives made by the Churches to undo the wrongs, but rather to point to the serious disproportion that separates them from the enormity of the oppression that brought them about. One may wonder whether, despite the new and humbler stance the Church has adopted *vis à vis* herself in the Council, she has inadvertently allowed a strain of the old triumphalism to live on, at least in relation to the Jewish people. One may cite in this respect the Vatican's cool policy toward the State of Israel, whose existence and meaning is so central to Jewish beliefs and hopes.

Question can also be put on the promulgation of the new positive teachings. To what extent have they been made to reach the Christian people? Sufficiently to bring them into the seminaries, classrooms, and pulpits, and in this way to the pews and thereby into the home? The final aim of the Jewish-Christian interface is not, or should not be, solely theological but also pastoral. Theological understanding is of great importance, but it is not the ultimate goal, which is rather the reconciliation of the Jewish and Christian peoples.

## JEWISH REACTIONS TO THE CROSS

Negative Jewish reactions to the Cross are not limited to its association with the deicide myth. Thanks to numerous conversations on *Oneg Shabbat*[4] about these reactions I was led to conclude that in many cases they derive from it, but not in all. Some of those with whom I spoke were under the impression that whenever Christians see the Cross, they always think of Jews as culprits – an eloquent testimony to the enduring efficacy of the deicidal accusation. Others claimed they simply saw it as a symbol of Christianity, Christianity sensed as the historic enemy of the Jewish People. There is no myth involved here. From the earliest days of Christian history, before the deicide notion had fully evolved, Jews were judged guilty of unbelief. Their refusal to accept Jesus as Messiah and accept baptism took a heavy toll on Jewish life. The deicide tradition aside, the charge of unbelief took on a life of its own and cast the Jews in a precarious position. Their supposedly stubborn disbelief in Jesus as Messiah, considered damnable in itself, was soon viewed as a challenge to the Christian faith and a source of temptation to Christians.

This latter reaction to the Cross presents a more serious ecumenical problem than that posed by the deicide myth, now well on its way out. That Christianity conducted itself as an enemy of the Jewish People cannot be questioned; that it remains that enemy today can be questioned, indeed denied; but that Jews should see it that way is quite another matter. It is noticeable that a goodly segment of Jewish leadership has kept its distance from the newly formed Jewish-Christian dialogue and has failed to join in the new spirit of friendship and cooperation that has characterized much of the upper levels of both Jewish and Christian leadership. Acutely aware of the millennial oppression of their forebears, these reluctant ones are not convinced that the historic enemy has so profoundly changed as to no longer see them as unbelievers or candidates for conversion. For the Christians, some of them believe, the dialogue is of necessity a vestibule of the baptistry. Many of them are willing, however, to wait and see.[5]

In sum, the Cross as an archetypal image of Jesus' death and of Christianity remains for many Jews a stumbling block on the road to Jewish-Christian reconciliation, and for Christians, by reason of the ambivalent significance it has acquired in history, an ecumenical problem of first importance. And for both it remains an opportunity to probe more deeply into what separates Christians and Jews both within and without the requirements of self-definition.

## A NEW SITUATION?

At this juncture the question becomes: given the failures of the past and difficulties of the present, what are the prospects for the future? Is it conceivable that the Cross, though posited at the very center of these failures and difficulties, may acquire a positive and healing role in our ongoing efforts of understanding and rapprochement? Must it always remain a bitter barrier between Jews and Christians? If not, what is needed to bring about this healing reversal? To find answers to questions such as these is the task before us. It is a considerable one. The reflections that follow, taken in its pursuit, are to be understood as an all too brief and tentative assay to offer some suggestions that may serve as pointers along the path toward a renewed theology of the Cross that will show forth a true visage of Christianity and turn the Cross, as Paul hoped, into a source of reconciliation and peace, especially among Jews and Christians.

## CHRISTIAN THEOLOGY OF THE CROSS

### A THEOLOGY OF SUFFERING

For the Christian, the theology of the Cross, a theology of suffering, traces its first roots to the Hebrew Scriptures. Israel's history is abundantly marked by this condition. Israel itself, a small and powerless people and nation, reveals the power of God. According to many exegetes, Isaiah 53 casts her in a redemptive role as God's suffering servant. The psalmists meanwhile sing of God's mercy toward the weak and oppressed.

Jesus follows in that tradition. The foundation stones of this theology are found in the life and death of Jesus as recorded in the Christian Scriptures. They are four: those sayings and actions of Jesus that exemplify suffering, self-sacrifice, humility and vicarious atonement. Already evident in his life, these marks are re-enacted in his death. Taken as a whole, they are seen as revelatory of Jesus' redemptive work. Jesus, it is important to emphasize, imposed this principle of humility and self-sacrifice upon his followers, promising that the humble "will be exalted" and urging whoever would follow him to "deny himself and take up his cross daily" (Lk. 9:23).

### THE CONTRIBUTION OF PAUL

It was given to Paul first to extract from the oral tradition elements for a full-fledged theology of the Cross. In numerous passages he extols the Cross, making it all but synonymous with Christianity. Not only is it made the central symbol of Christian soteriology, but of Christian living and spirituality as well. As did Jesus, Paul places a strong accent on the obligation of Christians to take up the Cross in the sense of accepting all suffering in imitation of Jesus. He himself, Paul tells us, is "crucified to the world" and "the world to him" (Gal. 6:14). In virtue of his/her mystical union with Him, the Christian too "has been crucified with Christ" (Rom. 6:6).

Applying this to himself, Paul educes a moral theology daunting in its demands and radical in its reversal of worldly values:

> So I willingly boast of my weakness instead, that the power of Christ may rest upon me. Therefore I am content with weakness, with mistreatment, with distress, with persecutions and difficulties for the sake of Christ; for when I am powerless then I am strong (2 Cor. 12-96-10).

We have here the core of a revolutionary moral Christian theology of voluntary powerlessness and reliance on the grace of God. It stands at the antipode of the *theologia gloriae*[6] that led in time to a triumphalistic apologetic and missionary impulse which held sway in so much of Christian history to the detriment of the Church's true mission.

Surprisingly, Paul, reflecting on a saying of Jesus to be recorded in John 12:32, goes on to see the Cross as a source of reconciliation of all things "in heaven and on earth" (Col. 1:20) and of Jews and Christians (Ephs. 2:16). And yet, so much does he consider the standards of the Cross to be at odds with the wisdom of the world (I Cor:17) that it is a "scandal" to Gentiles, and even a "stumbling block" to Jews. One recognizes here the ambivalence of Paul's thought concerning his own people. As his first hopes for their entry into the Church were dashed by their refusal, he came to see this as a "mystery" (Roms. 11:25) but intimates that the refusal was of divine provenance for the salvation of the Gentile world (Roms. 11:25, 28). Thus was the cross at once a source of reconciliation and yet a stumbling block in its path.

## POST NEW-TESTAMENT DEVELOPMENTS

Little substantive was added to the Pauline theology of the Cross throughout the next millennium and a half with the exception of Augustine's relating it to humankind's "fallen nature," remediable only by access to the limitless grace of Christ. It was left for Martin Luther to work out an elaborate theology in 1518 when he formulated his *theologia crucis*,[7] which he based largely on Paul's views. Postulating that all theology must be centered on Christ's redeeming death on the cross, the theology of the

Cross was made the central Christian teaching. He saw this *theologia crucis* as a negation of the *theologia gloriae* that preceded him, which sought God in the work in Creation and led to a soteriology that canonizes good works and righteousness. Such a theology he deemed as nonbiblical and triumphalistic. All theology, he postulated, must be centered on faith in God's redeeming love and human receptivity to his grace.

Luther's *theologia* waxed and then waned in Protestant thought. Others found it divisive. More recent times have been more receptive as non-Protestant theologians joined Protestant colleagues in reaffirming it and in exploring the idea of God suffering in His creatures. Twentieth century catastrophes, especially the Holocaust, have facilitated such a development. From a Roman Catholic standpoint Karl Rahner has affirmed the *theologia* in these words: "The Christian can fulfill his existence only within the context of Jesus' cross," yet holds that the cross must be subordinated to the "always greater unfathomable mystery of God," and allow for "following Jesus by committed action on behalf of the suffering and oppressed."[8]

## SOME CONTEMPORARY VIEWS

Some contemporary theologians have taken the subject in a radical direction. A. Roy Eckardt rejects the belief that the *theologia crucis* can overcome Christian triumphalism. As the source of the deicide myth, he holds, it disqualifies itself for that role. It has long been his conviction that the defeat of triumphalism devolves rather on discounting the Resurrection of Jesus, but more recently he has modified this view to allow for possible nontriumphalist affirmations of it.[9] It is true that some theologians have pressed the Resurrection into the cause of Christian apologetic, particularly in its controversy with the Synagogue. This only serves to demean it and enhance the triumphalist mindset. The message of the Resurrection is one of hope of eternal life, not of temporal triumphs. It may well, on the other hand, temper to some extent the dour message of suffering and self-sacrifice of the *theologia*. This is as it should be, for neither should stand in isolation from the other, and their necessary relationship need not be made to detract from the centrality of the Cross in Christian theology.

Paul van Buren ventures further in conceding no more than an accidental soteriological role to Jesus' death on the cross. Viewing the Crucifixion against the backdrop of the Holocaust, he finds it necessary to deprive it of its traditional theological eminence. Reduced to a "tragic accident" probably unforeseen by God, Jesus' death is made into an occasion for faith in a victory of God's love over sin and grafting the Gentiles into Israel's Covenant.[10]

These interpretations are wide of the aim of this essay to renew the *theologia* for purposes of reconciliation. It is improbable that they will recommend themselves to many Christian bodies, without whose acceptance the extensive ameliorations that are needed now would not be forthcoming.

## JEWISH CRITIQUE

Jewish theologians who have studied Christianity steer clear of commenting on Christian theology as such, but have had a considerable amount to say about its value and consequences, whether ethical, social, or psychological. One of the most forceful and penetrating among these is Rabbi Leo Baeck (1873-1956).[11] He considered Paul to be the founder of Christianity, not Jesus, whom he considered entirely within the precincts of Judaism. According to Baeck, who relied heavily on the rationalist criticism of his time, Paul's borrowings from Hellenistic mystery cults converted Christianity into an admixture of "romantic passivity" and ethical Judaism. He viewed Christianity's emphasis on faith, human weakness, and passivity to divine grace as an unfortunate departure from Judaism's emphasis on works, *mitzvot*, and life on earth. Many Jewish thinkers adopted this general interpretation of Judaism and Christianity, and many Christian theologians regard it as a misinterpretation of Paul and Christianity. Paul's acceptance of dependence on God and self-denial did not derive from mystery cultic mythology, but from human experience and the moral ideal which, he believed, Christians should strive to pursue, in imitation of Jesus' self-immolation for others. This Jewish critique of Christianity is obviously not receptive of Paul's theology of the Cross, but it is not out of harmony with those parts of his theology that speak of faith acting in love (Gal. 5:6) and in selfless service of others (Gal. 5:14) — which his critics missed.

## TOWARDS JEWISH-CHRISTIAN RECONCILIATION

## IS IT POSSIBLE?

Is it possible in view of this survey of the vicissitudes of the *theologia crucis* in history to approach in its light the question of reconciliation of the Jewish and Christian peoples? Many things militate against it. The spirit of the times would forbid it – a period that glorifies personal and collective autonomy and power and discards self-effacement as unhealthy, unproductive, even a pathology. To the contrary, it might be asked: is it not a proper function of Christian thought to be counter-cultural in all times? It may also be pointed out that the Christlike way this theology fosters manifests itself best in a courage and strength that defies the bravest exploits of secular heroes. The early Christians were hardly seen as wimps or losers. Nor were, to mention a merest few in our own time, the Bonhoeffers, Niemoellers, Jägerstaters, the Mother Teresas. If Christ is to be conjured up as a Prometheus, as he has by some, it must be in virtue of these self-effacing ones rather than the Constantines or crusaders who have exemplified the triumphalist strain in the Church. At all events, one can be certain that under the influence of an authentic theology of the Cross and its requirements for Christian living, Christian history would have been spared the deicide myth, replacement theology, the *in hoc signo vinces* motif that helped to launch the Constantine era,[12] the Crusades, forced baptisms and sermons, anti-Jewish legislation, the *auto da fe*, and the Christian contribution – indirect and unintended but real – to the Holocaust, in short, Christian antisemitism.

It is a sad and sobering irony that because of this lapse the people who suffered most grievously throughout Christian history was not the people to whom persecution was promised by its Founder but rather the people from which he came (Mt. 5:11, 10:23, 23:34; Jn. 15-20). Jews, I might add, were always curious when in Temple talks I told them that they have been our Simon of Cyrene (Mt. 27:32), forced to carry a cross destined for Christians. In explaining this reference I found it regrettable that it was unclear as well to Christians in the audience who, still unaware of what happened to Jews in Christian history, did not understand.

It can be seen in retrospect that in pursuit of its mission the Church could have taken two quite different directions: one particular, that of Christ's universal redemption; another along the path of an evangelization of a more tolerant and spiritually persuasive kind and of selfless service. It is also apparent that for the greater part of its history the former was taken. True, the inner path was also taken but in a secondary way, in such wise as to encourage it only for religious and saintly persons – always a minuscule minority. The theology of the Cross until now has been only partially fulfilled.

## CHRISTIAN FAILURE TO "TAKE UP THE CROSS"

Why is this? What happened? More than one reason can be given, to be sure, but few will escape the compass of the fact that Christianity has suffered from a failure in its teaching of a crucial component of the theology of the Cross - its moral implementation. The doctrine of Christ's redemptive sacrifice has been faithfully taught, but the moral and spiritual norms it imposes on the Church and on Christian life have been given short shrift. The "word of the Cross" (I Cor 1:18) calls the Church, its leadership and people, not only to proclaim its faith in Christ's sacrificial death on the Cross, but to take up its own cross and, in reliance on Christ's saving grace, manifest his power in humility, suffering and selfless service; *in fine*, to become a pilgrim Church and a pilgrim people, a "people of God" *in via*, on its way, *in via crucis*, its way of the cross. It was a way less traveled.

It is still the way ahead. One of the first destinations should be reconciliation with Judaism and the Jewish People, a reconciliation that will include genuine repentance and reparation. The price of this is no less than a transformation of the Christian mind and heart realized *in via crucis* along the lines laid down by Paul, Luther, Rahner, and others. And what is required of Jews? For the moment, nothing.[13] One can hope that eventually, if this transformation has taken place on a wide enough scale, Jews will have lost whatever fear or hatred of the Cross they may have had in virtue of their positive reaction to a new make of Christian. The observable first fruits of such a transformation in some Christians and its resultant in some Jews, that have made their appearance in the Jewish-Christian interface of the last quarter of a century, give good grounds for believing that our hopes are not a chimera.

## A FURTHER GOAL

A final question and a leap into the future: is reconciliation enough? Judaism and Christianity, Jews and Christians are possessed of a spiritual kinship. Worshipers of the same God, possessors of the same basic morality, and bonded by a parent/offspring relationship, they are of the same spiritual family. Specially chosen and covenanted by God, both, wittingly or not, are spiritual partners in the divine economy, each in a different way, to proclaim God's word to the whole human family.

If this be so, is mutual understanding and reconciliation of these two peoples a sufficient final goal? All of humanity is entitled to that. It is a law of nature, hence a law of God, that family members are held to a greater bond of love toward one another than that binding them to all humanity. Are not Jews and Christians spiritually held to a bond of familial love, a bond of special affection? Special affection of Christians for Jews and Jews for Christians! This road is a long one. Only the dream of its possibility can move us to correct our focus and quicken our pace. The day may not be that far off when Christians and Jews after centuries of alienation, having stood face to face in dialogue, will be united in fraternal partnership to do what they were always held to do, to bring forth God's reign upon earth.

## A POSTSCRIPT

In the course of a talk I was giving one evening in a Temple in Westchester I spied sitting in one of the front seats, the Jewish lady who several years earlier had divulged her negative feeling to me about the cross. After the talk we chatted. She told me she had become involved in Jewish-Christian circles. Apparently she had lost the discomfort she felt towards Christians. And she told me that the cross no longer made her shudder. It was so clear. It was not the cross she had feared, but Christians of whom the cross was only a symbol. She probably did not realize that her new Christian friends were something the Cross had wrought.

## ENDNOTES

1. "God wills it"
2. C.G. Jung, *Symbols of Transformation*. New York: Pantheon, 1956), pop. 233, 269 and passim.
3. "Grace perfects nature," a Latin scholastic theological adage.
4. "Joy of the Sabbath," a Hebrew phrase used to describe the social gathering after the Sabbath service.
5. Rabbi Eliezar Berkovits speaks for those who, declining to enter the dialogue, counsel silence. Holding that "honest fraternal dialogue now" is "emotionally impossible." he states: "In a hundred years, perhaps, depending on Christian deeds toward Jews, we may be emotionally ready for the dialogue." See his *Faith after the Holocaust* (New York: Ktav. 1973) p. 44.
6. "Theology of Glory," Luther's expression for the theology of Jesus' redemptive death, which he made the center of his entire theologies preceding him that glorified Christianity and the Church.
7. "Theology of the Cross," Luther's expression for the theology of Jesus' redemptive death, which he made the center of his entire theology.

8. Karl Rahner, *Dictionary of Theology* (New York: Crossroad, 1981) p. 107.

9. A. Roy Eckardt, "The *Shoah* and the Affirmation of the Resurrection of Jesus: A Revisionist Marginal Note" (Unpublished paper delivered at Annual Scholars Conference on the Church Struggle and the Holocaust, Philadelphia, March 1989) pp. 18 & 25.

10. Paul M. van Buren, *A Theology of the Jewish-Christian Reality, Part III: Christ in Context.* (San Francisco: Harper & Row, 1988) Ch. 7.

11. See Leo Baeck, *Judaism and Christianity* (Philadelphia: Jewish Publication Society of America, 1958, esp. Chs. 3, 4 & 5. For a critique by J. Louis Martyn, see *Jewish Perspectives on Christianity.* ed. Fritz A. Rothschild (New York: Crossroad, 1990) pp. 21-41.

12. In 312 C.E. Emperor Constantine won a decisive battle, which one can say opened the Constantinian era, an era of close collaboration of Church and State that was to last up to modern times. Constantine confessed to Eusebius, the Church historian, that before the battle he saw a cross in the sky with the inscription *in hoc signo vinces* (in this sign you will conquer). The Emperor ordered that the cross be marked on the shields of his almost entirely non-Christian army. See J. Stevenson, ed., A New Eusebius. (London: Camelot Press 1970) pp. 298-300.

13. Nothing, of course, except that those already involved, or inclined to be, continue patiently in dialogue and cooperative ventures with their all too few Christian colleagues.

# STATEMENT OF JAN KARSKI

Poland is ill served by the growing conflict over crosses placed in the grounds of the so-called "gravel pit" which constitutes an integral part of the Auschwitz site.

As we know, Polish authorities agreed to respect the principle, established through international dialogue, that the area of this damned soil should be free of religious connotations and there should be no signs or symbols of any religion or denomination – no crosses nor stars of David nor symbols of Islam or Buddhism.

There appear to be people in Poland without respect for their Country and the authority of the Church who, in violation of the position of the Bishop in charge of the diocese including Oswięcim (Auschwitz), bring crosses to the gravel pit. They can see that this brings pain to Jews for whom this place remains the largest cemetery in their history. Knowing this, they still do it.

These actions have nothing to do with faith or with religion. They are an expression of conceit, contempt, and desire to humble our "older brothers" in our joint faith in God. These feelings and actions are contrary to true Catholicism and they bring painful, acute shame because the use of religion and its symbols for political purposes is sacrilege.

It is also a sacrilege to cite the name of the Holy Father as justification for the political acts in Oswięcim and to quote his words "Defend the Cross." Those words, which are dear to the heart of every Christian and especially a Catholic, refer to the teachings flowing from the martyrdom of the Savior which is the bedrock of fidelity to the Church. It is impudence to use these words to justify humbling representatives of another religion.

These new crosses are a falsification of Christ's Cross and of the words, statements, and the intent of the Holy Father.

I never expected that, toward the end of my life, a part of which was devoted to a futile struggle to save "our older brothers" perishing in the Holocaust, I would live to see my countrymen raising blasphemously the sign of the cross against those through whom our God was revealed.

249

# THE NATIONAL POLISH AMERICAN-JEWISH AMERICAN COUNCIL

## Statement of the National Polish American-Jewish American Council on the Recent Placement of Crosses at the Auschwitz I Death Camp in Poland.

Aug. 5, 1998 - The National Polish American-Jewish American Council (NPAJAC) expresses its profound concerns about the placement last week of 50 crosses outside the Auschwitz I death camp in Poland.

While the Council recognizes that Auschwitz remains a place of special memory for both Jews and Poles, erection of these new crosses at the site is a provocation that will only drive a wedge between Polish Christians and worldwide Jewry. With this action, it will be all the more difficult to bring about a necessary and mutually beneficial "normalization" of relations between the two communities. Catholic members of NPAJAC also share the sentiment of many other church leaders around the world who view the use of the cross in this instance as a desecration of one of Christianity's most sacred symbols.

We urge Polish government authorities and church leaders in Poland and elsewhere to take effective action to help defuse this potentially volatile situation. Unless such provocative actions are met with an appropriate response, those who oppose reconciliation will be only further emboldened.

The placement of the crosses at Auschwitz I will further postpone efforts, initiated by the Polish government two years ago, to finalize a draft "Declaration" regarding development around and preservation of the death camp. The Declaration, whose ratification was postponed earlier this summer when a few Jewish groups regrettably withdrew their support for it, is a framework to respond constructively to provocations like the placement of the new crosses last week, and it represents a model of progress on Polish-Jewish relations.

The NPAJAC is committed to helping with the process of improving Polish-Jewish relations. In recent years, this process has moved along encouragingly on a number of fronts. But, to state the obvious, it is

251

not yet complete. NPAJAC stands ready to assist in efforts to overcome the tensions that arise, including the present one, and to promote better understanding between the communities, whose intertwined histories date back nearly a millennium. We call on others of good will to join us in this endeavor.

# LETTER OF POPE JOHN PAUL II
# TO THE CARMELITE SISTERS

On 9 April 1993 the Holy Father sent the following letter to the Carmelite Sisters.

Dear Sisters,

"...Love is my vocation. Oh, yes, I have found my own place in the Church... ...The Church has a heart... this heart burns with intense love... I have come to see love as the essence of my vocation... In the heart of the Church, my Mother, I shall be love" (*Manuscrits autobiographiques*, Lisieux 1957, 227-229).

These words of the holy Carmelite of Lisieux speak of the essence of the vocation of each of Her Carmelite sisters: of each of you. You came to Oświęcim to be love in the heart of the Church. Is there any need to explain how very necessary it is for the heart of the Church to beat at this very place? How much the love that Christ had for man to the very end is needed here? How much it is needed here, where for years hatred and contempt for man raged and gathered the horrid harvest of destruction and death among men belonging to so many nations?

It is now the will of the Church that you should move to another place in this same Oświęcim. It is up to each of you to decide to continue to live the Carmelite life here (in Auschwitz) in your present community or to return to your home cloister. This is certainly a moment of test for each of you. I ask Christ the crucified and risen from the dead to let each of you know His will and particular vocation on the Carmelite way of life.

Oświęcim, and all that is connected with it as the tragic legacy of Europe and mankind, continues to be a Carmelite task. In particular, what remains of this task is all that is connected with the annihilation camp "Auschwitz-Birkenau" in the memory of nations: in the memory of sons and daughters of Israel, all that is connected with the history of Poles, with the history of our Fatherland. In what way the future will grow out of this most painful past depends largely on whether "this love that is more powerful than death" will be on guard at the threshold of Oświęcim. Dear Sisters, the mystery of this redeeming love, the love that saves the world, was entrusted in a special way to you. And fifty years after a horrible war, a war which produced Oświęcim besides other things, how very much our modern world continues to be threatened by this hatred!

Dear Carmelite Sisters! Accept the "*gaudium paschale*" that animates the Church at Easter time. Accept as well the blessing in the name of the Father, the Son, and the Holy Ghost – in the name of Jesus Christ who conquered the world (see J 16, 33).

The Vatican, 9 April 1993.
John Paul II, (Pope)

# AFTERWORD

The theological and political upheaval unleashed by the episode of the Cross and crosses at Auschwitz is the most serious threat to Catholic-Jewish relations in Poland since the convening of Vatican II.* Instead of fulfilling the promise of fresh winds blowing away the detritus accumulated by centuries of the teaching of contempt and the theology of supersession, the controversy that ensued over the cross and crosses exposed the continued existence of disregard for the Other. The fact that people of good will on both sides of the Catholic Jewish dialogue resolved to persevere amidst the turbulence is a sign of great hope, as are the existence and activity of the Polish Council of Christians and Jews (CCJ) and various declarations by the Episcopate in Poland. In the following pages, we will present an overview which both addresses the political resolution of the crisis and which reflects on the remaining underlying issues which have yet to be fully confronted.

On the political level, the situation of the "baby" crosses, some three hundred in number, was resolved when the Polish Parliament passed the Act for the Protection of Former Nazi Extermination Camps in May, 1999. Consequently, these crosses, many bearing the inscription – "only under this cross, only under this symbol, Poland is Poland and a Pole is a Pole" – planted by the right-wing nationalist and antisemite Kazimierz Switon and his followers, were immediately removed. This commendable act occurred shortly before Pope John Paul II's eighth pilgrimage to Poland. The process to resolve the controversy involved talks between the government and the church, although the official action was taken by the government rather than by the church. The Jewish community was apprised of the situation but, according to Stanislaw Krajewski, co-chairperson of the CCJ, "had no decisive role." These crosses are currently stored in a Franciscan convent not far from Auschwitz.

* Editors' note: This was the situation prior to the Jedwabne controversy which appears to conform to the crisis pattern of Polish Catholic-Jewish interchange in Poland. Important steps forward in the dialogue are continually put in the background by unresolved theological issues and competing historical memory.

The so-called papal cross, located in the garden of the former Carmelite convent remains. Its history, no less than its future, speaks volumes about the possibilities and the perils involved in Catholic-Jewish dialogue. Erected in 1979 when John Paul II celebrated mass at Auschwitz-Birkenau, the cross had to be sufficiently large in order to be seen by the multitude gathered at the spot. Nine years later the cross was surreptitiously moved to the gravel pit at Auschwitz where one hundred and fifty Poles had been murdered by the Nazis. Although the cross was never consecrated by the pope, it has been embraced by extreme nationalists as a symbol of resistance, reasserting thus the monolithic notion of an exclusive Polish Roman Catholic identity. In the experience of these national extremists, first the Nazis and then the Communists prohibited displaying the cross, not to mention denying its salvific message. However, they are unable to discern the distinctive concerns of the Jewish people and wrongly claim that the Jews are continuing the anti-Catholicism and anti-Polonism of the previous totalitarian regimes.

Plans are currently being discussed which call for the planting of high trees in order to hide the cross from the view of those visiting Auschwitz. At first sight this plan appears to offer something to both sides; the cross remains, yet it does not offend Jewish religious sensibilities. However, upon further reflection, it is deeply flawed for at least two reasons. Trees *cover over* indeed camouflage rather than confront the pain of the Other. The pain of the church is the pain of the persecutor. The pain of the Jews is the pain of the church's victims. Further, hiding, covering over – or covering up – reverts to the pre-Vatican II pattern of behavior of the Roman Church. Dialogue, in the astute phrase of David Patterson, "requires difference." If Catholic Jewish dialogue is to continue to mature, it must in certain crucial instances openly agree to disagree.

For Christianity the cross symbolizes redemption, rebirth, and overcoming sin. Both individuals and the world itself are redeemed. For Judaism the cross has no such meaning. Rather, it represents an inverted sword at the point of which Jews were humiliated, murdered, exiled, or forcibly converted. Elie Wiesel poetically expresses this situation in his novel *A Beggar in Jerusalem*. There, Shlomo, one of the many Hasidim – in this case a blind seer – populating Weisel's tales, says about Jesus "You think you are suffering for my sake and for my brothers', yet we are the ones who will be made to suffer for you, because of you." He follows up this stark statement by painting "A picture of the future which made him (Jesus) see the innumerable victims persecuted and crushed under the sign

of his law."[1] Asked about this passage by an interviewer, the Nobel Peace
Laureate observes, "I suggest that (Jesus) did not know, that he could not
have known, what his disciples would do in his name."

While this is not the place to rehash in detail the lachrymose history
of Jewish persecution at the hands of the Roman church, it is appropriate to
recall three historical eras, each marked by the murderous triumphalism of
the cross.[2] The Crusades involved mass murders of Jews at the hands of
Christian warriors on their way to drive out the infidels (Muslims) from the
Holy land. Capturing Jerusalem, God's soldiers set fire to a synagogue
which was packed with Jews. A Jewish chronicler of the time refers to the
cross as an "evil sign."   The medieval period witnessed a similar
phenomenon. A cross in thirteenth century England was engraved with
texts containing phrases such as "Jews — Christ's assassins." During the
Inquisition prisoners condemned to death were compelled to march
through the streets wearing yellow robes covered by a black cross.

What, one may ask, is the point of raising old hatreds in light of the
demise of what James Carroll terms the Constantinian church? Considering
where the Catholic-Jewish dialogue was at the turn of the twentieth century,
the situation one hundred or so years later has changed dramatically for the
better. Yet old enmity is not easily banished. Symbols, like nations and
peoples, have a history. The cross is clearly an inter religious problem and a
stumbling block for Catholic — Jewish dialogue in Poland. And elsewhere.
Wisely distinguishing between intention and symbolism, Carroll trenchantly
describes the issue of the cross at the largest Jewish cemetery in the world.
He writes: "The cross at Auschwitz, transcending whatever benign
intention attaches to it, embodies supersessionism, medieval absolutism, the
cult of martyrdom, the violence of God, the ancient hatred of Jews, and the
Christian betrayal of Jesus Christ."[3] Carroll's pointed observation
underscores the generalized Jewish concern that the cross at this particular
death camp is an attempt to "Christianize the *Shoah*." Given what the cross
embodies as the central symbol of Christianity, it is an entirely inappropriate
way to memorialize the million Jews murdered in Auschwitz-Birkenau.

The conflict also revealed with great clarity the fact of competing
historical narratives. Monica Adamczk-Garbowska terms this competition a
"martyrdom rivalry."[4] This martyrdom competition exists on two levels.
There is, first and foremost, the issue of Auschwitz and the Holocaust. The
belief is that if the suffering of one side is stressed, it will necessarily
minimize the tragedy of the other. There is as well the historical sense of

Poles and Jews. Poland views itself as innocent among the nations, a victim of both the Nazis and the Communists. Further, the Jews, in this narrative, betrayed Poland by aligning themselves with the Communists. In addition, the Jews are accused of anti-Polonism.

Jews, for their part, view Poland as a Catholic nation which is at its core antisemitic. Consequently, the Church is seen as the primary teacher of anti-Judaism. As Konstanty Gebert observes, in the view of many Jews, "the Church should acknowledge its sins of the past, express contrition and remain vigilant in condemning and combating contemporary antisemitism, first of all in its own ranks."[5] Moreover, Poles are viewed as insensitive to the enormity of Jewish loss. The demographics here are also revealing. There are approximately only 3500 Jews comprising the Polish religious community, in the midst of an estimated 35 million Polish Catholics. Consequently, as Gebert notes, "it is the Church that sets both the religious and the inter-religious agenda."[6]

The conflict over the crosses and, more recently, the heated debate surrounding the murder of Jews by their Polish neighbors in the towns of Radzilow and Jedwabne, has brought out both the best and the worst in Polish response to their historical relationship to the Jews. Exemplifying the worst are statements by certain high Church officials, such as Bishop Stanislow Stefanek of Limza — the district where both towns are located — and the Reverend Henryk Jankowski. These men contend that the Poles are innocent and that charges of murder are merely an American attempt to defame Poles. Responding to Jan T. Gross's 2001 book *Neighbors* which discloses the incontrovertible evidence of the fact that it was Poles and not German Nazis who murdered the Jews of Jedwabne, the mayor of Radzilow contends the book was written based on a single story. "I can," attests the mayor, "invent any story right now." Perhaps fittingly, the best response came from Aleksander Kwasniewski, President of Poland who observed: "There are indeed black stains on our history and we will no longer be able to ignore them."

There are certain significant positive developments in Polish-Catholic Jewish relations. As noted earlier the Catholic Jewish dialogue has managed to survive and continues in the face of the acrimony surrounding the cross and crosses controversy. Further, the Auschwitz Museum now conducts seminars for Holocaust teachers in Poland that are far more comprehensive than those offered at any time during the post-war period. These seminars include a detailed study of the Jewish fate under National Socialism's occupation of Poland and Poland's own complex responses during the *Shoah*. In addition, Poland commemorates A Day of Judaism which is dedicated to study of biblical texts and an awareness of the vital role Jews have played in Polish history, although the events of this day are primarily by and for intellectuals. There is also a Jewish culture week, and the Jewish Historical Institute in Warsaw plays an educative role in addition to housing a precious collection of Judaica.

Dialogues have also developed between participants in the March of the Living — Jewish teenagers from around the world — and their Polish Catholic peers. In the year of 2000 the inaugural March of Remembrance and Hope brought some three hundred college students, most non-Jewish, from around the globe to Poland. Within the context of this new enterprise dialogue and discussion played a significant role. Important letters condemning antisemitism and confessing wartime sins against the Jewish people have been written by the Polish Episcopate. Moreover, the phenomenon of "New Jews," is playing a role in contemporary Poland. New Jews are those who discover that their own biological parents were Jewish. These parents who knew the Nazis were going to kill them gave their infants to Catholics so that the children might live. Jews, for their part, have begun to understand better the history of Polish response during the *Shoah* and to recognize the efforts of those who are sincere about engaging in dialogue.

Yet political distortions, religious fanaticism, and dislike of the Other continue to cloud the Polish interreligious landscape. Many years ago Emil Fackenheim, the distinguished Jewish Philosopher of Religion, wrote of the 614th Commandment. By this he meant that Jews should not cease being Jewish. For if they did so, they would be awarding Hitler — who wished to exterminate all Jews and everything Jewish — a posthumous victory. Today, the irony is that the Cross and crosses, not to mention other controversies between Poles and Jews, are in effect awarding such a victory to the preachers of exclusionary hatred. While it is still too early to say with certainty which path Poland will take, it is no exaggeration to contend that what happens in the crucible of Polish Catholic-Jewish relations over time will go a long way in determining whether the Church worldwide and the Jewish people can move forward in a meaningful dialogue.

## ENDNOTES

1. Elie Wiesel. *A Beggar in Jerusalem*. Translated by Elie Wiesel and Lily Edelman (New York: Random House, 1970), p. 56.

2. We are indebted for the particulars in this paragraph to Rabbi Michael Hilton's article, "The Shadow of the Cross," in *SIDIC* vol. xxiv, No. 1, 1991, English Edition, pp. 3-5.

3. James Carroll. *Constantine's Sword: The Church and the Jews* (Boston: Houghton Mifflin Company, 2001), p. 603.

4. Monika Adamczyk-Garbowska. "Poles, Jews and Auschwitz: A Controversy Over Historical Memory," in *Polish and Polish American Studies Occasional Papers*, No. 7, 1999, p. 6.

5. Konstanty Gebert, "Parallel Monologues: Catholics, Jews and Jedwabne," in *Jews and Christians in Conversation: Crossing Cultures and Generations*. Edited by E. Kessler, J. Pawlikowski, J. Banki  (Cambridge: Orchard Academic, 2002), p. 144. Gebert cites the demographics in his chapter.

6. Op. cit., p. 145.


ALB
SEN

# INDEX

Jacob Neusner

*The Aggadic Role in Halakhic Discourses.* Lanham. February 2001. University Press of America. Academic Studies in Ancient Judaism series. Volume I

*The Aggadic Role in Halakhic Discourses.* Lanham. February 2001. University Press of America. Academic Studies in Ancient Judaism series. Volume II

*The Aggadic Role in Halakhic Discourses.* Lanham. February 2001. University Press of America. Academic Studies in Ancient Judaism series. Volume III

*A Theological Commentary to the Midrash.* Lanham. April 2001. University Press of America. Academic Studies in Ancient Judaism series. Volume I. *Pesiqta deRab Kahana.*

*A Theological Commentary to the Midrash.* Lanham. March 2001. University Press of America. Academic Studies in Ancient Judaism series. - Volume II. *Genesis Raba.*

*A Theological Commentary to the Midrash.* Lanham. April 2001. University Press of America. Academic Studies in Ancient Judaism series. Volume III. *Song of Songs Rabbah*

*A Theological Commentary to the Midrash.* Lanham. April 2001. University Press of America. Academic Studies in Ancient Judaism series. Volume IV. *Leviticus Rabbah*

A Theological Commentary to the Midrash. Lanham. June 2001. University Press of America. Academic Studies in Ancient Judaism series. Volume V *Lamentations Rabbati*

*A Theological Commentary to the Midrash.* June 2001. University Press of America. Academic Studies in Ancient Judaism series.Volume VI. *Ruth Rabbah and Esther Rabbah I*

*A Theological Commentary to the Midrash.* June 2001. University Press of America. Academic Studies in Ancient Judaism series.Volume VII. *Sifra*

A Theological Commentary to the Midrash. July 2001. University Press of America. Academic Studies in Ancient Judaism series.Volume VIII. *Sifré to Numbers and Sifré to Deuteronomy*

A Theological Commentary to the Midrash. August 2001. University Press of America. Academic Studies in Ancient Judaism series.Volume IX. *Mekhilta Attributed to Rabbi Ishmael*

*The Unity of Rabbinic Discourse.* January 2001. University Press of America. Academic Studies in Ancient Judaism series. Volume I: *Aggadah in the Halakhah*

*The Unity of Rabbinic Discourse.* February 2001. University Press of America. Academic Studies in Ancient Judaism series. Volume II: *Halakhah in the Aggadah*

*The Unity of Rabbinic Discourse.* February 2001. University Press of America. Academic Studies in Ancient Judaism series. Volume III: *Halakhah and Aggadah in Concert*

*Texts without Boundaries. Protocols of Non-Documentary Writing in the Rabbinic Canon,* Lanham, 2002: University Press of America. Academic Studies in Ancient Judaism series. Volume Two. *Sifra*

*Texts without Boundaries. Protocols of Non-Documentary Writing in the Rabbinic Canon,* Lanham, 2003: University Press of America. Academic Studies in Ancient Judaism series. Volume Three. *Sifré to Numbers.*

*Texts without Boundaries. Protocols of Non-Documentary Writing in the Rabbinic Canon,* Lanham, 2003: University Press of America. Academic Studies in Ancient Judaism series. Volume Four. *Sifré to Deuteronomy.*

*Texts without Boundaries. Protocols of Non-Documentary Writing in the Rabbinic Canon,* Lanham, 2004: University Press of America. Academic Studies in Ancient Judaism series. Volume Five. *Genesis Rabbah.*

*Texts without Boundaries. Protocols of Non-Documentary Writing in the Rabbinic Canon,* Lanham, 2004: University Press of America. Academic Studies in Ancient Judaism series. Volume Six. *Leviticus Rabbah.*

*Texts without Boundaries. Protocols of Non-Documentary Writing in the Rabbinic Canon,* Lanham, 2004: University Press of America. Academic Studies in Ancient Judaism series. Volume Seven. *Pesiqta deRab Kahana.*

*Texts without Boundaries. Protocols of Non-Documentary Writing in the Rabbinic Canon,* Lanham, 2004: University Press of America. Academic Studies in Ancient Judaism series. Volume Eight. *Esther Rabbah and Ruth Rabbah.*

*Texts without Boundaries. Protocols of Non-Documentary Writing in the Rabbinic Canon,* Lanham, 2004: University Press of America. Academic Studies in Ancient Judaism series. Volume Nine. *Song of Songs Rabbah.*

*Texts without Boundaries. Protocols of Non-Documentary Writing in the Rabbinic Canon,* Lanham, 2004: University Press of America. Academic Studies in Ancient Judaism series. Volume Ten. *Lamentations Rabbah.*

*Texts without Boundaries. Protocols of Non-Documentary Writing in the Rabbinic Canon,* Lanham, 2004: University Press of America. Academic Studies in Ancient Judaism series. Volume Eleven. *Mekhilta Attributed to Rabbi Ishmael.*

*Texts without Boundaries. Protocols of Non-Documentary Writing in the Rabbinic Canon,* Lanham, 2004: University Press of America. Academic Studies in Ancient Judaism series. Volume Twelve. *Abot deRabbi Natan.*